Who Are We?

OTHER BOOKS BY JOHN H. WESTERHOFF III

Values for Tomorrow's Children
A Colloquy in Christian Education (ed)
Generation to Generation
    (with Gwen Kennedy Neville)
Tomorrow's Church
Will Our Children Have Faith?
McGuffey and His Readers
Learning Through Liturgy
    (with Gwen Kennedy Neville)
The Churchly Ministry in Higher Education (ed)

Who Are We?

The Quest for a Religious Education

Edited by

JOHN H. WESTERHOFF, III

on the occasion of the Religious Education
Association's 75th Anniversary

Religious Education Press
Birmingham Alabama

Library of Congress Cataloging in Publication Data
Main entry under title:
Who are we? : In search of an identity.

    Includes bibliographical references.
    1. Religious education—Addresses, essays, lectures.
I. Westerhoff, John H. II. Religious Education
Association.
BL42.W47   207   78-12392
ISBN 0-89135-014-4

Religious Educatin Press, Inc.
1531 Wellington Road
Birmingham, Alabama 35209
2 3 4 5 6 7 8 9 10

*Religious Education Press publishes books and educational materials exclusively
in religious education and in areas closely related to religious education. It is
committed to enhancing and professionalizing religious education through the
publication of significant scholarly and popular works.*

Dedicated
to
H. Shelton Smith: friend, colleague, and
predecessor at Duke
Robert Wood Lynn: mentor and friend at
Columbia and Union Theological Seminary;

and to

Henry F. Cope (1906-1923); Frank G. Ward
(1923-24); George Albert Coe (1924-26);
Laird T. Hites (1926-1929, 1935-1948);
Joseph M. Artman (1929-1934); Leonard
Stidley (1948-1958); Randolph Crump Mil-
ler (1958-1978); and Acting Editor Paul H.
Vieth (1959-60, 1966-67, and 1970).

I acknowledge with gratitude the permission of The Religious Education Association, 409 Prospect St., New Haven,
Connecticut, 06510, to reprint articles
from the journal, *Religious Education,* as
indicated in the introduction to each essay. (Note: all titles of authors refer to their
position at the time the article was published. Where persons are also presently
teaching, reference is made to their present positions.)

Contents

Who Are We?
An Introduction

JOHN H. WESTERHOFF, III
Professor of Religion and Education
Duke University Divinity School

Two decades ago, I joined the Religious Education Association. Today I serve on its board of directors and as editor-elect of its journal, *Religious Education*. Impressed by its past, grateful for its present, and hopeful for its future, I thought it appropriate to edit an anniversary volume celebrating its significant contribution to seventy-five years of American religious and educational history. That decision was easier than the next: What should this anthology contain? Should I focus on a theme such as public education; major contributions by its Roman Catholic, Jewish, and Protestant members; historical emphases such as character education; or social issues of continuing special concern to the REA, e.g., economic justice and world peace?

Two things were clear. First, this book was to be a testimony to the influence of the Religious Education Association and a reminder of the contributions of its journal, *Religious Education*. And second, it was to be a book with present and continuing value. I therefore, concluded that this anniversary volume should address the most pressing issue facing us today, namely, the search for an identity and a constituency.

While exploring these issues, I discovered that the history of the REA can best be understood through an awareness of the REA's always present quest for identity and allies. Convinced that a knowledge of this story could contribute positively to our present discussion and search for identity, this book was born. My hope is that it will prove of interest and value not only to the members of the Religious Education Association, but to a vast number of lay persons and clergy who, in the confusion of our modern world, are striving to be faithful to their tradition, the future of their religious communities and human kind.

To begin, 1903 witnessed the birth of the Religious Education Association and 1906 its journal, *Religious Education*. Intended to be a movement more than an institution, its mission seemed clear, at least at the beginning: to unify the efforts of all those agencies engaged in religious, moral, and value education; to stimulate and aid all such efforts; to reform the Sunday School; to create new agencies or other means where necessary; to broaden the nation's understanding of religious education; and to generate new thought in this foundational aspect of national life. Intended to be both ecumenical and international, the REA was spearheaded by university and college presidents, seminary deans and professors. A desire for national identity and purpose amid a host of new problems resulting from national expansion and consciousness, urbanization, and industrialization occupied the nation's leaders. Only religion, they believed, could provide the country with necessary foundations. And only a unified, reformed, educational program could provide a satisfactory means for achieving national unity and purpose. Religious education, almost all agreed, was the answer to our nation's greatest need. Thus an elite group of theologically and socially liberal, white, male, Protestant intellectuals took the lead and organized the REA. At that moment they had a clear sense of identity and purpose. They sought others to join them, naively believing that all Roman Catholics, Jews, women, blacks, conservatives, and nonintellectuals from around the world shared their goals and agreed on their methods.

For some seventy-two years *Religious Education* has been the voice of similar folk. Except, however, for the earliest years, when those who made up its membership shared a clear sense of purpose, the association has experienced one identity crisis after another, though today's appears to be the worst. Even the names used to identify its constituency have continually changed, though with the exception of the gradual addition of women, blacks, Roman Catholics, Jews, and Canadians, the membership has remained essentially older liberal intellectuals. While the name of the association and the journal has been constant throughout the years, you will find in the journal the words religious education, religious instruction, Christian (Jewish) education, Christian nurture, Christian instruction, church (synagogue) education, ecumenical education, and catechesis. Though the name religious education has been used most frequently, there has been no complete or consistent agreement on what those words mean or to what they refer. Today there is less concurrence than ever before. While always in search of an identity, today we can not even agree on a name by which to be identified.

It will not be easy to resolve that question, but hopefully these essays will provide a context for doing so. At least, it will help us gain a greater awareness of ourselves and our past understandings.

Since, however, we live in an historical land, it may not appear obvious that this historical quest is relevant, so permit me to retell a story from George MacLeod's book, *Only*

One Way Left. It is a pathetic story of an army boxing tournament in France. Between two bouts they lead round the ring a soldier who has lost his memory. They hoped that someone would recognize him and assist in his cure. None did. In total frustration, the man cried, "Will nobody tell me who I am?" He had lost his identity because he had lost his memory. The story of his life had been eliminated. If only someone could help him recall his history he would know who he was.

"We humans are in history as a fish is in water," wrote H. Richard Niebhur. We are our history and so we need to know what went before us. Most of our present convictions have their roots in our past. Unless we know others' history it is difficult to understand them or their conviction.

John Dewey is reported to have told a seminar at Columbia University, "I have learned to take all my troubles back to Plato." Familiarity with the past is a necessary resource for contemporary life. To be unaware of our roots is to be victim of both the present and the past. We will always know who we ourselves are in the mirror of history.

The more comprehensive the knowledge of our inheritance, the less likely we are to imagine that we have to begin our quest for understanding from scratch, the less likely we are to take one aspect of our tradition over-seriously, the less likely we are to romanticize the present. An understanding of our past functions to stretch our minds, to free us from the ruts of past mistakes and to aid us in transcending the fashion of our generation. Further, it can liberate us from those contemporary myth-makers who, in their desire to influence us, use history for their own purposes.

The founding convention of the Religious Education Association was one of the outstanding events of the twentieth century. Three thousand person from the United States, Canada, and four other countries assembled in Chicago on Tuesday evening, February 10, 1903 under the leadership of Dr. William Rainey Harper, president of the University of Chicago and first president of the REA. Three years later the journal, *Religious Education*, was born. Today it holds the honor of being the oldest, and most prestigious publication of its kind. Within its pages are revealed seventy-two years of history, the history of a loose association of liberal Protestant, Roman Catholic and Jewish educators in search of an identity and a constituency. What follows, therefore, is a collection of essays by various national leaders in the Religious Education Association representing different periods and positions. Regretfully, the picture presented is not as complete as might be desired. There are periods when few Roman Catholic or Jewish educators wrote for the journal. Further, those who did were not always representative of their communities. I therefore must apologize if this book appears to slight the position of Jewish educators. Equally significant is the absence of opinion by that large segment of the American religious population who have never associated with the REA. Hopefully the future will be different from the past, but I have tried to reflect honestly opinions expressed in *Religious Education* rather than give a complete picture of any particular religious body.

Fortunately today the scene has changed. Significant numbers of Jewish, Roman Catholic, and Protestant educators comprise the REA. There are university and seminary faculty, but also national educational leaders and local practitioners. Both women and men, blacks and whites are participants. Though still essentially liberal intellectuals, greater diversity of opinion exists within the association than ever before. Roman Catholics are discussing the differences between religious education, Christian education, and catechesis. Convictions vary on which of these names should be normative. A similar discussion has arisen within Judaism; for example, although Jewish educators have not thought it important to make an issue of names, some emphasize schooling and others the family, ritual, and community life. Most Protestant, Roman Catholic, and Jewish writers in the REA today share a commitment to pluralism. Identity with openness is their common goal. They are concerned with the transmission of their tradition, the perpetuation of faith, the nature of community and religious identity. But they are also seriously committed to an open, ecumenical, society. They are concerned with conserving their own understandings and ways, just as they are committed to reform and change. And thus the continuing struggle for an identity and name can best be understood in terms of these polar needs and commitments. Religious education appears to emphasize openness, catechesis identity, Church education conservation, Christian education change. Where do our Jewish brothers and sisters fit? What name is best? Who are we? Our contemporary quest for an identity and a constituency is the most significant issue facing us. The past can enlighten. However, the issue is greater than agreement on a name. Our crisis of self-understanding and our fuzziness of identity is essentially theological. It is this awareness that makes the decision on a name so difficult.

Ian Knox in his important book, *Above or Within?* (Religious Education Press, 1977) isolates the central ideological issues underlying the religious, Christian (Jewish), church (synagogue) education, catechesis debate. He asks does God *erupt* into human affairs from within the world itself, or does God *erupt* into human affairs from above and outside the world? Knox presents a threefold typology: the "immanentists" to correspond to the liberal movement in early twentieth century American Protestantism and some recent Catholic thought, the "transcendists" who correspond to the orthodox and post-liberal movements in Protestant theology and the more recent kerygmatic approach among Catholics, and the "integrationists" who affirm the paradox created by the other two positions and seek a basis for integration.

The "immanentists" affirm the immanence or this wordly presence of God, the significance of natural experience and the natural growth and development of persons. The "transcendists" affirm the transcendence or supreme otherness of God, the significance of revealed supernatural word of God and the importance of revelations' transmission. The first takes its clue logically from the social sciences and the second from theology.

On the issue of human nature another set of poles exist. There are the "environmentalists" who tend to side with the "transcendentists" on theological issues and the "maturationists" who typically share convictions with the "immanentists". And, of course, there are those who desire to be "integrationists."

While Pato stressed the training of children for moral life and Augustine stressed the importance of early training for later moral development, it was not until the seventeenth century that children came to be recognized as distinct from adults. With the genesis of this acknowledgement came attempts to influence human nature and society through child training. To accomplish this end the desire to understand growth and behavior of children emerged. New questions surfaced: Were children naturally evil or good until corrupted by society; more important, were children naturally anything at all? Were human characteristics inherited or learned? Did human beings actively develop according to some internal order or did persons merely react to their environment as it impinged upon them? Was truth knowable by everyone or was truth communicated through special means to particular persons and groups?

Beginning in the seventeenth century, an "environmentalist" viewpoint dominated. Influenced by Newtonian physics (all actions are caused by prior actions) educators looked for the causes of behavior outside the child. British philosophers, John Locke and David Hume provided a foundation for the thesis that children are nothing but a product of their environment. All knowledge, they asserted, results from experience. An infant is a blank slate on which the environment (experience) makes impressions. Beliefs, character, and moral behavior, therefore, are determined by nurture and instruction. Persons are essentially passive. Thinking, feeling, and willing are best understood in terms of environmental cause and behavioral effect.

A decade after Hume the German philosopher, Kant presented a different point of view. Kant believed that human beings were active, purposive organisms. Influenced by the biological sciences more than the physical sciences, he held the position that all organisms (including humans) were ordered by built-in principles of growth. That is, children were born with all that was necessary to organize and make sense of the world. In the 18th century the French philosopher, Rousseau, described children as active, self-developing beings, not merely passive recipients of environmental influences. Indeed, he asserted that children would seek what is needed from their environment during each step of their natural growth. Believing that children would unfold naturally, if allowed to do so, he asserted that children should be encouraged to make active use of their environment and be permitted to follow their own course of development. At best an environment can nourish or limit the natural growth of processes, for children are driven by an internal tendency to develop fully. The environment simply provides the material necessary for the developing self; it does not determine the thinking, feeling or willing of persons. Nature, not nurture is determinant.

By the close of the eighteenth century these two poles were firmly established. On one side were the environmentists or behaviorists who emphasized the importance of the environment and cultural transmission for the life and thought of persons. On the other side were the maturationists or developmentists, who emphasized human nature and natural development for persons' life and thought. Social scientists and educators have continued to line up on either one side or the other. There have been those who affirm the importance of nurture and cultural transmission for human understanding and those who assert the importance of human nature, genetics, and heredity. Similarly the history of the REA is a history of the continuing debate between these polls and attempts to either mediate a middle road between them or assert their paradoxical interrelationship.

During the earlier years of the REA the maturationist and immanentist positions dominated and religious education was the name. In the late 30s and 40s the environmentist and transcendist positions dominated and Christian education surfaced to importance. Religious education emphasized nature. The task of education was to provide an environment for the natural growth of faith and life. Revelation too was natural, available equally to all. Indeed, God revealed himself through the educational process. Education for religious living was simply good education. Nevertheless, the religious educational programs which emerged from these understandings failed to reach the social goal which their advocated believed would accompany genuine religious living; namely, the elimination of poverty and the establishment of peace; neither did economic/social/racial justice for all result. The attempt to create environments where the natural growth and development of latent personal and religious capacities could evolve was not satisfactory. Indeed, the myopic concern for the development of personality through experience in which the divine essence could unfold naturally created new problems. Religious education's optimism was shaken.

As a result, a theological renaissance within Protestantism emerged which stressed a distinctive heritage and a special (unnatural) revelation. These new convictions gave birth in Protestantism to Christian education. A new emphasis on instruction evolved and Christian education became deliberate, planned, conscious, teaching and learning activities taking place in the church at a definite time and place. God revealed himself in particular ways, to particular folk, at particular times. Knowledge of this revelation was essential to life and it could only be acquired if it was transmitted from one generation to the next. A new emphasis on the content of the tradition took the form of doctrines and dogmas (ideas) to be given and received. But a catechism presenting right answers to the right questions did not seem to result in more faithful communities. Growth in faith did not appear to be achieved through the instructional process. Similarly, Roman Catholics experienced similar polarities, though at different times and in different expressions a kerygmatic approach placed emphasis on the content of the tradition, ignoring, for all practical purposes, present experience. In response, some placed undue emphasis on present experience and neglected the tradition.

Today some Roman Catholics, Protestants, and Jews have, in reaction, returned to the maturationist-immanentist points of view, others defend the environmentist-transcendist positions, and some strive for something half-way between. But neither the cultural transmission-behaviorist nor the maturational-developmentist position seem to be able to provide us with a satisfactory foundation. Neither the immanentist nor the transcendist position seem to be able to provide us with a satisfactory understanding of God or revelation. Could the truth be found in a paradox, namely that both positions, though they appear to negate each other, are true, depending on what question we ask?

In any case, it is important as we search for an identity that we do so by exploring the foundations which undergird these various positions. There is more to the question whether or not we'll answer to the name religious education

Christian (Jewish) education, church (synagogue) education, or catechesis. Behind each of these names, both historically and presently, are theological assumptions about
the nature of human life and revelation. Perhaps that is why
our historic debates over a name have assumed such importance and consumed so much time in the seventy-five
year history of the REA.

Before we turn to that seventy-five years of searching we
need to reflect on our own convictions. What do we believe?
Why? Is the knowledge of ultimate truth possible for all
regardless of their upbringing? Is there within a person at
birth a sense of goodness, truth, and beauty? Are people,
when they are born, creative, filled with potential, ready for
actualization if they are but put into an environment which
encourages their natural growth and development? Are we
essentially good and in need only of a free environment
where we might develop in those ways which are basic to
our nature? Or is it true that we are nothing at birth except
the possibility of becoming what we are influenced to become and all our understandings and ways are dependent
upon the environment in which we live, the experiences we
have, and the truths we are taught. Are truth, goodness and
beauty dependent upon the culture in which we live and the
people with whom we associate? Which is it: a wordly presence of God or supreme otherness? Are we dependent on
forces in our culture or beyond it for all that we know? Are
we free or determined, the producers of our culture or the
products of our culture? Is religion in general of value or is
its value in particular expressions, e.g., Judaism, Christianity, Islam? Is education a helpful category? Is instruction or nurture? Is catechesis or catechetics? Whatever
words we use, they have connotations and meanings — can
we give old words new meanings? All words carry some

meanings. The matter of a name is more than semantics. Each possible name reflects some distinctive variance in our understanding of who we are and what we are to be about. The need for identity is, as always, without a doubt a pressing problem. A decision of a name should not be taken lightly or agreed upon too quickly. Too much is at stake, but perhaps the wisdom and ignorance of the past can save us from errors and inspire us to better solutions. The decision, or course, is pressing; it is also ours. The struggles of our foreparents can provide us with insights necessary for this day and for tomorrow. Read on!

1. Religious Education as a Part of General Education

GEORGE ALBERT COE
Professor, Northwestern University Evanston, Illinois

At the turn of the century a concern for the integration of education and religion was shared by a significant number of well-known, progressive educators and liberal protestant church persons. Convinced that religion and education belong together, they founded the Religious Education Association. George Albert Coe, surely the most important figure in the history of what is best understood as a movement, expressed its earliest understandings. Coe assumed that religion was neither given nor transmitted, but rather a fundamental aspect of personality which needed to unfold naturally. A place, therefore, was to be found for religion within general education, just as education was a proper concern of religion. Typically, this natural and essential unity of education and religion was understood best as liberal, mainline, protestant Christianity. Together, the church, the home, and the public schools shared a common purpose, namely to have "every child grow up Christian and never know themselves as being otherwise," a position first asserted by Horace Bushnell in a quite different context in Christian Nurture (1847). *A new century in American history had opened; a new name—religious education—born, a new movement begun.*

The modern conception of religious education takes the form of an argument. True education, it says, must develop all the normal capacities of the mind; religion is one of these normal capacities; therefore true education includes edu-

Religious Education Association, Proceedings First Convention, 1903, pp. 44-52.

cation in religion. If, for any reason, the state does not impart religious training, then the home and the church must assume the whole task. This task is no mere appendix to general education, but an essential part thereof. It is not a special or professional matter which, like training in the fine arts, may be left to individual taste or ambition. Religious education must be provided for all children, and institutions that provide it for any children are organs of the general educational system.

This view is modern in the sense that a new awakening to it is upon us; it is modern in the sense that the exclusion of religious instruction from the public schools has given it peculiar emphasis and peculiar form; yet, in one form or another, it is as old as civilization. The theory that there can be any education that does not include religion; the theory that looks upon our so-called secular schools as a scheme of general education, leaving religious training as a mere side issue, is so new as to be almost bizarre. If, therefore, any new idea is before us for our judgment, the question should be formulated as follows: What shall we think of the strange notion that men can be truly educated without reference to the development of their religious nature?

It is well, however, to think through the old idea in order to see whether it is, in any full sense, a modern idea also. In the present state of educational philosophy and of religious thought, can we make good the assertion that sound general education must include religion? If so, what shall we think of the education, commonly called general, that leaves religion out? What follows, also, with respect to the present relative isolation of religious education from our school system and our school methods?

The central fact of the modern educational movement is recognition of the child as a determining factor in the whole educational scheme. The child is a living organism, a being that grows from within by assimilation, not from without by accretion. Therefore the laws of the child-mind yield laws for educating the child, laws as to method, and laws as to material. Education is not to press the child into any pre-arranged mold, but to bring out his normal powers in their own natural order.

Religious education has commonly proceeded from the opposite point of view, namely, from a fixed system of religion to which the child is to be shaped. If, then, religion is to find any place in a general scheme of education under modern conditions, some kind of settlement must be effected between these opposing points of view. If we start from the modern philosophy of education, our question is this: Is the human being essentially religious, or only adventitiously so? Does religious nurture develop something already there in the child, or does it merely attach religion to the child, or the child to religion? On the other hand, if we start from the standpoint of religion, our question is: Does not all education aim to fit the child for some goal or destiny; and, if so, how does religious education differ from any other except through its definition of the goal?

That the child has a religious nature can be asserted with a degree of scientific positiveness that was never possible before the present day. First, every theory that makes religion a mere by-product of history has been almost universally abandoned. Religion has come up out of the mind of man as a natural response to universal experience. There is debate as to the content, the utility, and the significance of this response, but none as to its naturalness. The psychology of the day finds that religion is as deeply rooted in human nature as any of the higher instincts or impulses that distinguish man from lower orders of life.

The idea that religion belongs to man as such has been

reinforced in recent years by accumulating evidence that the development of the human individual runs parallel, in a general way, to the evolution of man. The individual is said to recapitulate the history of his race. It follows that the mighty power and pervasiveness of religion in general history are to be looked for in miniature in child-life.

Observation confirms this presumption. The kindergarten, the highest outward expression of our knowledge of child-nature, is squarely built upon the religiousness of the child. Fröbel's whole plan of education revolved around the thought that God is a present reality within us and within nature about us, and that the end of education is to make us conscious of his presence. This was a philosophical idea, of course, but to Fröbel's eye, and according to the experience of kindergartners, the child freely, joyously responds to it.

The same observation has been made within the home circle. What is that wondrous reverence and sense of dependence with which little children look up to their parents, sometimes actually believing that the father is God, but the first stage of the feeling of absolute dependence which Schleiermacher declared to be the essence of religion? The appetite of children for fairytales, wonderstories, and heroic legends reveals the very same impulse that once peopled the woodlands, the mountains, and the sea with supernatural beings, heard in the thunder the voice of the stormgod, beheld in the rising sun the very face of divinity, and traced our human pedigree back to demigods.

The evidence becomes piercingly luminous in the period of adolescence, when childhood culminates and pauses before settling into the fixed forms of manhood. Adolescence reveals in the blossom the seeds that were germinating through infancy and childhood. What distinctly human quality—one not shared with the brutes—is more characteristic of adolescence than susceptibility to the ideal longings that culminate in religion? Interfused with the hero worship, the romanticism, the truth and beauty seeking, the self-consciousness of youth, is a reaching out after something more satisfying than all that our eyes see and our hands handle.

The philosophy of religion goes one step farther, and declares that analysis of human consciousness in its three phases—the true, the good, and the beautiful—reveals the idea of God as implicit in the whole of our conscious life.

Here religious education takes its stand. It declares, with all the authority of the history of the race, with all the authority of sound observation and analysis, that religion is an essential factor of the human personality, and that, therefore, a place must be found for religious education within general education.

We reach this conclusion from the pedagogical point of view. But there is also a religious point of view. The pedagogue says: "Bring out what is already in the child." Religion says: "Bring the child into obedience to the will of God." Apparently education is guided by what the child already is, whereas religion prescribes what he must become. Can we unite these two points of view?

The case is not different for religious education from what it is for education universally. The reason why schools exist at all is threefold: because children cannot remain children; because what happens to them during childhood affects their maturity for good or ill; and because adults know which is the better life and can help children attain it. What adults know of the good life does and must preside over all education whatsoever. The material put before the child is always selected, and it should be adapted not only to the child's spontaneous interests, but also to producing the kind of man we wish him to be.

At this point the educational reform has been somewhat halting. Is the end of education knowledge, or culture, or power? Is it intellectual or ethical? Is it individual or social? Just at present there is a flood-tide of sentiment that asserts that the end is neither knowledge, nor culture, nor power as such, nor anything else that is merely individual, but rather social adjustment and efficiency. This is a favorable moment for religion to lift up her voice and proclaim that within her hand is the final meaning of life, and that to her belongs, not only a place, but the supreme place, in determining the end of education.

The point of view of the-child-that-is and the point of view of the-man-he-should-become are reconciled through the insight that the later self is preformed in the earlier. It is possible to make education ethical because the child's nature is ethical; social because it is social. The ethical authority to which the child is taught to bow is already within the child himself. It is the same with religious education; it is the same with specifically Christian education. God has made us in his own image and likeness; he has formed us for himself, and there is a sense in which, as one of the Fathers said, the soul is naturally Christian.

At this point religious thought transfigures the whole idea of education. The chief factor in the process is no longer the text-book; it is no longer the teacher; it is God who preforms the child for himself, plants within him the religious impulse, and grants to parents and teachers the privilege of cooperating to bring the child to a divine destiny. The time is not far behind us when men failed to connect the thought of childhood or thought of education with the thought of God. They put education and religion in sharp antithesis, making one a human process, the other divine. Even today there is distrust of religious education lest it shall leave conversion and religious experience out of the account. But in reality infancy, childhood, and adolescence are themselves a divinely appointed school of personal religion, a school in which the divine Spirit is prime mover and chief factor. Religion does not flow from the teacher to the child; it is not given, or communicated, or impressed, merely from without; it is a vital impulse, and its source is the source of all light and life. In the normal unfolding of a child's soul we behold the work of the Logos who gives himself to every man coming into the world. When the Logos comes to a child, he comes to his own, and it is in the profoundest sense natural that the child should increasingly receive him as the powers of the personality enlarge.

The thought of God works a further transformation in our thoughts of education. For God's will compasses all the ends, his presence suffuses all the means, and his power works in all the processes of it. Accordingly, religious education is not a part of general education, it *is* general education. It is the whole of which our so-called secular education is only a part or a phase. Religious education alone takes account of the whole personality, of all its powers, all its duties, all its possibilities, and of the ultimate reality of the environment. The special hours, places, and material employed in religious training do not stand for any mere department; they represent the inner meaning of education and of life in their totality.

Our practical problem, therefore, is greater than that of organizing a good Sunday school and promoting religion in the home. The spirit of religion must be infused into the whole educational organism. Religion has not separated itself from general education, but public education has separated itself from the vine of which it is a branch. Yet not wholly, for there are leaders of public instruction who see that the end of education is one with the end of life, and that, though religious instruction be excluded from the schools, the spirit of religion should pervade the whole system. The time has not come, it is not very near, when the public school can resume the work of specific religious instruction. We must first learn more of Christian union. But we are needlessly squeamish regarding the limits of the moral and spiritual functions of our school system. The system exists as an expression of the ideals of our civilization. In the most democratic state there is no reason why ideals that are common to the people should not be expressed in the people's schools, even though some citizens should disapprove. We shall never secure an ideal school system by consulting the citizen who has the fewest ideals. Why not assume that some principles of the spiritual life are already settled, and that these principles are to control our schools? Why should not moral training be made to approach nearer and nearer to the fully unified ideal that is found in our religion?

On the other hand, it behooves the home and the church, realizing that they are members of the general educational organism, to relate their work more closely to that of the public school, the high school, and the college. Religious education is not peculiar in method, but only in its aim and in the material as determined by the aim. All the results of modern progress in educational philosophy, methods, and organization belong to the home and the church as much as to the state schools.

Existing organs and methods of religious training—the Sunday school, the young people's society, the junior and intermediate societies, the Young Men's Christian Associations, the catechism, the lesson systems and lesson helps—arose, for the most part, in response to special needs, and were adopted with no clear consciousness of their possible place in a general scheme of education. This is not a matter of reproach at all. On the contrary, these things have all pursued the normal course of development, which consists first of all in doing the thing that is immediately needed, the theory being left for later working out. But when the theory has been worked out, then the organ that arose in an incidental way may attain to higher usefulness through understanding of its nature, laws, and relations.

This self-conscious, fully reflective step must now be taken. There is a great body of pedagogical philosophy that must be assimilated. There are principles of teaching that must be observed. There is knowledge of the child mind that must be utilized. There are riches of knowledge in many directions that are waiting to be consecrated to Christ in the service of children and young people.

We cannot longer neglect these things and remain guiltless. The light has dawned, and we must love light rather than darkness. Both the home and the church must rise to their privilege of being parts of the general organism of education. They must realize that they are under as much obligation as the principal or the teachers in a public school to study the child, to master the material and methods of education, and to acquire skill in the educational process. Vastly more time and vastly more money must be devoted to this service, and we must never regard either home or church as normally successful until it is no longer the exception but the rule for children to "grow up Christians, and never to know themselves as being otherwise."

2. Bringing All The Moral and Religious Forces Into Effective Educational Unity

WASHINGTON GLADDEN
Pastor of the First Congregational Church
Columbus, Ohio

During the first quarter of the century the context of religious education was broadly conceived. The Religious Education Association divided its educational concerns into a variety of departments: universities and colleges, theological seminaries, churches and pastors, Sunday schools, fraternal and social organizations, teacher training, young people's societies, libraries, foreign missions, arts and music, Christian associations, summer assemblies, correspondence institutions and the press. Sharing common understandings of religion and education, university presidents (e.g., William Rainey Harper of Chicago), college professors (e.g., John Dewey of Columbia Teacher's College), lay persons (e.g., Jane Addams of Hull House), and pastors (e.g., Washington Gladden) united together to frame the future of a movement which aimed to influence American life and history. Gladden, like the others, identified religion with character and morality; an effective educational unity of the religious and moral forces of the country. While still consistent with earlier understandings, religious education began to take on specific content and direction, consistent with liberal theology's concern for social justice and progressive education's commitment to moral and character education.

Religious Education Association: Education and National Character (Fifth Convention) 1908, pp. 33-42.

The religious forces of the community — what are they?

The churches, of course, with their affiliated agencies — the Sunday schools, the Young Men's and the Young Women's Christian Associations, the King's Sons and Daughters, the Salvation Army and the Volunteers, and a part of the social settlement. The dintinctively religious colleges and schools would also come into this category.

The Christian home, of course, is a religious force — the first and the mightiest of religious forces. And I am inclined to believe that many homes which give but little outward sign of being Christian homes would be unfairly treated if we denied to them any religious character. Very feeble and defective is the religious influence in many of them, but from few of them is it altogether absent. Even the roughest and most degraded people, when they stand in the presence of the sacred mystery of parenthood; when they look into the eyes of those round about whom heaven lies, and press to their bosoms such as are of the Kingdom of Heaven, have some revelations made to them, and there are few among them who are not sometimes in the praying mood. These altars are often terribly desecrated, but I am disposed to decline discrimination, and to reckon the homes of the people among the religious agencies.

What are the moral forces? Can we make any list or classification of them? What shall we say of the schools? Are they moral agencies? Originally they were regarded as religious agencies. The first public schools in America were intended to teach the children the elements of religion. The whole of the public instruction was for a long time affected with a deeply religious character. That interest is now pretty thoroughly eliminated from public-school instruction; and we have learned, perhaps too well, to regard the public school as having aims which are chiefly intellectual.

But I am sure that this estimate is under correction, and that most educators now clearly see that character is the product which our schools must be expected to produce. The one fact which we must insist upon in all our administration is that our schools shall be primarily and essentially moral agencies; that, no matter what their intellectual achievements may be, they shall be deemed to have wholly failed of their highest function if they do not give us good men and women.

The press — is that a moral agency? In its worst estate it is far from that, in its best estate there are few moral agencies more efficient. In the days when newspapers were owned and edited by individuals they were often powerful instruments of righteousness; even in these days they have not all lost the prophetic function. One might name not a few daily and weekly newspapers, and a good number of monthly magazines whose services to good morals are of the highest value.

We have also a variety of organizations in most of our communities whose objects are avowedly moral, such as temperance organizations, societies for the suppression of vice, rescue homes for women, and the like; and those settlements which are not professedly religious in their aims are all primarily moral agencies, since the interests of character are paramount in all their work, and the relief of suffering and the enlightenment of ignorance are held subservient to the building up of manhood and womanhood. The same thing might be said about the charity organization societies; for the modern charity is distinguished by the emphasis which it places on the invigoration of the character of those to whom it ministers.

What shall we say of the institution which includes them all — the civil government — the political organization of the state or the city? If we will be thorough in our thinking we must say that the state is first of all a religious, a divine institution, since it springs out of an impulse divinely implanted in the human soul. And if we admit that its function is to establish justice, we can hardly hesitate to say with Hegel that it is a moral organization, for justice is the primary element of morality. That is moral conduct by which a man realizes himself, completes his manhood; and the rights which the state maintains and protects are simply the opportunities of self-realization. Civil government, when rightly conceived, is therefore the one supreme and crowning expression of morality which the world contains, and we must never suffer this conception of it to be blurred or lowered on behalf of any mere economic or materialistic interpretation.

Our problem is to bring these religious and moral forces into effective educational unity. The churches of all creeds, with their progeny of religious institutions; the homes, the schools, the colleges, the newspapers and magazines, the various organizations for human betterment, the governments of the nation and the state and the city which include them all — how can we get them all to cooperate for the purpose of education? That seems, indeed, a very large contract. Yet when we stop to reflect upon the essential functions of all these agencies, the question does not, after all, seem so visionary. For the truth is that the proper work of all these religious and moral institutions and organizations is largely the work of education. That, at first blush, may not be so evident; but a little reflection will make it clear.

The periodical press, in all its types and varieties, deems itself charged with an educational function. Even those philanthropic and reformatory agencies of which we have spoken do their best work along educational lines. The temperance societies succeed only by enlightening the public mind with respect to the physiological and economic and moral effects of strong drink, and of the drink traffic. The settlements are not only frankly and broadly educational in their institutional work, with clubs and classes and lectures, but the entire conception of their function is that of teaching, by precept and example, a better manner of life. The home, to the children growing up in it, is ideally a school of method. The best home does far more for the education of its inmates than all other institutions put together. The best home furnishes to the children protection, shelter, sustenance; but, after all, its greatest service to them is in teaching and the training which are properly included in the category of education. Watch the intercourse of a wide-awake child with a thoughtful mother for a day, and see how large a proportion of all would be reckoned as contributions to the child's education.

The church is also, primarily, an educational institution. We are sometimes inclined to emphasize rather its rescue work, and that, of course, must never be lost sight of. The church is in the world to save souls, we say, and that is true; only we must remember that souls are just people — men, women and children. Our business is to save them; but in this we are the followers of Jesus, and the title by which Jesus was best known as teacher. His followers were his disciples — learners; and the word in which he submerged his message as "repent," which means "change your mind," get a new idea of what life means. That was his way of saving men. He put a new idea of the meaning of life into their minds, and got them to choose it. That is the greatest work that any teacher ever does for a pupil.

This, surely, is the main business of the church. It has not always remembered its commission; it has often put the emphasis elsewhere; but the one thing that the world wants of the church today is to come right back to first principles, and take up the work where Jesus left it off, and teach men the way of life, just he taught it, in the sermon on the mount. If we could only get men to accept the teaching of Jesus, and live by it, all our troubles, national and international, would soon be at an end. I hope that we are beginning to see that this is the main business of the church, and when we do see it, the educational function of the church will soon take the rank which Jesus gave it.

Is this other great institution of civil government, in any sense, an educational institution? It would seem that it must be; for in this country at least it has arrogated to itself the supreme educational prerogative, and holds itself responsible for the education of all the children and the youth. Of course, there are other functions of the state besides those which are distinctly educational; but the fact that education is an integral and prominent part of its high prerogative can hardly be questioned. And this interest appears not only in its assumption of the care of public education, but also in all the administration of public affairs. An enlightened government is always educating the people; it is teaching them the laws of health; it is suggesting to them methods of thrift; it is refining their tastes, by producing for them parks and pleasure grounds, free libraries and galleries; it is leading them to great cooperations in the provision for their needs. Take the government of a city such as Glasgow or Berlin; how much is done outside of the schools, for the education of the people?

In truth we may say that the greatest rulers that the world has known were distinguished by their work for the education of the people. Moses, Lycurgus, Confucius, Marcus

Aurelius, Alfred the Great, Charlemagne, Peter of Russia
— were not these preeminently teachers of men?

In a very important sense it is true that the main work of
the great political leader in a democracy is the work of
education. To get right ideas into the minds of the people;
to teach them to see things as they are and to deal with them
intelligently, is the best part of his high calling.

How large and deep was the concern of Washington as
expressed in all his state papers, and notably in his farewell
address, that the people should rightly value the liberties
which they had won, and sacredly keep the compact of their
unity. No man has ever more clearly discerned the truth
that the life of the nation is in its ruling ideas; that as a
nation thinketh in its heart, so is it.

What did this nation most need when the great struggle
of the Civil War drew on? It needed to be taught what to
think about slavery and freedom; about the meaning and
genius of our government; about the compacts of the
Constitution; about complications and perils which the nation was then confronting. It had many teachers, but wisest,
clearest, most convincing of them all was Abraham Lincoln.
It was his great gift of exposition which came out so strongly
in his debate with Douglas and in his Cooper Institute
speech that drew the people to him; and through all the
days of the war the greatest service that he rendered to the
nation was in the illumination of the minds of the nation, in
his inaugurals, letters, speeches. He made it all plain to us.
He helped us to see things as they were. That is why we
loved and trusted him. That is why the people were held
together for the great struggle.

What does this nation most need in the critical times
through which it is now passing? It needs education in the
principles of social justice. It needs to be taught how these

principles apply to our complex industrial and commercial life. A great many things have been going on among us, the nature of which the people at large do not clearly comprehend. A great many subtle and veiled injustices have been weaving themselves into our business life, and the cunning and the strong have been able to enrich themselves at the expense of the rest of us. There is need that all this should be brought into the light and made plain to the comprehension of the common people. We all believe in justice, in fair play, in the square deal; but we need to be taught how these principles apply to the great and complicated transactions of modern industrial life. I think that it was the supreme obligation of the man at the head of the nation in this hour to make the people understand these things. That obligation he has faithfully discharged. No more effective teaching has ever been done in this country. The people do understand these things today, thanks to Theodore Roosevelt. And they are not likely to forget the man who has led them into the light and shown them the path of national safety and honor.

If, then, all these religious and moral agencies and forces of society — the home, the church, the school, the state, and all the rest — are in their very nature educational forces, it ought not to be impossible to bring them into effective educational unity. But how?

Could we agree upon our ideals? It seems to me that there is already some approximation to an agreement upon ideals. Could we not unite in saying that the chief business of education in all these fields is to assist men to realize themselves, to complete their manhood? Is not this what the church means by saving men? Can the home set before itself any higher destiny for the children growing up in it? Might not the school recognize this as the statement of its aim? And how better could the state define its highest duty to its citizens? Could we not all set this before us as the thing to be believed in and striven for—that every man shall have a chance to be a man — to become what God meant him to be? Could we not agree that all our teaching and training shall keep that end steadily in view?

This would mean, of course, that we should pledge ourselves to see that the obstacles should be cleared from every man's path and the gates of opportunity set open before him. It would mean that the strong should not be permitted to prey upon the weak, or use them for their own aggrandizement.

It does not seem to me to be asking too much when we ask the moral and religious forces of the community to come to a fair understanding about this; but when they have done it they will have taken a long step toward unity.

But they will need to go further. For no man, alone, can complete his manhood. That great achievement requires the cooperation of a great many people. It is by the constant interplay of thought and feeling, of teaching and learning, of giving and receiving, of leading and being led, of yielding and resisting, of loving and hating, that character is wrought out and manhood is perfected. The elements of belief, of impulse, of mental habit, of moral tendency, of habitual judgment, which form what we call the character of every one of us, are largely the contribution to our lives of other lives. No man liveth to himself. No man builds his own manhood out of materials furnished by himself. A self-made man is a conception as unscientific as perpetual motion.

What, now, should be the law of this intellectual and spiritual commerce on which the entire product of character depends. I shall not be venturing upon any novelty if I say that it ought to be the law of friendship; that all our exchanges and communications one with another should proceed upon the basis of friendship; that the right relation of human beings is that in which each finds his joy in giving as much as he can to all with whom he has to do, and in sharing his best with all to whom he can be of any service.

This is Christ's law of life, and I believe that it is the true law — the law by which both the individual and society are brought to perfection.

There is one more path to unity, the path which leads into the presence of him who is the archetype of all our ideals, and the Being in whom our moral obligation and our religious affections are united. Religion and morality are not twain but one. The religion which is not moral is superstition, and the morality which is not religious is dead, being alone. If we will agree upon this, and will steadily and persistently stand for it, we will soon find ourselves walking in the straight path that leads to righteousness and unity. There is no morality worth the name which is not rooted and grounded in the law of him whom we call God, and worship. All these moral and religious forces have their source in God, and are vital and efficient only as they come into relation to him.

When we are united to him we can not be divided from each other. There may be diversity of laws, but there can be no antagonism. If these religious and moral forces are really religious and moral, they will be sure to come into harmony. Is it too much to hope that all these good people who are seeking to promote the interests of morality and religion may begin soon to work toward that end? The one way to that end is to fill the world with a Christlike friendship. The church of the living God should understand what has been committed to her. The three agencies that make for righteousness in our land today are the church, the state, and the home. Upon each of these today a deadly attack is made by forces that seek to undermine them.

None of them can win this battle alone; they must stand together and fight for their lives. The worth and sacredness of the individual, the royal law of brotherhood, the divineness of humanity are all-essential elements in the higher moral and spiritual life of the nation.

3. The Meaning of Religious Education

FREDERICK TRACY
Professor in the University of Toronto

*From its genesis, the religious education movement aimed
to be ecumenical and international. While neither were
realized during its first fifty years, Frederick Tracy, a Cana-
dian, is a rare representative of this desire. Like Coe, Tracy
linked religion and education. The end shared by both he
assumed to be the fullness and perfection of human character,
a potential given to all at birth. Each person is naturally
religious, and religion (properly understood) is to be the
supreme concern of all human beings. The salvation of the
soul is a vital process taking place naturally, through experience, within the spirit of every human being. Education's
essential role, therefore, is to liberate persons from everything
which hinders this human potential from developing and
unfolding. As such, religious education is best understood as a
complex process uniting instruction, training, and nurture to
aid in a person's becoming. Solidly established in the educational philosophy of Rousseau and Dewey, and sympathetic to
both Protestant liberal theology and "modern psychology,"
Tracy defends his contention that religious education is a
public concern shared equally and similarly by school, church,
home, and community. It appeared as if a discipline, a field of
practice, a body of practitioners had begun to emerge.*

In the consideration of this topic we have to deal with two
of the greatest words in human speech, and with two of the
greatest conceptions in human thought. The one is religion

Religious Education, XVII (February 1922) pp. 3-8.

and the other is education. If both terms are properly understood it is hardly an exaggeration to say that within the compass of their meaning you may find the things that constitute man's supreme vocation, the central purpose of his being. So far as we can make out, man is the only mundane creature capable of either religion or education; and the records which he has left behind him in every age of the world furnish abundant evidence not only that he is capable of both, but that they play a very large part in his life and absorb a very large share of his attention. It is moreover a matter of history that religion and education are regarded by most men as having a very close connection with each other. In spite of the fact that some educated persons are not religious and some religious persons are not educated, and do not wish to be, it remains true that the great teachers, in every age of the world, have been for the most part devout and godly men, and that the outstanding prophets of religious faith have valued learning above rubies, and have sought for it as one seeks for hid treasure. The conviction is widespread that religion and education are not enemies, but staunch allies.

But we must go deeper than that; for the connection between these two things is widely conceived to be more than a mere alliance or affiliation. It is believed to be so close and vital that you may bring them together within the compass of a single notion. In the phrasing of my topic, for example, the one is predicated on the other, and the two terms are blended in a single term, "religious education," whose meaning I am expected to discuss. The assumption clearly is that religion and education belong together, and that there is a real sense in which the term "religious education" may be legitimately employed.

Now it seems to me that in order to accomplish the task

that is before us we must determine for ourselves what we mean by "religion" and what we mean by "education." You are well aware that both these have been the subjects of ceaseless discussion and investigation during many centuries, that men's notions about them have been repeatedly reshaped and restated, and that those whose opinions carry most weight are now fairly unanimous on at least one or two points, which are of fundamental importance.

Perhaps the most significant feature of our progress in these matters might be described by saying that in our judgments of value the emphasis has gradually shifted until now it bears most heavily upon those things that belong to the spirit and the inner life of man. Personality and character are looked upon as having inherent and intrinsic value; all other things as having derivative and instrumental value. The ultimate standard of worth is an ideal of personal worth, and all other values are dependent upon and tributary to the values that lie wrapped up in personality. As a direct result of this, in the field of education we have long since come to see that the curriculum should be made for the pupil and not the pupil for the curriculum, and that courses of study should be selected and prescribed primarily and principally with a view to the making of character and their perfecting of human personality. Having achieved this much in the way of progress, we awake to the fact that we have simply been moving over to the standpoint of Jesus, whose character is the embodiment of this ideal, whose life is the supreme example of it, whose teaching contains the irrefutable logic of it, and whose death on the cross was the price that had to be paid for its worldwide realization.

The most important result of this shifting of the emphasis is that the whole matter is conceived less mechani-

cally and more vitally than in the days of yore. Education on
the one hand, and salvation on the other, are now thought
of, not so much as formal transactions, like buying goods
over a counter, but rather as vital processes taking place
within the spirit of a man; processes which are best described by saying, not that he obtains something worth
while, but that he becomes something worth while. The
metaphors employed to describe the essence of the matter
have undergone a change that is highly significant. The
process of education was commonly thought of in former
days as the process of obtaining a lot of useful knowledge.
This knowledge came from without, and the pupil got
possession of it — or as much of it as he could — and stored
it away in his mind against the day when he could turn it to
good account.

Religion was thought of in a similar fashion. The great
thing was to get "salvation." Salvation was regarded as
something which a man might obtain, if he were prepared
to fulfill the conditions or pay the price. Or, if salvation was
free, it was because someone else had fulfilled the conditions or paid the price on his behalf.

There were other metaphors, of course, under which the
essential nature of religion and education were expressed,
and other ways of setting forth the peculiar advantages of
religion and of education respectively. Men have not hesi-
tated to urge the claims of education on the ground of the
relief from toil and poverty which it is supposed to bring;
and men have not scrupled to urge the claims of religion as
the most reliable means of escape from impending disaster,
and the surest way of securing personal safety and happi-
ness, either here or hereafter. Under such metaphors as the
lifeboat, the lifeline, the court of justice, the canceled debt,
and the ransomed slave, men have done their best to ex-

press the meaning of this great word "salvation," and have only partially succeeded, even as you and I shall only partially succeed.

For I am by no means claiming that these ways of speaking are false. I am only claiming that they are inadequate. The world moves forward. New occasions teach new duties. The new wine bursts the old bottles. The vocabulary of one age is not competent to utter the thoughts of another age. There is valuable truth in every one of these old formulae, but none of them contains the whole truth. And if exclusive attention is given to any of them by itself, it is apt to become misleading and mischievous. There is no doubt that the metaphors of the cabinet, the lifeboat, and the court of justice, have been overworked, to the detriment of our educational and religious enterprises. As we learn, slowly and painfully, the lesson that personal character is the greatest thing in the world, and that there would be no profit to a man if he should gain the whole world and fail to find himself, the defects to which I have referred are being gradually remedied, so that the controlling purpose in modern education has come to be the emancipation of the individual from everything that would hinder him from entering upon the heritage that lies potential within the depths of his own being and becoming all that his Creator intended him to be. In like manner it may be said that the controlling purpose in present-day evangelism is that the soul shall be delivered, not so much from impending calamity from without as from the canker that would eat away its life from within; that the soul-tissue shall be made clean and pure and strong; that holiness (which is just wholeness, or soul-health) shall be attained; that the divine life, as we see it in Jesus, shall flow freely through the veins of our humanity, and that human life and character shall realize their divine possibilities. "Soul-saving," says a distinguished Oxford scholar, "is really soul-making," and if we catch the significance of that remark it will give us a very broad hint as to the meaning of religious education.

But let us be a little more explicit. "The fullness and perfection of personal character" is a splendid phrase, but as it stands it suffers from vagueness. Can we, by any added word, make it more definite? What is meant by personality?

That question, of course, is a very profound and difficult one, but for the present it will be sufficient to point out that we are not dealing with some mysterious entity, lying outside of the concrete activities of the soul's life, but with the living principle that operates and functions through those activities — through thought and feeling and will; a principle, indeed, that has its very being and life in and through those activities and nowhere else. Not in feeling alone, nor in thinking alone, nor in will alone, but in all of them together. For modern psychology has discovered the complete interrelation and interdependence of these forms of the mind's energy, within the unity of the personal life. And so the "fullness and perfection of personal character" means the complete and healthy development of the powers of thought, of feeling, and of will, in the closest relation with one another; and hence it follows that education (which aims at the realization of that healthy development) is not merely instruction, nor merely training, nor merely nurture; but all of these, woven together in the unity of a single though highly complex process.

We may speak in the same way of the religious life. I am aware, of course, that this subject has its mystic or transcendental side, where there is endless room for abstract speculation. But it has also its concrete and empirical side; that is to say, religion shows itself in the thinking, the feeling, and the conduct, of actual persons living their actual lives in the world. For religion is neither something outside of these, an alien plus, nor does it realize itself in any one of them apart from the others. Religion is not merely a matter of the intellect, though intellect is essential to it, and no religion is possible except to rational beings. Religion is not merely a matter of will, much less of mere habitual behavior, and yet behavior is essential to it, and the main effort of true evangelism is to persuade and enlist the will. Religion is not "morality touched with emotion," though morality constitutes perhaps four-fifths of its actual content, and it arouses the deepest emotions of which we are capable. A man's religion is found in the quality of his thinking, feeling, and behavior, and in the way in which these are organized about a common center and directed towards a true ideal. "Let thought and feeling and will be exercised in the highest way about the highest objects, and you have religion. Religion is neither apart from life nor a part of life, but life, at its highest and best."

From this point of view, religious education means the culture and training of the intellect, the emotions, and the will, so that they shall function in the highest way about the highest objects and in the most wholesome harmony, so that the pupil shall know the true, appreciate the beautiful, and will the good; so that he shall be at one with the Divine, and, what is the same thing, at one with his own ideal self, rejecting and repudiating his worse and lower self, and bringing into being that higher unity and reconcilement in which all life and love, all purpose and endeavor, all things within and without, are "bound with golden chains about the feet of God."

There is still another point, of very great importance. When I speak of "the fullness and perfection of personal character," I have in mind an ideal, not yet realized, but in process of realization. And this serves to remind us that in religion and education alike we have to do with capacities that are unfolding, with processes of growth, with something that has not yet attained, neither is already perfect, but which is capable of advancing towards perfection, and whose very life consists in such advance. Herein lies the challenge and the charm of all educational work. The soul of a child is not created mature, but immature. It is not a finished product, like a cabinet as it leaves the factory, but a vital principle that has before it the glorious vocation of realizing itself and entering into the possession of that inheritance which lies within its own being. The soul's task is to become more and more completely the master of its own powers, and to make continually higher attainments in thinking what is true, in appreciating what is beautiful, and in loving and willing what is good. The metaphor of the cabinet with its pigeon-holes gives place to the metaphor of the tree planted by the rivers of water, whose development is not by additions from without but by continuous unfoldings from within. And the task of all education, whether called religious or not, is to foster and facilitate that development by every possible means. And all education that contributes to this end is in the broad sense religious education.

Several important deductions follow. For example, it follows that salvation, though from one point of view a transaction that may take place at a definite moment of time (a man goes into a meeting "lost" and comes out "saved") is nevertheless from another point of view the business of a lifetime. In one sense it is completed in a moment; in another sense it is forever incomplete, but always approaching completion. Soul-saving is really soul-making. I know that crises may occur; that there may be moments of great and weighty decision. Such moments mark the focus points of spiritual adjustment. And yet if salvation is the building of life and character and the adjustment of thought and feeling and conduct about a divine center, then this adjustment may and should be going on continually. And while in some lives the initial adjustment is no doubt sudden and revolutionary, in other lives, that are spent in an atmosphere charged with godliness, the adjustment is continual and progressive. And the latter type of Christian experience is usually more satisfactory on the whole than the former. Indeed we may go further and say that even in the case where there is a marked and sudden conversion, there must also be continuous and progressive adjustment to the Divine center and ideal. Otherwise the focus point of religious experience loses its value, and the last state of that convert is likely to be worse than the first.

Again, it follows that salvation is not so much a prize to be awarded at the end of a long, arduous struggle, as a reward that lies in the struggle itself. This principle holds everywhere. The real reward of all genuine labor lies in the joy of producing; the wages are merely a token of the value which the community places on the product. The real student does not have to wait for his reward until the results of the examinations are published, or until he kneels before the Chancellor to receive his degree. He begins to reap his reward in the very first hour of diligent study. The degree is merely the official mark by which the University records its esimate of his attainments, an estimate which may sometimes be erroneous. "The rank is but the guinea's stamp." And so it is, most emphatically, in the religious life. Its full rewards, no doubt, will occupy the measureless experiences of eternity, but those rewards begin to be reaped in the very first occupation of the soul of a little child with the things that are true and lovely and of good report.

This leads easily and logically to my last remark, namely, that just as there is an education appropriate to each period of the pupil's life, so there is a religious experience appropriate to each period of his life. No small part of the task of the teacher consists in finding out how to adjust the curriculum and the method of teaching to each stage of the pupil's progress, so that he shall achieve and attain to the very best that he is capable of within that stage, and at the same time become most perfectly fitted to enter on the next. Each period is looked upon not only as a preparation for the next, but also as having its own value in itself. So it is also in the matter of religious experience. Corresponding to each period in the life of the individual there are ideas, groups of concepts, feelings, and forms of activity, appropriate to that period, constituting its perfection and value, and at the same time the best preparation for the period that follows. Professor Coe has written a book on *The Religion of a Mature Mind*. He would cordially endorse me in saying that there is also a religion of the immature mind. And the latter is just as real and just as valuable as the former. The child at any given age can be genuinely religious, within the range of ideas, feelings and activities, that are psychologically possible at that age. To ask less of him than this is to rob him of his spiritual birthright. To ask more of him— to try to force on him the religious concepts and the religious phraseology that belong to maturity; to expect him to have the experiences proper to adult life and to repeat the formulae in which those experiences are expressed— is to school him in religious pedantry and cant, and to train him for membership in that class, already much too large, who remain all their lives satisfied to put words in the place of ideas, and shibboleths in the place of realities.

If we have been on firm ground thus far, the meaning and the value of religious education should now be fairly clear. Religion, properly understood, is man's supreme concern. It is not a part of life, much less an adjunct of life; it is life itself, in its wholeness and perfection. But the wholeness and perfection of life is a divine ideal, which continually rebukes and challenges the actual life, and lures it on to become more and other than it is at any given moment. This progress upward takes place always in accordance with the laws of human growth. "First the blade, etc." The whole affair is both natural and supernatural at the same time. Some of us may be prone to forget the former, others to overlook the latter. To keep in touch with both; to have ever before us the divine ideal on the one hand, and the actual human life of thought and feeling and conduct on the other; and to know how to guide the one towards the other; this is the equipment we need for the work of religious education, which now turns out to be nothing else than the fine art of helping the pupil to be the very best that he is capable of being, and to exercise to the full the prerogatives that are his, at every stage of his development. And the reward is ours, not merely at the end, but at the beginning, and at every step of the way.

4. Perspectives on Religious Education

While the membership of the REA may have had a growing sense of identity, twenty years after the birth of the Religious Education Association the question was still being asked, what makes education religious: Is religious education, education which is religious, education in religion, or both? Three of the earliest and best known professors of religious education (a new academic title within theological schools) score the numerous prevailing misunderstandings and then restate the purpose of religious education, established at the 1905 Boston Convention of the Religious Education Association (almost two decades earlier), namely, "to inspire the educational forces of our country with the religious ideal: to inspire the religious forces of our country with the educational ideal: and to keep before the public mind the ideal of religious education in the sense of its need and value."

What Makes Education Religious?

ARTHUR BENNET

Professor, Boston University School of Religious Education

The educative process involves three fundamental considerations: (1) What is the nature of the mind? Is it passive or active; recipient or agent; a mechanism or a motivation; an it or a personality? (2) What is the end of education? Is it the liberation of internal potentialities, or the appropriation of external stimuli; the realization of what we want to do, or the performance of what should be done? Is it a

Religious Education XVIII, (April 1923), pp. 88-95.

becoming, a being or a doing? (3) The nature of the mind and the end of education determine the means. This educational means must take cognizance of the child's native equipment as the subjective means, and educational values, curricula, methods, discipline, and the teacher as the objective elements.

Given the answers to these philosophical presuppositions of education, with their implications reasonably well established in secular school science and practice — when is education religious?

Religion relates life to God. Hence, education is religious when its conceptions, aims, and methods are conceived, motivated, and directed in terms of religious idealism. Varying ideas of God, man, and duty give varying ideas of the function of education. The conception of God as our Father places personality as man's nature with functions of intellection, affection, and volition as the nature of our inheritance from the Supreme Personality. Born of God, "in him we live and move and have our being."

Religious consciousness functions first as feeling, second, as imagination, third, as insight. Development takes place in this order. If development stops with feeling, mysticism results. If arrested with imagination, forms of idolatry ensue. If growth and development continue up through these stages into the stage of conceptual thinking, it gives rise to reflective and speculative groups of thinkers. Religious education must make its appropriate stimulation and contribution to these successive stages. Feeling complexes, which are at first instinctive, affect imagination complexes and these complexes in turn lead up to reflective consciousness with its varying concomitants. That which is built into the brain in an affective way predetermines conduct. Feelingful consciousness leads to thoughtful consciousness.

Just as thinking goes back and reinforces sense-perception, so conception goes back and gives validity to religious feeling and imagination.

What is the aim of religious education? The Mohammedan answers that it is to make a follower of Islam. The Buddhist says that it is to make a devotee to Buddha. The Hebrew holds that it is to make a servant of God. Christianity holds that it is the development of personality after its Teacher, that God may be glorified in the extension of his spiritual kingdom. This makes religion the basis of morality and motivates conduct in terms of responsibility to creator and creatures. Education to be Christian interprets the aims of life in terms of Christian idealism, breathing through it all the meanings, attitudes, and the principles of its Exemplar.

Given, a mind created after the nature of God and conceived as destined to do free service to him, how may this end be attained? First, by the recognition of the fact of the child's legacy. His inheritance, normally, gives him spiritual legacies destined for dynamic endeavor. *Nurture* then becomes the key to unlock nature. The formative agency of the home, in the fixation of right reactions, becomes the precursor of the informative agency known as the school. It must select and train the worthy impulses and make such reactions automatic, inhibiting the unworthy and predetermining the initiation of right habits by wholesome social, intellectual, and religious environment. Equipped with impulses, feelings, and instincts with all of their potential implications, the home and the church, before the school age, should unite in training in religion through suggestion and positive direction.

Up to about the age of nine the child is only a little human being, on the road toward responsibility, unmoral and unreligious, being inducted into the mysteries of the world; and the home is the first responsible agency for his direction. If the training toward obedience to proper authority, toward right responses and attitudes in meeting daily situations are linked up with appropriate feeling associates, these all count for religion. Neglected or misdirected they may constitute the *impedimenta* to spiritual attainment. Christianity is a *way of life*. Religion is caught through the forces of imitation. Out of the home are the real issues of life.

The three institutions of a democracy are the home, the church, and the school. If the ideal for our country is a Christian democracy, for this realization larger responsibility must rest upon the home and, the church. Christianity is a spirit and an atmosphere of life. Therefore the home with its helpfulness, affection, sacrifice, confidence, and aspiration, with its inner endearments and its secret pain, its wonder stories, music, art, nature mysteries, worship, and spiritual enlightenments, must direct the inner forces of life. The church and the church school not only give their sanctions to the home but give additional forms of religious association, expression, and instruction. Homes cannot afford to risk the religious culture of children to the necessarily more or less passive attitude of public education. Religion demands the stressing of all the forces which go toward making Christian life and practice. The church is really the place for worship with its devotions, communions, liturgies, music, dramas, pageants, and celebrations. Therefore it should have the church school with its organization, classification, promotion, and curricula standards. Its housing and mechanics should harmonize with the best standards but meet the purposes of religious instruction and training. There is no need of unnecessary duplication. But the church school should select the materials for its curricula, determine its methods and choose its teachers with direct reference to the needs of religion. It should accept the findings of scientific pedagogy as valid in related fields of knowledge, at the same time modify or adapt these methods to the nature of its own materials and to the needs of the child. Much of the teaching in our public schools and colleges has real religious value. We like to believe that they are Christian, nominally so, at least. Whenever knowledge is developed in terms of religious concepts, whenever motives are construed in terms of the Christian ethnic, whenever conduct is evaluated in terms of duty to man or responsibility to God, life is being construed in terms of religion. Conceding this, there is the patently admissible fact that this influence is largely passive, fragmentary, occasional, and incidental, if not negligible. As related to the possible connections the number of instances suffer in comparison to the opportunities. Facts must have their connectional value to religion *emphasized* to cure our spiritual poverty. Matters of fact must be translated into matters of *worth*. Materialism must be spiritualized.

Religious education must ever have the Bible and all that goes along with it of related literature, history, biography, science, and philosophy, as furnishing the heart and core of its curricula. Comparative religions, ethics, church, and denominational history, the study of social, racial, and industrial problems from the standpoint of Christian ideals furnish abundant materials for the enrichment of courses of study from the cradle roll to the maturest adult class. To be religious education, the materials must be selected with reference to religious culture. Such materials help to stimulate and clarify thinking about life motivation, achievement, duty, and destiny. A graded curricula will keep spiritual enlightenment in direct and growing contact with scientific and philosophical knowledge. Without this contact they grow apart with a bias. Such loss defeats the aims of cooperative effort and Christian solidarity.

The class management, control, and instruction must be conceived in terms of the Christian ideal. The dictum "as the teacher is so is the school" applies with especial forcefulness. The teacher's indirect influence must give validity to positive instruction. To all that modern education has contributed in standardizing the qualifications of the teacher religious education must accept with the additional demand that the teacher must be *what he professes*. To teach conduct, is to live after a pattern. Christian personality plus professional training constitute the equation for the teacher in the church school. The recitation may be conducted after any of the standard forms, but unless it is permeated with the spirit of good will, stimulated through social motivation and directed toward worthy ends by a competent, attractive instructor, the vital contact for religion is lost. The very best method may be followed and still no worthy end for religion be attained. There should be the motivation of religion, for religion and by religion — for religion is life lived for God.

What Makes Education Religious?

LUTHER A. WEIGLE
Professor of Christian Nurture, The Divinity School, Yale University

Education is naturally and normally religious. If, for any reason, it loses religious content and motive, it becomes a rival to religion. Like religion, education is interested primarily in the development of persons, and is concerned with the discovery and perpetuation of the highest values of human life. Like religion, it may be conceived in terms too individualistic, but is rightly social in content and method. Like religion, it may be conceived too narrowly as but a part or segment of life; but it is in reality inclusive, consisting not so much in specific, particular kinds of activity as in a direction of interest that may characterize any and all of human action and motivate the whole of life. Education has reference to the human conditions, religion to the divine initiative, which make possible the fulfillment of Jesus' purpose: "I am come that they may have life, and may have it abundantly."

Religion and education, like religion and morality, have at times been partly sundered and have even, to some extent, worked at cross-purposes with respect to the immediate ends in view. But such sundering or opposition is always partial and temporary. It can not be permanent, if religion be true or if truth and right be the goal both of religion and of education.

The present sundering of religion is due principally to: (1) the tendency to conceive education as the function primarily, or even, solely, of the state; (2) the world's preoccupation with particular facts and processes, in the name of science, invention, industry, trade, and government, to the relative neglect of thought and belief concerning the character of the universe and the meaning of life as a whole; (3) the divisive sectarianism and partisanship which cripple organized religion in our time; (4) the assumption, on the part of many religious people, that instruction is the whole of religious education and that the Bible is the sole textbook of religious instruction; and (5) the actual ignorance which leads some adherents of religion to conceive its interests in terms inadequate to the developing life of men and even in some respects opposed to the interests of education.

Education becomes religious:

(1) When it becomes completely rational — that is, when it is no longer content merely to describe, count, and couple particular facts, to cultivate particular aptitudes and to create particular bonds between situations and active responses; but presses on, above these and including these, to a synthesis of belief, conduct, and character which has explicit reference to the Whole of which human life is a dependent part.

(2) When it rises within, expresses and mediates group-life which is religiously motivated, and takes as its own method the induction of that life by processes of fellowship and participation, free and responsible.

(3) When it is conscious of the presence, power, and love of God as the ultimate condition and supreme motive of human life, which includes and integrates all lesser values and motives whose proximate end is some form of human welfare.

(4) When it avails itself, as an intellectual, moral, and spiritual resource, of the whole range of the religious experience of the race, as this is recorded in the literature which is our heritage and is communicated by those who, however distant, are our fellows. As such a resource, we Christians accord supreme value to the religious experience recorded, in the Bible, if this is interpreted in the light of Christ, in whom, we believe, there dwells the fullness of the Godhead bodily.

We who are interested in the present movement toward a

better integration of religion and education fear two great groups of dangers — those involved in a merely secular education on the one hand, and those involved in a non-educational religion on the other hand. At the risk of being misunderstood, and with a view to stimulating discussion, may I suggest, without elaboration, that certain tendencies, present here and there within our own movement, may involve dangers?

These are:

(1) The tendency to identify religion with ethics, religious experience with social-mindedness, minimizing or reducing to mere symbol its metaphysical or doctrinal content.

(2) The tendency to contrast religious education with evangelism. We may properly contrast religious education with revivalism, Christian nurture with reliance upon conversion and rescue. But the terms "evangelism," "evangelistic," and "evangelical" are too meaningful to be surrendered. They connote the Gospel of Jesus Christ, which is the Gospel of the divine initiative. Any method that makes the Gospel effective is evangelistic; and no methods are better adapted to this end than those of Christian nurture and education. Not evangelism *or* religious education, but evangelism *through* religious education, will meet the world's need.

(3) One is at times uneasy lest the present reaction against material-centered curricula — which is a quite proper and needed reaction — and the development of project methods of teaching in this as in other fields of education, may possibly lead to a new abuse of the Bible. Our fathers used it as a collection of proof-texts for dogmas. Are we in danger of using it just as an ethical case-book or a collection of proof-texts to illumine projects?

What is "Religious" Education?

GEORGE A. COE
Professor, Teacher's College, Columbia University,
and Union Theological Seminary

The problem concerns the qualifying adjective. Why do
we have education *plus* "religious" education? The first we
take for granted, but the second must stand and render an
account of itself. When we of today think "education" —
whether we have in mind mental training, or knowledge, or
culture, or efficiency — no religious connotations are assumed; religion enters as a *plus*.

To say how this has come about would require an analysis
of several of the prime factors in modern culture. One
would have to consider the renaissance, with its feeling for
literary values utterly uncolored by either Christianity or
Judaism; the scientific movement, painfully winning freedom from restrictions imposed in the name of religion; the
modern state, gradually emancipating itself from ecclesiastical dictation, and, at the very moment when it expands its
educational functions, asserting itself more and more as
religiously nonpartisan or even secular; the absorption of
the modern mind in the mastery of nature's forces under
the guidance of science and invention; and finally, through
the extension and multiplication of human contacts, the
growing realization that, in spite of religious diversity, we
men have many and profound interests in common.

Our educational situation is not a creation of philosophic

reflection, but of complicated historic forces. In philosophy the concept "religion" is one. Conceivably some single tap root is the source of every faith and of every cult, but what we encounter in ordinary practice is neither a concept nor a tap root; not religion, but religions many and contradictory. Even within what goes under a single name, as Judaism, or Christianity, or Protestantism, we find irreconcilable oppositions. Philosophers may tell us that religion should be the inclusive concern of men, that it should sum up the meaning of all worthy interests and give them unity; yet religion, as it is consciously practiced, has not in any large measure thus interpreted and asserted itself. Instead, on the whole it accepts the position of a special interest merely coordinate with other interests that are capable of standing alone. For it operates in and through limited societies called churches or denominations; it is locally housed in church or synagog buildings; its characteristic acts occur on days specially set apart therefor; its thought-content, as a rule, assumes to be separate from thought in general in respect to origin, grounds, and application; even its ethics not seldom lacks contact with the major motive forces that dominate the work of the world.

This, on the whole, is religion, "as is," and religion as it is determines the education that is given in the name of religion. Hence it is that in actual practice the differentia of religious education will be found in one or more of the following processes: Instruction in the contents of an ancient sacred literature, as the Old Testament, the New Testament, or the Koran; indoctrination in one or another of the separate party systems of thought or belief; habituation to the worship of a particular communion; initiation into membership in one of these communions; and inculcation of ancient, for the most part highly generalized, rules of conduct, such as the Ten Commandments, that have nothing to say about current forms of organized right and organized wrong.

Is the "gentle reader" dissatisfied, perhaps exasperated, with the outcome of this cold-blooded, unsympathetic, merely empirical analysis? Well, so is the "gentle" writer! Probably my readers and I have experienced in the modern religious-education enterprise some of the greatest thrills of life; we have felt in it the inspiration of something broadly human, progressive, and unifying. Surely we are not devotees of anything as divisive, abstract, and anachronistic as that which I have described! We tend, therefore, to define "religious" education, not by its history, not by its actual status as objectively determined, but by hopes, ideals, possibilities that we labor to make actual. To us the most religious thing in religious education is the vision that it fosters: visions of a new collective ordering of life, of a new experience of "Immanu-El" — "God is with us" — and of a new kind of initiation of children into religious fellowship. What we now put the children through is not religious enough; therefore it does not suffice for a definition.

This implies — whether or not we are clearly aware of the implication — that for us who are thus-minded religious education is or ought to be a process in which religion, even in the act of transmitting itself to the young, reconstructs itself. Appreciation of the past is of course a necessary and constant part of education, but unless appreciation is likewise a judging that distinguishes the wheat from the tares, then, under the name of religion, irreligion infects the mind of the young. There can be no adequate teaching of the young that is not at the same time repentance and confession on the part of their elders. The older generation does indeed know something of the way of life, has indeed wisdom that is indispensable to the young. Some of the institutions of civilization deserve the loving loyalty of the new generation. Yet, dare we assume that any knowledge, wisdom, or institution of ours is sufficient for the new day? Have we anything whatever to offer that deserves unquestioning acceptance? Is our religion itself good enough? Surely we of the generation that is passing away have bungled every great human interest. Not one of the essentials of a reasonable human life — health, food, education, freedom of speech, economic justice, peace — not one of these is assured to the children of any nation, no matter what its prevalent religion may be! How dare we, then, assume that we can teach children how to live? Must we not humble ourselves, rather, saying to the oncoming generation, "This is the best we have; it is worth something, but it is only a clumsy approximation to real living. Take it, use what you can of it, but above all things rebuild it into something better!"

An early interpreter of Christianity ascribes to Jesus these words: "I have yet many things to say unto you, but you cannot bear them now." One may count oneself a disciple of this same Jesus not merely because of what he said and did, but still more because, implicit in his doings and sayings, is a permanent starting point and motive for judging and progressively rejudging human life, the Christian life included. He did not tell us all essential truth; we cannot tell all of it to the children who are committed to us. Blessed are the teachers who lead the young to listen to the Spirit of Truth who has ever and ever unprecedented things to say.

Can there be any doubt as to which phases of our civilization and of our religions most loudly call for reconstruction through education? The woes that are already upon us prescribe our duty. We have sown the wind, and now the whirlwind is beginning to rise. We adults have not yet learned how to prevent war, or how to secure even the rudiments of justice to those whom we declare to be of infinite value in the sight of God. How far, then, are we, who do not yet love the brother whom we have seen, really acquainted with God, whom we have not seen? Do we really know how to worship? The intended implication of these questions is that the reconstruction of our collective life, and the reconstruction of our religions, constitute not two problems but one. The differentia of religious education, when it is most radically religious, will be that it comprehensively and uncompromisingly interprets life as friendship or ethical love.

The education that the state provides does not do this. The state, as it now is, asserts its own sovereignty, which means, in practice, insisting upon the finality of its own arbitrary will and of its own self-interest, as against the will and the interests of the rest of the world. World brotherhood is not and cannot be the educational ideal of a political power that is represented in world affairs by diplomacy and warships. As statecraft is not understood and practiced, nationalism is of the essence of it, and the patriotism that such statecraft inculcates in the young is inevitably infected therewith. Even as between fellow citizens the education that the state provides does not uncompromisingly teach brotherhood. Our industrial and economic system inherently and of necessity breeds injustice and strife, yet the state schools, instead of laying the axe at the root of the tree, are teaching the young how to water its roots and how to gather its more pleasant fruits. Let not the point of these remarks be missed. The Public schools do teach fairness as defined by the rules of the game, moderation in the use of inherently destructive forces, and amelioration of misery that the system produces. They are doing, moreover, an immeasurably important work in developing tolerance, respect for one another, neighborly good will, and the spirit of cooperation. The point is that, in the nature of the case—and this is not the fault of the teachers—state schools cannot go the whole length; they cannot achieve either the comprehensiveness or the uncompromisingness that make social education unambiguously religious.

How far the churches are able to go in this direction, this is not the place to say. But it is appropriate to remark that here is the crucial test of the religiousness of the church school. Of course, any sort of religion can be intense, and success in religious education can be estimated upon any sort of base. Doubtless jazz is music, and musical skill and appreciation might be measured at this esthetic level. Doubtless, too, those who said, "Lord, Lord," were intensely and sincerely religious. If they had been acquainted with modern record systems, they might have exhibited the results of their kind of religious education in statistical tables of the number of pupils, the state of their vocal cords, and the frequency, distinctness, loudness, and unanimity with which the essential words, "Lord, Lord," were spoken. But, as the esthetic quality of jazz is not finally judged by persons who receive their musical education in the modern dance, so the final measure of religious education is not to be found in religion prancing in a paddock, but in religion out in the fields plowing, sowing, and reaping.

The problem of the world's work, let me repeat, is all one with the problem of religious life and religious education. I am quite willing to approach religious education through the idea, or rather the experience, of God, but only on condition that an ethically great enough God and a suffi-

ciently dynamic experience of God are assumed. Where do
we have this experience? Is it a modern fad, or is it an
ancient inspiration, that finds God where goods are produced to feed and clothe the sons of God rather than for
profit and power; where sickness is prevented as well as
relieved; where opportunity for all prevails over special
privilege; where injustice and oppression give way to justice
and freedom; where the narrowness of individualism, of
class, of denomination, of nation is being outgrown; wherever, in short, friendship or ethical love is gaining a more
comprehensive or a more uncompromising control of life?
If this is the great present sign of "God-with-us," then, too,
when it is incorporated into education, it is the great sign
that education is there and then religious.

5. A Curriculum for Character and Religious Education in a Changing Culture

WILLIAM CLAYTON BOWER
Professor of Religious Education in The University of Chicago

By 1930, the religious education movement had reached an important turning point in its history. William Clayton Bower is representative of the period. A prolific writer, Bower exemplifies religious education's identity with what was known as character education–a process oriented toward aiding self-realizing persons to function in social groups as intelligent, effective personalities. Religion and morals were still important aspects of character development, but religion had been essentially secularized and the content of education isolated in contemporary experience and process. The early understandings of the religious education movement have moved to their furthest extreme. Religious education has become simply and solely good education.

Any adequate program of character and religious education must take into account the fundamental and rapid changes through which our contemporaneous culture is passing. This factor of change is not unique in current culture. It is a part of the historic process. Indeed, it is from the fact of change that history derives its chief significance. Change, however, is more thoroughgoing and rapid in contemporaneous culture than it has been in the past because of the growing complexity and differentiation of modern life and the multiplicity of factors that are opera-

Religious Education XXV (February 1930), pp. 127-133.

tive in it. The factors that are chiefly responsible for the changes in current culture are science, industry, and the experiment in the democratic way of life, with their corresponding reconstruction of the relations, functions, and structures of social living.

PERSONALITY THE OBJECTIVE OF CHARACTER AND RELIGIOUS EDUCATION

Within this milieu of a changing culture, education itself is undergoing profound changes. In no aspect of education are these changes more thoroughgoing than in the manner of conceiving the objective of education. While there is a decided lag of general practice behind educational theory, it is obvious that the pronounced trend in educational thinking is away from conceiving the end of education to be the transmission of the accumulated knowledge of the past. Less obviously, but nevertheless decidedly, the trend is away from conceiving the objective of education in terms of training in adult-predetermined ideals, traits, and habits and of the preparation of the young to take their place in a remote adult society. That this latter conception is still entrenched in educational theory is evidenced by the fact that there is still a considerable body of current literature devoted to the exposition both of this concept of the end of education and of the techniques that proceed upon this assumption.

The trend in educational thinking, however, that is gathering momentum in America is in the direction of conceiving of education as a process oriented toward self-realizing *persons* functioning in social groups. The objective of education so conceived is the assisting of persons to achieve an intelligent and effective personality.

If this conception of the objective of education is valid for any type of education whatsoever, it is in a unique sense a valid objective. for character and religious education are concerned with assisting growing persons to achieve a certain kind of personality—personality possessing moral and spiritual qualities. In this respect a distinction is to be made between personality and character. Personality is a more or less stable organization of physical qualities, impulses, habits, ideas, attitudes, and purposes subjected to assessment and reconstruction in terms of moral and spiritual values. Character and religious education are thus not primarily concerned with the imposition of inherited knowledge or behavior patterns upon more or less passive and receptive subjects of education by means of the traditional techniques of instruction or training. Character and religion are of the very essence of inwardness. They are concerned with ethical and spiritual values as the inner motivation and controls of behavior. If these motives and controls are to be effectively operative they must be self-chosen. Character in its deepest sense is an achievement on the part of self-realizing persons.

From this point of view it is assumed that character is not a system of ethical principles. It is a *way of life*—a quality that is involved in the responses which growing persons make to the concrete and day-by-day situations which they face in the normal processes of adjusting themselves to their material and social world—in the family, in the school, in the community, in the church, in civic activities, in recreation and in esthetic enjoyment. So also religion is not a system of intellectual beliefs, of practices or emotional attitudes in isolation from the concrete movement of practical experience, but a quality of all the experiences which emerge from all the relations and functions of life. When morality and religion are dissociated from the normal range of concrete situations in all the areas of experience, they lose their essential qualities as morality and religion.

PROCEDURE DETERMINED BY PROCESSES OF PERSONALITY DEVELOPMENT

From this approach the procedures in character and religious education are determined by the way in which personality is achieved by self-realizing persons. This procedure is very different from that by which knowledge as an end in itself is transmitted, or adult predetermined traits, ideals, or habits are inculcated.

It is now well understood that persons realize themselves in and through the experiences which they have. The procedure, in consequence, calls for a technique by which growing persons may be assisted to become objectively aware of their experiences in their full content, to understand them, to criticize and evaluate them, to discover the factors in their control and to form choices about them which may be organized and integrated into dominant life-purposes. The school thus becomes a laboratory which reaches out into every area of adjustment within which the experience of learners is involved and which brings these experiences in for interpretation, analysis, assessment and reconstruction in terms of the highest values and achievements of the race and of the new demands of the changing situation. In a changing world and a changing culture, the good life cannot be lived by precedent alone. In the dynamic and creative experience of the living members of society and of the ongoing experience of the race, values are constantly undergoing reconstruction, and new values are in process of formation. It is the function of a creative education to help growing persons to discover these values and to put them to work in the reconstruction of experience as well as to make available to them the cherished and tested values of the receding past.

Moreover, the procedure of character and religious education must be comprehensive enough to include all the factors that enter into the determination of personality. The experience by which persons realize themselves includes the physio-chemical factors that are involved in physical health. The first step in helping persons to achieve moral and spiritual character may well be concerned with the proper functioning of the glands, with proper metabolism and with the normal action of the automatic system. This program calls for the techniques of health and medicine.

It must include the inner drives and emotional tensions that arise out of conflicts in the adjustment process. Many of these conflicts and emotional conditionings go on below the conscious level of experience. This factor calls for the techniques of the psychiatrist.

So also with the factors concerned with the adjustment of the individual to group life with its organized patterns of social behavior. The social psychologist well understands that the self is largely a social product. The social factor operates to a considerable extent below the conscious level of experience. One of the first steps in assisting persons to achieve a high-grade personality may well concern itself with the proper adjustment of group relationships.

Thus the factors that determine personality range all the way from those involved in physical and mental health through adequate social adjustment to the factors of intelligence and self-evaluation of forms of behavior that issue in selective behavior in the light of organized purposes. No program of character and religious education can be considered adequate which fails to include all of them in its procedure. The orientation of character education toward persons and the assisting of persons to achieve a quality of personality in keeping with the highest self-chosen values thus provides the connecting tissue that integrates the hitherto more or less isolated techniques of these several disciplines into a whole and continuous process to which each makes its contribution. Physical and mental health, social adjustment to group life, and forming of intelligent and evaluating judgments about experience become functional with reference to their supreme end—a sound, intelligent, social, moral, and spiritual personality.

CONTENT AND METHOD INSEPARABLE

From this approach the content and method of character and religious education become inseparable. The content becomes the full content of experience as that experience undergoes interpretation, enrichment and control in terms of the best moral and spiritual values of the long and tested experience of the race and of the moral and spiritual values that are emergent in the new experience of the evolving present situation. Method, on the other hand, becomes the procedure by which the learner interprets his experience, discovers its moral and spiritual values, and seizes upon the factors of its control.

In character and religious education, as in all other practical enterprises, the stuff of the experience and the manner of dealing with it are only different aspects of an undifferentiated process. They can be separated only in thought; never in the process itself. In its total and integrated form, the content of the experience and control of it are merged in an activity—a behavior pattern.

It is, therefore, not only possible, but probably more fruitful, to think in terms of what may be called curriculum content and curriculum procedure—a terminology quite different from that which connoted a logically organized "course of study" or a catalog of isolated traits, ideals, and habits to be "taught."

SPECIFIC CONTENT OF EXPERIENCE

The specific content of moral and religious education thus becomes the specific content of experience in the process of undergoing interpretation, enrichment, and control in terms of moral and spiritual values.

An understanding of that content can perhaps best be arrived at by isolating a unit of experience and analyzing it into its component parts as it undergoes reconstruction.

The smallest identifiable unit of experience has for its *terminus a quo* an identifiable situation and for its *terminus ad quem* an identifiable response. In the process of resolution that lies between the situation and the response which the total person makes to a total situation are operative all the factors that in any way condition the response, be they physical, psychiatric, social, intellectual, or valuational. In its completed form the response constitutes a mode of behavior or a behavior pattern. The unit of learning thus becomes a unit of experience moving from an identifiable situation to an identifiable response with its twofold aspects of content and procedure. The sum of these responses becomes the total behavior pattern of a given person's character. In a form organized for educational purposes, the sum of these situation-response units, comprehending the entire range of the learner's experience, constitutes the curriculum of moral and religious education.

If, now, the content of a unit of experience as it undergoes interpretation, enrichment and control is further analyzed, it becomes clear that it consists of three elements.

The first of these elements of content consists in the situation itself with all the factors involved. This situation may be very simple when there are few stimuli operative, as when one is greeted with a hearty "Good morning" from a passing friend. Or it may be very complex where many stimuli complexly organized are present, as in the case of racial adjustment, the choice of a vocation, or arriving at a satisfactory philosophy of life. But whether simple or complex, every experience has as its beginning point an identifiable situation capable of evoking a response from the person involved.

This, obviously, has the effect of reversing the traditional concept of curriculum as well as of procedure. The traditional curriculum has as its content the accumulated and logically organized bodies of social experience schematized in blocks of subject-matter, such as history, literature, language, mathematics, philosophy, and the physical and social sciences. The procedure began with the mastery of that historical subject-matter. The procedure that is here proposed begins with the current experience in which the growing person is involved. When, however, current experience is analyzed it is clear that the primary element in its content is the situation which immediately confronts one and to which some sort of response is about to be made. The records of racial experience, as we shall presently see, constitute an essential part of the content of that experience as it undergoes reconstruction; but instead of its being the first element of content in current experience undergoing reconstruction, racial experience is, in fact, the last element of content.

This discovery of the primary element in the content of experience, as well as the beginning point in educational procedure, is particularly significant with reference to an educational procedure suitable to a changing culture. The situation that constitutes the primary content of education arises within a current experience of persons or groups. The situation embodies within itself the factors of change in an ongoing social experience, so that an educational process so conceived deals with the new elements of an evolving experience as part of the basic data of education. The content of the situation itself consists of all the factors that are involved in it, and also of the organization of all these several factors into a total situation.

The second element of content in an experience undergoing reconstruction is the learner's own past experience to which he first turns as a resource for dealing with the situation. This past experience of the learner consists of the accumulated results of past responses to situations and includes as its content habits, ideas, preferential attitudes, skills, and sets of the personality. Much of the knowledge it contains is factual; much of it is extremely tentative and untested; some of it may be merely assumption. Some of the attitudes may be objective and factual; others may be weighted with prejudice. Some of the skills may be exceedingly accurate and dependable; others may be extremely faulty. But whether ample or meager, factual or prejudiced, dependable or imperfect, this store of knowledge, habits and attitudes is the first resource to which the person turns for materials and techniques for dealing with the situations that confront him.

The third element of content in an experience undergoing reconstruction is the accumulated store of racial experience. This exists in part in the form of the great tradition of literature, science, history, and art. Much of it persists in social viewpoints and customs that furnish the patterns to social behavior. Much of it survives in social institutions which are the result of long and sometimes quite unconscious social experimentation. In this racial experience is a fund of resources that vastly outruns the limited experience of the individual.

It helps one to appreciate the function and value of racial experience when he understands its origin and nature. At one time every fragment of this vast accumulation of knowledge, achievements, techniques, standards, and customs was an outcome of an identifiable historical situation. That is to say, it was itself once current personal or social experience. Its meanings, techniques, and values in this manner became parts of the already accumulating store of meanings, techniques, and values. There is, therefore, nothing sacred attaching to these inherited traditions. Their validity in no case rises above the specific and concrete experiences out of which they arose. Their age and incorporation into the impressive body of tradition invests them with an extraneous and fictitious value. Consequently their age and general acceptance in the past should not in any way exempt them from reexamination in the light of fresh experience and the demands of contemporaneous living. What is now current experience, and therefore likely to be undervalued, will in time become part of ancient tradition and invested with the authority and prestige which age and usage confer.

In this fund of racial experience are preserved impressive accumulations of organized knowledge that represent the meanings that have grown up out of the long human experiment with life. Here are to be found techniques for dealing with situations that in their collective and organized form constitute the complicated technology of society. Here also are to be found the organized values which have grown up within each area of experience and which constitute its canons of judgment regarding modes of behavior. Here are to be found social behavior patterns with their sanctions of group constraint.

The content of racial experience is of incalculable value as a resource for interpreting current personal and social experience, for evaluating it, and for seizing upon the factors of its control. It is, however, functional with reference to current personal and social experience, and not to be thought of as an end in itself, as was true when the subject-matter of racial experience was thought of as constituting the curriculum and when its assimilation was thought of as the appropriate procedure in education. The worth of racial experience is to be judged by its relevancy to current experience, the social and cultural levels upon which its ideas, techniques, and values arose, and its correspondence to the requirements of a complex and evolving modern social situation.

Racial experience, like the learner's own past experience, is a mixture of the true and the false, of the tested and the tentative, of the factual and assumptions, of objectivity and prejudice. Consequently, as a resource for dealing with current experience, it needs to be subjected to rigid criticism and evaluation and to be utilized with discrimination and selection. It is not the function of education to transmit the knowledge and behavior patterns of the past. It is the function of education to make these available for the utilization of self-realizing persons and groups in dealing selectively and creatively with current experience. Similarly, it is not the function of character education to teach ideals, traits, or habits. It is the function of character education to assist self-realizing persons to achieve moral and spiritual personality. Ideals, traits, habits, and knowledge are functional to personality—resources in assisting contemporary persons and groups in arriving at appropriate conduct outcomes to present situations.

It is a mistake, therefore, to assume that education is either knowledge-centered or child-centered. Education takes place at the point where current personal and social experience and racial experience are brought into interrelation, and where each is thereby subjected to evaluation and reconstruction. Social experience, on the one hand, makes possible the better understanding, assessment, and more certain control of current experience. Current experience, on the other hand, tests and reorganizes past experience. In the light of the fresh experience of the present evolving situation, many of the results of an earlier and more primitive experience become irrelevant to modern life; much of that past experience must be rejected as discredited by later discoveries; many of its values and standards are inadequate to the demands of contemporaneous culture.

To make education child-centered is to subject it to the caprice, the limitations and the superficiality of the immediate. To center it in the knowledge, standards and behavior patterns of the past is to load education with tradition and precedent, and to render it backward-looking, imitative, and appreciative. Education is a concern of civilization which has a long future as well as a long past. In the forward-moving point of current personal and social experience, the life, culture, and achievement of the race are renewing themselves in an evolving experience. It is the business of education to make that current experience creative in helping living persons to be aware of it, to understand its meaning, to discover its values that are in process of reconstruction and formation, to project purposes worthy of the best experience of the past and to perfect and discover techniques for carrying them through to fruitful issues in personal and social behavior.

CHARACTER AND RELIGIOUS EDUCATION THROUGH CREATIVE EXPERIENCE

Creative experience! Under some such formula as this are to be discovered the techniques or methods of character and religious education for a changing culture. In the light of the foregoing considerations, it is clear that the procedure by which self-realizing persons deal with the content of their experience as it undergoes reconstruction is quite as important as the content itself. In fact, from the standpoint of education for a changing culture, the procedure is more important than the content. The content of human experience has changed from the beginning—at first relatively slowly, but with increasing rapidity as the present if approached. Change in content of knowledge, techniques, and standards is extremely rapid in contemporaneous experience and will become increasingly rapid and complex.

The procedure demanded of education under such conditions of change is one, not for reliving the experience of the past, but for the continuous reconstruction of current experience with the aid of such insight and values as the past may offer as resources for meeting present situations fruitfully.

The technique of creative experience our contemporary

culture has itself produced. It is the technique of the scientific method. Basically, it is the experimental procedure. It involves analysis of the factors involved in experience, reflective thinking regarding outcomes and processes in the light of their consequences, and the effective application of purposive control to the practical issues of living. Moreover, this aware and creative experience must objectively take account of the full content of the person's experience, including its organic, its psychiatric, and its social factors as data in the process of conscious reconstruction with the aid of the knowledge and techniques that belong to these factors.

The steps of this procedure may be stated somewhat as follows: helping self-realizing persons to become objectively aware of the situations they face, to analyze these situations for factors and possible outcomes, to search and evaluate their own past experience and the experience of the race as sources of understanding, techniques, and standards, to discover the moral and spiritual values resident in these situations, to form appreciations concerning them, to choose the best outcomes in conduct in the light of the best experience of the race and of the demands of the present situation, to experiment with the chosen outcomes in the actual conduct of life, to generalize these outcomes so that they will be available for all similar situations, and to integrate the units of behavior into a consistent and dependable total behavior pattern. The sequence of steps will by no means always be that suggested here. The resolution of a situation may sometimes begin with an unsatisfactory outcome in conduct. Sometimes it may have its beginning with contact with persons or social groups or the outstanding facts of social experience. But in any event these steps of the scientific procedure will in one way or another be involved.

In such a procedure of creative experience, the growing person himself must increasingly come into control of the creative process up to the limits of his capacity and experience. Otherwise, it cannot be a creative experience. Consequently there are two methods—a method of the learner by which he secures the understanding, enrichment, and control of his own experience as a method of selective behavior, and a method of the teacher by which, through understanding guidance, he helps the learner successfully to take the steps necessary to the control of his own experience.

In this way education as a social process is lifted from the levels of authority, imposition of adult-predetermined knowledge, standards, and manipulation, to the level of human engineering—of a guided experiment in living in a changing world which is still in the making, with unlimited possibilities concerning which the precedents of the past are only prophecies of the future.

6. Jewish Religious Education

ABRAHAM FRANZBLAU
Principal Hebrew Union College School for Teachers in
New York City

Regretfully, it was not until 1930 that a distinctive Jewish voice in religious education was to be heard. A few liberal Jewish educators influenced by John Dewey belonged to the REA; typically they expressed anxiety over the wedding of religious education and the public schools. All too little conversation on this issue surfaced and when it did the parties spoke more to each other than with each other. In Abraham Franzblau's rare essay we get a glimmer of the diverse understandings of religious education shared by the Jewish community. All tend to be different than those expressed by the Protestant-dominated religious education association. For example, character education is not a Jewish priority. They, rather, express a concern for survival, the transmission of their tradition, the induction of persons into their community, the nurturing of Jewish understandings and ways. At the beginning it appears that Jewish religious educators, while emphasizing schooling, were essentially concerned with intentional socialization of persons into the faith of the Jewish community.

It is difficult to speak on this subject because of the diversity of meanings which the term Jewish religious education has had in the past and has today.

In the Biblical period, when education was entirely informal, parents gave their children instruction in those crafts necessary for earning a livelihood, taught them the simple morality of the times and inculcated, through actual practice, whatever religious customs were observed. The

Religious Education XXV (May 1930), pp. 427-430.

priests developed the symbolism of sacrifice and taught the law, and the psalmists developed and taught the poetry of religious expression. Prophets thundered their message from the market places to whatever crowds would gather to listen. Not until the time of the scribes were those earlier traditions written down, which were to be the foundation of later Jewish education.

In the Talmudic period, as the Jew strove to "build a fence around the law," religious practices and ceremonials multiplied and the law became, in increasing degree, the basis of all Jewish life. Religious education became formal, with the law as the subject of instruction.

In the medieval period, when persecution hemmed in the Jew and forced him to retreat to his own inner spiritual strongholds, all of life was religiously motivated and the Talmud, with its various codes and commentaries, served as the exclusive guide and arbiter of conduct. Here the religious education of the child was begun in his cradle when he heard the Jewish melodies his mother sang to him as lullabies. His first toddling steps brought him into contact with things Jewish, and among his first lispings was the phrase, "The Torah was commanded to us by Moses as the heritage of the congregation of Jacob." Rich religious rituals met him at every step. Prayer was a vital and integral part of life. Every meal was a religious rite; every Sabbath, a day of beauty, with peace and content resting upon the hearth, regardless of the storms which might be raging without. Here, devotion to study was the highest good, and wordly pursuits were engaged in merely to supply the meager sustenance without which the study of Torah would be impossible. The ideal of the Jewish home, with its uncompromising emphasis upon chastity and virtue, with its jealous guardianship of the obligations of parenthood and the duties of childhood, provided all that was needed in character training. There was thus no formal religious education in our modern sense of the term; but all education in the home and the school was deeply religious.

Coming to modern times, we find that emancipation, civil, political, and economic, broke down the walls of isolation and separatism which cut the Jew off from the non-Jewish world. Secular education became the basic education, and religious education was relegated to a subsidiary and purely supplementary plane.

It is equally difficult to speak with singleness of meaning about Jewish religious education today, because of the many differing outlooks and points of view which prevail. In addition to the more commonly known groupings of Orthodoxy, Conservatism and Reform, there are Nationalist groups, Yiddishists groups and Radical Laborites, and so forth, among whom ideals of Jewish education vary, from the advocacy of the strictest adherence to tradition, to outspoken departure from all religious objectives, with emphasis solely upon the racial and national aspects of Judaism. Among Orthodox Jews today, religious education aims largely to secure adherence to tradition and observance of the traditional rites and customs of Judaism. Adherence to tradition is regarded as a discipline which contains all the necessary elements of character determination. Character objectives thus motivate all of this education, although they do not appear formally in the curriculum.

Among Conservative Jews, we find less emphasis upon mere adherence to tradition and more upon nationalistic objectives and cultural ideals. Palestine looms very large in the program of religious education among Conservative

Jews. Character objectives are basic but still informal, as far as the curriculum is concerned.

Among Reform Jews, education has been focused very sharply upon the achievement of ethical, moral, and religious values. The curriculum has shaped itself definitely around these objectives, to the exclusion of the greater part of the subject matter of the traditional Jewish school. Except among Reform Jews, there has been little emphasis upon character training as a formal objective of Jewish religious education. There is a very sound reason for this. As a small minority living in the midst of a vast majority which was often subtly if not outspokenly hostile, the problem of survival has always been the basic problem of religious education among the Jews; and it continues to be the basic problem today. In the face of this problem, all other objectives become of secondary importance.

The building of character is a function of the home and of the social environment. The religious school has too little time and too few facilities at its disposal to do very much in this direction. Character cannot be built by enunciating precepts. Hartshorne and May have shown that character is much more than the knowledge of right and wrong, and that "integration is in itself a great accomplishment."

Neither can the teaching of religion be accomplished as easily as we imagine. Too frequently we present religious ideas which are far too abstract for the children to grasp, with little appreciation of their basic urges, impulses, and interests. By the time the child is old enough to understand what we teach, he has frequently been completely antagonized.

How, then, shall the aims of Jewish education be stated? As I see it, the aims of Jewish education are to achieve the adjustment of the Jew to himself, to the environment and to the cosmos, and to provide the means for rich, creative Jewish living.

Adjustment of the Jew to himself involves the acceptance by the individual of the fact of his Jewishness. This is necessary for the establishment of an inner harmony or balance of personality. As long as being a Jew automatically imposes certain inevitable social, economic, and other handicaps, we cannot achieve an adequate adjustment to Judaism until the individual is taught to accept these handicaps and rise above them. Much of the equally undesirable "superiority" and "inferiority" attitudes found among Jews can be traced to failure to make this adjustment. Jewish education has a definite task in this direction.

With reference to the environment, there are two aspects to which Jewish education must adjust, the Jewish and the non-Jewish. Adjustment to the Jewish environment involves, first, the transmission of the Jewish cultural heritage. This includes knowledge of our common past, or the history of the Jewish people, knowledge of our common literary heritage—that is, the Bible and the post-Biblical literature—knowledge of our common religious practices and knowledge of our common ideals.

Secondly, it involves the induction of the individual into actual participation in Jewish life. This implies the practice of ceremonies, participation in worship, and membership in religious institutions. It also implies participation in Jewish communal activites of philanthropic, educational, and social nature. It also implies the stimulation of Jewish cultural activity along the lines of both individual creativity and support of cultural movements.

Participation in these phases of Jewish life is not a thing toward which children naturally turn by themselves. Nor can it be achieved through routine practice. Forcing children to attend adult services will not train them in worship. Neither will the routine collection of small sums of charity money Sunday morning train them in habits of philanthropy. For these, as well as for all other phases of participation in Jewish life, we must prepare gradually, through a graded curriculum of instruction. We must begin with activities which are interesting and intelligible to the very young child and keep in pace with the development of the child as he grows toward maturity. Ideal participation in Jewish activities as an adult can come only as the logical culmination of participation in suitable and related activities as a child.

The adjustment of the Jew to the non-Jewish environment requires an adequate comprehension of his place in that environment. It implies the achievement of a state of harmony or balance between the centrifugal forces which impels the Jew to obliterate himself in the stream of the life and culture of the dominant environment, and the centripetal forces which impel him to create protective barriers between himself and the dominant environment. It is only when the Jew participates whole-heartedly and sympathetically in American life, fulfilling all his obligations as a citizen and contributing to American culture the best that is within him, while at the same time remaining loyal to his Jewish religious and cultural traditions, that genuine adjustment can be said to exist. This cannot be achieved without setting up definite educational objectives with that end in view.

It is in the final phase, that of adjustment to the cosmos, that Judaism as a religion can play its greatest role, in the scheme of education. This phase of education must aim to answer some of the great cosmic questions which rise in the minds of men. It must afford relief from the doubts with which we are beset. It must translate knowledge of the Jewish religion and its ideals into urges and impulses which will integrate the individual into the greater world. It must set up a goal which will give meaning to all existence, and it must make the individual conscious of the divine in life and permeate all living with this consciousness. This phase of religious education must be raised out of the elementary grades of the religious school into the high school grades and the, as yet fragmentary, system of adult religious education. It permits of most adequate treatment during the period of maturity. Any system of religious education which bases itself on the assumption that it can completely and satisfactorily teach this phase of religion before Confirmation cherishes a delusion.

These are the aims of Jewish religious education as I see them. To accomplish them, the cooperation of both home and school is essential. We also need a well-organized system of adult religious education, for the cultural enrichment of the parents themselves, and for the sake of the unification of the character values of the home. Our system of religious education must be continuous, ranging from the kindergarten age through the adult years. Our schools must have adequate physical facilities, adequately trained teaching staffs, more sessions per week, and a rich program of extra-curricular activities. For the youth of late high school and college age, the religious school must offer a broad program, including opportunities for devotional, education, communal, and recreational activities.

The problem of religious education transcends the limits of congregational organization and deserves to be a matter of cooperative communal concern within each denomination. On the basis of such an organization, I believe our objectives could be quite readily achieved.

7. Is Religious Education to Become a Science?

NEVIN C. HARNER
Professor of Christian Education, The Theological Seminary of the Reformed Church of the United States in Lancaster

One of the major contributions of the REA, to religion and education, has been in the area of research. Especially important is the work of Hartshorne and May in character education. Through their pioneering work a clear identity for the REA began to take shape. Religious education, sharing the outlooks and technique of contemporary social science, had begun to emerge as a distinctive discipline. Indeed, Harner contends that religious education must become a science so that it can command respect, better cope with the world, and achieve its aims. But more important, religious education needed to become a science because the scientific spirit was understood as being deeply religious. Religious education had begun to emerge as a highly specialized form of education, a discipline, a profession with a highly secularized frame of reference.

Religious education, as we know it today, is in many respects merely the continuation of Sunday school and church work of fifty years ago. It is in no sense an entirely new departure. Generally speaking, it seeks the same ends as were sought by the Sunday school workers of 1880. It uses the same Bible. It sings in large part the same hymns. It utilizes not a few of the same organizations. It works with the same human nature. Its indebtedness to those who have gone before is everywhere manifest.

Yet, notwithstanding these many points of similarity,

Religious Education XXVII (March 1932), pp. 202-208.

there are quite obviously points of difference. Religious education is something distinctive. A new spirit breathes through it. The church has witnessed nothing exactly like it before. And if it is asked wherein its distinctive quality lies, the answer must be: "It smacks of modern science. At this point there is a newness about it; namely, that it has taken over in large part the technique, the outlook, the atmosphere, and the vocabulary of science." A session of a church school where the newer religious education is being carried on is strangely suggestive of a laboratory. An observer could step from the one to the other without sense of shock. Present-day conferences are very largely taken up with the consideration of research and experimentation, or else with the elucidation of some method of hypothesis which has lately come over the horizon. One cannot at present take up a professional (note the word) journal of religious education without having eye and mind assaulted by statistical tables, means, standard deviations, and coefficients of correlation. Here, then, is a trend which is boldly distinctive of the new movement. Religious education might with fair justification be described as the offspring of the union of religious idealism with scientific method.

To observe this tendency is to raise a question of serious moment. How shall we regard this leaning toward science? Is it to be hailed as a great forward step, or deplored as a denial of the faith? Is it the occasion for the joy of a great Doxology, or the sorrow and foreboding of a Miserere? It is imperative that the issue be faced now while the movement is still in its infancy. If we wait long, its character will be firmly set, and then it will be too late.

As we endeavor to forecast the probable future of religious education, shall we visualize it as standing ultimately on the same footing as chemistry, physics, astronomy, engineering, and medicine? Will it, like them, make much of *observation?* Will it focus its attention increasingly upon every spot where human life is in process of growth—a group of boys in the street, a family gathered for the evening meal, a class session in Sunday school? Are we to expect it—and help it—to analyze these observations with a view to discovering wtat makes life grow, what retards it, and what kind of growth is best? Will it, at times, assemble thousands of such observations and deal with them statistically after the manner of Hartshorne and May in the Character Education Inquiry in the attempt to discover the general principles which are concealed in the welter of particular cases? And are we to picture it as making much of *experimentation?* Will it try out this way of conducting a worship service, and that way of disciplining children, and the various ways of dealing with delinquent boys? And are we to suppose that the day will arrive when it will have at its disposal *a sizable body of validated facts*, comparable to the accumulated knowledge of medical science, for example? Shall we imagine it saying to ministers, Sunday school teachers, playground directors, judges of juvenile courts: "Here are things which we *know* concerning the making and unmaking of religious personality? In these volumes are the accumulated results of our observation and experimentation. You can depend upon his medical library." Will such a picture ever be a reality? Will our ecclesiastical meetings be given over in part to the consideration of what scientific workers in the Kingdom have found to be effective, as is the case with medical congresses to day? And, if science should come to dominate not only religious education but the work of the church as a whole, would the cause of religion be helped or hindered thereby?

A generation or so ago the answer would have been

ridiculously easy. We would have dismissed the whole mat-ter as an idle dream. We would have said that the field of religious education was utterly inaccessible to scientific method. To begin with, human personality is so infinitely complex that we can scarcely define it—much less give a scientific account of it. It is the ever-present mystery which beggars all our powers of description and analysis. It mani-fests itself in a thousand ways and is the product of ten thousand antecedents. It is unthinkable that its workings should be reduced to a science. And goodness is an equal mystery. We think we know it when we see it, but it is like the wind which bloweth where it listeth. We can not tell whence it cometh nor whither it goeth. Some personalities achieve goodness, and some wickedness, and the reasons in both bases are largely unknown. And if human personality and goodness are mysteries, then religion is the mystery of mysteries. It is the life of God in the soul of man. It is the bond between the finite and the infinite. It is clearly, there-fore, the height of presumption to hope that in realms such as these we shall ever be able to proceed with the same sureness of step as that which now obtains in astronomy or in medicine. How shall we, for example, determine by observation and experimentation precisely that amount of parental affection which is best for children—not one grain too much nor one too little? How shall we ascertain the exact extent of self-guidance which will be best for girls fifteen years old? Can we know honesty as physicians know digestion? Can we with the scalpel of the intellect dissect the process of conversation until all its details are laid bare before us?

Such would have been our ready answer fifty years or more ago at a time when psychology was still mental philosophy and pedagogy was studied scarcely more than spiritualism is today, but not so in our day. The evidence to the contrary is too strong. Indeed, in the light of the experience of the last generation, it is foolhardy to venture to set limits beyond which science cannot go. One of the most glamorous pages of human history is the story of scientific achievement in the closing years of the nineteenth century and the opening decades of the twentieth. Who would have dreamed fifty years ago that two scientists in the realm of human personality would spend five years of their lives plus the labors of a number of expert assistants in studying deceit and kindred phases of character, and that in the study of deception alone they would administer 171,594 tests requiring an average of four hours of time from each of 10,865 boys and girls? In the judgment of an eminent psychologist, these two investigators, Hartshorne and May, made more progress in the measurement of human conduct in three years than was made in ten years by the earlier students of the measurement of intelligence. As a result, these scientists are able to tell us with certainty some facts about deception. They inform us that among children deception increases with age—the cheating ratio for children 9 years old being .35, for 13 years old, .50. This information, we believe, is as reliable as medical knowledge concerning the relative prevalence of measles at the several ages. They tell us that deception decreases with intelligence—the cheating ratio of exceptionally bright children being .25 and that of exceptionally dull children being .55. They tell us that the most important single factor in influencing deception in public school is the way the classroom group feels about the matter of cheating. The correlation or relationship in cheating among friends in the same class is .73; among friends not in the same class, .16; among classmates who are not especial friends, .60. These are only a few items taken from but one of a host of researches.

Who would have dreamed fifty years ago that we would know today the approximate relationship between nervous excitability and bodily acidity? Or, that we would know how old children must be before 75 percent of them will comprehend without special instruction the meaning of the Parable of the Sower? Or, the mathematical chances of reclaiming delinquent boys through correctional institutions and through fosterhomes? The science of human welfare, which is the science of the abundant life, has gone forward by leaps and bounds. Much of it has been prosecuted without the slightest hope of material gain. The very existence of these achievements serves to renew our faith in the idealism of mankind. And it becomes increasingly apparent in the light of these past achievements that it is impossible for us to say that religious education cannot become a science, if it wills to do so. It can, if it wills it, and if we will it. The major question, therefore, is not a can but a should.

Before setting forth the considerations which point to the desirability and even the absolute necessity of religious education to become a science, it is essential that an important distinction be made. We must separate sciences which deal only with things from sciences which deal with people as well as things. Chemistry, physics, astronomy, engineering, obviously deal only with things. Medicine, education—both secular and religious homiletics, deal not only with drugs and textbooks and sermonic material, but—what is more important—with people. Their whole purpose is to change people. Hence, a too exclusive attention to the thing-side of their respective fields without due attention to the people-side must doom them to certain failure. A doctor, who became so absorbed in his drugs or his surgical technique that he regarded his patients as mere opportunities for the practice of his narrowly conceived science, would sometimes be actually less successful than the old family physician, whose medical library was hopelessly out of date but whose warm human sympathies were entirely up to the minute. Likewise, a religious educator, whose interest in projects and the discussion method and worship techniques so usurped his attention that he had no room left for a passion to help boys and girls under God, would in all probability be inferior to a Sunday school teacher of the old school, who was blissfully ignorant of the latest methods but eternally grounded in love for God and man.

There is then a distinct sense in which religious education, if it becomes a science, is not to be forced into the mold of those sciences which have no human interest. It is precisely at this point that our greatest danger lurks, a danger so momentous that it may undo all the good which is potential in the application of the scientific method of religious education. It is at this point, we believe, that many ministers and churchmen have feared the scientific leanings of religious education, and rightly so. Their judgments have been altogether sound when they said they preferred an oldline Sunday school teacher to a modern technician. But, let it be noted, if in the first blush of our new emphasis upon research and technique we become coldly scientific, the cure is not less but more science. The very mark of a true science is to take all factors into consideration and to base its technique upon a balanced view of the whole. Therefore, any Sunday school teacher who is so absorbed in conducting a perfect discussion that she forgets the boys and girls for whom the discussion exists is in so far forth not scientific.

She is attending to only one element in the situation, and the least important element at that. She is thinking so much of the thing-side of her science that she overlooks entirely the people-side. She is forgetting that love for children, a genuine desire to do them good, is the supreme pedagogical technique. It has more power to touch growing lives than the discussion method can ever have. (In all probability, the statement just made could be validated by the methods of scientific research.) There is no substitute for a transparent love for people and a consuming passion for the Kingdom of God. These must at all costs be retained as integral parts of the whole in the development of religious education into a science.

And there is no good reason for believing that these two interests are incompatible. It never occurs to us, for example, that the more skillful physician is necessarily prone to be less anxious to heal his patients for their own sake. On the contrary, if he really cares for his patients, his mounting successes begotten of his scientific skill may serve to fan his joy in service to a fever heat until it fills his life from center to circumference. It is not, then, a case of "either-or" but a case of "both-and."

Having thus faced an insidious danger, we are now in a position to attend to certain considerations which seem to point irresistibly to the conclusion that religious education—and the work of the church in general—must become a science if it is to fulfill its destiny. These considerations exist because human nature is what it is, because life is what it is, and because our twentieth century civilization is what it is. There are four of them.

In the first place, religious education must become a science in order to combat the opposing forces of unrighteousness which themselves make such elaborate use of the methods of science. The children of light must fight the children of darkness with their own weapons if they entertain any hope whatsoever of winning the battle. There is no better example of the point in question than the motion-picture industry. This gigantic and offtimes unscrupulous enterprise is laying a host of sciences under tribute in order to fill its coffers. (If ten thousand human personalities are left mutilated by the wayside, that is none of its concern.) The sciences of music and acoustics, of electricity, of machinery, of architecture, of advertising (which is at root psychology) are combined by master minds and hands to make a mighty appeal to our young people. Can a Sunday school whose officers and teachers make their preparation on their way to the church successfully offset its influence? Slipshod methods, uncritically adopted and indifferently executed, have never yet triumphed over painstaking diligence.

Or, consider with what scientific thoroughness the enterprise of war is carried on, both on the battlefield and at the home base. Indeed, it is a well-known fact that many of the sciences received a decided impetus from the World War. Aviation, chemistry, physics, engineering, bateriology, medicine, and even psychiatry moved forward with ten-league boots under the stress of war. The thought-power of the nation was mobilized in order to make war. It would indeed be glorious if a future historian could look back upon our age and note that the sciences received a decided impetus from the church, by virtue of the extensive use made of them in the interests of a kingdom not of this world. Is it inconceivable that with high emotion we might mobilize the thought-power of the world in the service of peace? The foregoing are but two instances out of many wherein activities which are more or less detrimental to human well-being are being carried on with scientific precision. The clear inference is that if religious education is to make any headway in the opposite direction, it must do likewise.

In the second place, religious education must become a science in order to cope successfully with a world so complex that it makes and unmakes life in a thousand and one unforeseen ways. Our modern civilization of great cities, rapid transportation, radios, television, world-wide contacts, lower and higher education and gigantic industrial concerns has complicated endlessly the task of building the City of God. Compare the simplicity of a provincial town in the early nineteenth century. There the growth of a human personality was a relatively simple matter. It was conditioned by a home, a school perhaps, an occupation, a church, and neighbors. But now an American boy's taste in music is determined by a song from the NBC studios in Chicago. His outlook upon life is colored by a public school teacher whose philosophy is derived from Columbia University. His playlife is dominated by a schoolmate from southern Italy. His diet and consequently his health are affected ultimately by the importation of Russian coal, inasmuch as his father's steadiness of employment is the indirect result thereof. And his home is in the strangest and loneliest and newest place in the world—a large city. How, then, shall we proceed to secure the abundant life for an American boy? Who is sufficient unto these things in a day when lives are being made and marred by tremendous underground forces which are at least as difficult to understand and cope with as the mythical dragons of the Middle Ages?

Here is the modern city, a new social phenomenon of whose meaning for human life we know next to nothing. A recent investigation in Chicago has found that, if the city is divided into concentric circles beginning with the Loop and extending to the better-class suburban areas, each circle has its own distinctive rate of delinquency. Immediately outside the Loop is an area of tumble-down warehouses where one boy out of four becomes a delinquent. Adjacent to it is an area of mixed immigrant populations where one boy out of five becomes delinquent. The percentages gradually drop until in the outer edges of the urban area the proportion is only one out of fifty. What are we going to do about it? We do not know. Here is our gigantic industrial system, which, it is safe to say, is not understood by anyone from the president to the humblest citizen. Recently it played a cruel trick upon us, throwing several millions of men out of work, but no one knows precisely why it did it or what we should do about it. We know that this system is doing something to us as human beings but we have little idea what or why or how. A sense of helplessness overwhelms us as we confront the complex determinants of human life today. One thing seems clear; namely, that the only way out is to tackle social and religious engineering with the same scientific thoroughness as has been applied thus far to mechanical and industrial engineering. A Sunday school class which undertakes to develop religious character today must think and experiment and labor incessantly. It is a matter of life and death. Religious education must become a science in order to cope successfully with an infinitely complex world.

Again, religious education must become a science in order to command the allegiance and the intellectual respect of an educated constituency. The several realms of life have taken over one by one the scientific method. Medicine is now a science. It was not always so. Agriculture is a science, and a most careful one. Housekeeping is rapidly becoming a science. Transportation, manufacturing, merchandising, investment, secular education—all are now using in varying degrees the methods of science. The church, therefore, is face to face with a generation which has been educated to expect things to be done in a most careful manner, and to look lightly upon any life-area which does not set for itself high standards of study and workmanship. It seems probable that a part of the present indifference of the more highly educated classes to the church is due precisely to the uncritical, unscientific manner in which we often carry on our work. The contrast with other realms of life is too clear. We simply fail to command their intellectual respect. Doctor Coe, in speaking of our customary practice, says: "—the main tradition of religious education, Christian as well as non-Christian, as far as knowledge and thinking are concerned, is that of exercising intelligence to a very limited degree and then stopping—often not only stopping, but blocking the way to further use."

It behooves us, therefore, as churchmen and religious educators, to set standards of precision and thoroughness which shall compel the respect of trained minds and challenge their powers to the full. The church has long done this in some departments of her activity. There is no scientific discipline more exacting than that of biblical scholarship, for example. A long line of brilliant scholars have matched their intellects against the minute and highly technical problems in the fields of biblical introduction and textual criticism, feeling that here they had foemen worthy of their steel. Great profit has accrued to the church from this policy. With equal justification may she now follow the same strategy in the field of personal and social advantage to challenge a high school principal to the position of teacher of a Sunday school class as to a task into which he can pour all his faculties of critical analysis and thorough-going research without at all exhausting its possibilities. She can only gain, if a factory executive can accept the superintendency of a Sunday school with the consciousness that his new position will involve problems much more difficult than any encountered in his business life, upon which much less has been done, and in which infinitely more is at stake. Her position will be strengthened if she can give the student for the ministry to feel that his chosen profession contains possibilities for aduous mental discipline which are second to none, and that he need make no apologies for his choice to his college chum who is now in law school or medical college. These possibilities are as yet only partially realized. It is our privilege to realize them more fully to the end that we may command the unqualified intellectual respect of a twentieth century constituency.

And, finally, religious education must become a science in order that it may be truly religious, because the scientific spirit is ultimately deeply religious. It is religious on the manward side. As Doctor Coe has so well pointed out, the scientific method is the only basis for true intellectual fellowship between man and man. In the spirit of science there is no trace of dogmatism. I do not override your view because I can, nor do you disallow mine because your personality is the stronger. No, both of us are under bonds to the truth and the truth alone. Under this overarching quest for something higher than ourselves we meet in mutual respect. Under this stimulus of a search for reality, the teacher and his class, a minister and his people, elders and deacons, Sunday school officers and teachers advance to new heights of fellowship wherein each is free to "draw the thing as he sees it for the God of things as they are."

And the scientific spirit is religious, also, on the Godward

side. In this spirit lies the promise of a new kind of fellowship between man and his God. For what we call science,
rightly understood, is nothing more nor less than our child-
like attempts to discover and use facts of life which the
Almighty ordained eons ago. Science is not always so interpreted—of that we are well aware—but it and we would
be the richer for the religious interpretation. Religious
education has the solemn right to view it in this light. The
scientific method, thus, becomes one way by which we lay
ourselves open to God's revelation. We can discover no
truth that is not his truth. And, having discovered it, we use
it to accomplish ends which are his ends. To the scientific
religious educator it can be said, as it was said of old: "Work
out your own salvation with fear and trembling, for it is God
which worketh in you both to will and to do of his good
pleasure."

Is religious education, then, to become a science? Fully
conscious of the dangers involved, we answer that it can,
and it must.

8. Let Religious Educators Reckon With The Barthians

H. SHELTON SMITH
Professor of Religious Education, Duke University
Divinity School

In the late 30s and early 40s religious education (as understood by the REA) had moved from an aspect of all education, to a specific discipline, a field of endeavor conducted primarily in churches, synagogues, and parochial schools and concerned for the moral character of children and youth. Undergirded by modern psychology, modern pedagogy (schooling-instruction), and liberal Protestant theology, the movement appeared secure and almost sure on its identity. It seemed as if, however, liberal theology and the progressive education movement had moved so far to an extreme that it had reached the end of its influence. In theology, a new concern for orthodoxy returned and challenged the prevailing understandings and ways. Smith, himself an important figure in the early days of the REA, simply raised a question that was heard as an extreme judgment. Unable to hear his mediating voice between the earlier concerns of religious education for the social world and neoorthodoxy's concern for the tradition, the movement was split asunder. Neither side in the controversy could understand him. The forces for change were too severe. The social situation (a war and a depression) had destroyed an earlier social optimism. The liberal leaders of the movement had grown old and younger leaders sought after a new name, Christian education. The long, slow struggle for an identity had collapsed. Could a new identity surface? Could the REA, an ecumenical group of liberal Protestants, Catholics, and Jews survive? If so, would it ever again have the sense of movement or would be become an institution which shared common concerns but went in different directions?

Religious Education XXIV (January 1934), pp. 45-51.

Religious educators must reckon with Barthianism. For one reason, this movement, although still in its teens, is the capturing topic of theological talk in Europe. More recently it has awakened interest among Christians of the Orient. When, in 1928, Dr. Douglas Horton translated for American readers Barth's *Das Wort Gottes und die Theologie*, Barthianism had scarcely been heard of on this side of the Atlantic.[1] Today it is one of the livest subjects of debate in seminaries, and within a short while it must extend its interest to the ministry at large. Simply as a matter of being intelligent, religious educators should get acquainted with Barth.

In the second place, there is much truth to what Barthians are saying. To dismiss the movement, as some have done, as being a mere postwar reaction, is stupid. Of course Barthianism arose during those chaotic war years. Likewise it has spread during a postwar period of socio-economic catastrophe. But what of it? If one's body should reveal a dangerous disease at a moment of severe physical shock, would this fact make the disease any less grave or the pain any less real? Barthianism as an articulated movement may prove to be *ad-interim*. But even so, this is no reason for refusing to consider the merits of the movement. It is my candid judgment that if one will ponder Barth's *Epistle to the Romans* in the spirit in which it was written, one will find himself wrestling with the key issues that vexed the soul of Paul. Here is no valley of dry bones!

There are those who would also dismiss the movement on the ground that it is a recrudescence of Fundamentalism. Probably not a few tired liberals and frayed traditionalists will use Barthianism as a bridge over which to pass into the camp of Fundamentalist security. But those who thus retreat from the contemporary scene will put themselves beyond the pale of Barth's theological tent. If Barth shakes off the dust of his feet against Modernists, he pulls down a mountain upon the heads of Fundamentalists.

For yet another reason Barthianism should concern religious educators. The leaders of this revolt have definitely "spotted" religious educators as being on the wrong theological track. One of Barth's most devoted English followers, Dr. John McConnachie, has recently brought out a volume in which he says: "The whole system of religious education, which is being pursued, is built on certain presuppositions which cannot be reconciled with the teaching of the New Testament." In his latest edition of *Dogmatics* (1932), Barth points out the great importance of Christian education. But the sort of "evangelical pedagogics" which he and others emphasize runs at crosscurrents with liberal religious education in America. Religious educators may not welcome the sharp shafts of Barthian criticism. Nevertheless, all is not well with religious education. This is no time to shut our eyes to light from any source. The first evidence of decay in any movement is at the point where its protagonists resent or ignore criticism.

Nothing is more important to Barthians than to rescue religion from the slough of Humanist subjectivism. Under the combined influences of philosophical idealism, historicism, evolutionism, and psychologism, God has, they think, been progressively dethroned while man has progressively elevated himself until he has superseded God. For theocentric culture, liberalism has substituted anthropocentric culture; for the rule of God, the rule of man. Under this process, religion has experienced a steady loss of all the characteristic theocentric content of the Christian faith. Thus Barth repeats again and again: "Men are men, and God is God."[3] Doctrines of immanence that would break down this wall of partition all good Barthians vigorously reject. There is no way, they urge, to unite man and God in terms of the continuity of nature.

Another aspect of Barthian thought focuses on the nature of natural man. It is here, perhaps, that Barthians diverge most widely from the position of liberal Christianity. Probably no man of the latter part of the nineteenth century did more to popularize the modernist view of man, as related to religion, than Henry Drummond. His two leading works, *The Ascent of Man* and *Natural Law in the Spiritual World*, had an enormous circulation both in England and America. Working within the perspectives of biological and cultural evolution, to which both Darwin and Spencer had made celebrated contributions, Drummond pictured man as the apex of life, the end to which the "whole creation moves." Under the glamor of progress, poets like Tennyson and Browning mused: "nothing walks with aimless feet"; "All's well with the world." The divinity of man was, in their judgment, reflected in man's conquest over nature, in his scientific discoveries, in his growing devotion to philanthropy, and in his achievement of political and economic freedom. Speaking of his Sunday talks which he gave in churches, Drummond says: " . . . I discovered myself enunciating Spiritual Law in the exact terms of Biology and Physics."[4] Writing of the application of the principle of continuity to every aspect of man's world, Drummond says: "It will be the splendid task of the theology of the future to take off the mask and disclose to a waning scepticism the naturalness of the supernatural."[5]

Against this view of man and of his relation to the supernatural, Barthians rebel with vehemence. Mrs. Browning may sing, "Earth's crammed with heaven," but not so Barthians. For to them such romanticisms spring out of an idealism that is blinded to important realities. Thus Barth writes: "Caught up in the struggle for existence—eating, drinking, sleeping, yes, above all, sleeping! marrying and giving in marriage—men stand midway between life and death. Immersed in the flux of time and history, fleshly, they are not righteous before God . . . What men account righteous and valuable is, as such *flesh*, which, in God's sight, is unrighteous and valueless."[6]

To many, this will appear to be only the wail of a pessimist. But Barth reminds any such that he and his associates "are moved neither by pessimism, nor by the desire of tormenting themselves, nor by any pleasure in mere negation; they are moved by a grim horror of illusion; by a determination to bow before no empty tabernacle."[7] In any event, much of what the Barthians are saying sounds peculiarly like Paul, who said, "O wretched man that I am, who shall deliver me from the body of this death?" When liberal religion lost this realistic awareness of death in the midst of time, it surrendered an important aspect of realism in Pauline Christianity. Harnack's definition of the Christian religion as "eternal life in the midst of time"[8] is, for Barth, the illusion under which liberal anthropologists labor. It is such who see in all our programs of social action the Kingdom of God.

The two aspects of Barthian thought already considered are but preliminary to what may be regarded as the movement's most central concern; namely, the problem of revelation. As long as supernatural modes of religious thought prevailed the problem of revelation met with no unsurmountable difficulties. Ever since the Renaissance, however, supernaturalistic world-patterns have been slowly dissolved under the growing belief in the adequacy of the scientific approach to reality. The success of this way of thinking has rendered the old apologetics of a special revelation invalid. Schleiermacher, the "father of modern theology," instituted a type of thought with respect to religion which, under the subsequent developments of men like Ritschl, Herrmann, and Troeltsch led to the extinction of the Christian revelation as a unique, discontinuous event in history. For Schleiermacher, Jesus is distinguishable from other historical characters only "by the constant potency of his God-consciousness."[9] The nature of revelation is understood more significantly as that which functions in "the region of the higher self-consciousness."[10] God, the "universal fountain of life," reveals himself in man's nobler self-consciousness. Working upon this legacy, Ritschlians made the moral self-consciousness of Jesus the basis upon which to testify to the finality of his revelation. It remained for Troeltsch, the historian, to consummate the meaning, implicit in liberal thought since Schleiermacher, and to identify God with eternal world-reason, immanent within man and man's culture, and working out his purposes through the ethical creativity of man. The divine purpose is everywhere at work, and it is man's unique distinction as well as privilege to participate in the moral enterprises of God, thereby furthering the Kingdom of God.

Against this view of Christian revelation Barthians war with might and main. Modern theology, they say, took a false trail under the leadership of Schleiermacher. He and subsequent modernists betrayed the essence of Christianity into the hands of theological relativists, with the result that the Christian Faith as portrayed in the Bible and in the Reformation, has been all but liquidated. Let us, Barthians say, discard the approach of the modernists and take a new start, for nothing less than this will save Protestantism from the ravages of Humanism.

In their approach to a new solution, Barthians are not overawed by science. On the contrary, Professor Emil Brunner, who is perhaps the best systematizer of the movement, says: "The kind of truth which is to be found in the realm, and by the means, of science is relatively un-important; for it deals with the external aspect of things. . . . Even the sciences that investigate the essence of things in the most thorough-going way, such as theoretical physics, do nothing more than produce an accurate time-table indicating where and when future events will take place."[11] When, therefore, the objector says, "Christian faith in revelation contradicts modern science," this is cheerfully granted without in the least upsetting Barthians.

Barthians also reject the epistemological approach to God under the aspect of divine immanence. "A religion," says Brunner, "based on such a conception of God is monis-tic and optimistic. It asserts an unbroken unity and contin-uity of God and the natural existence of man. God and the world experience are not contradictory; nor are the experi-ence of the world and the Ego different from God. The world in its being is divine and the essence of the Ego is God-like."[12] Man comes to know God only in response to that which comes to him from without, not by way of self-consciousness acting upon man's better self within.

How, then, may one apprehend God in salvation? Knowledge of God, Barth himself admits, "is not accessible to our perception: it can neither be dug out of what is unconsciously within us, nor apprehended by devout con-templation, nor made known by the manipulation of occult psychic powers. These exercises, indeed, render it the more inaccessible. It can neither be taught nor handed down by tradition, nor is it a subject of research. Were it capable of such treatment, it would not be universally significant, it would not be the righteousness of God for the whole world, salvation for all men."[13] Knowledge that is revelational, redemptive, saving, must come to man from without, from the holy Other. God's chosen way to reveal himself is through Christ, the Eternal Word. The process of the revelation involves divine invasion of the human. Brunner puts the matter squarely thus: "It is obvious that the entire New Testament in all its parts, where it speaks of Jesus the Christ, means by this name an event which is not only gradually but fundamentally above all other events, and one which essentially can happen only once."[14] Barthians anticipate the kind of criticism that will be leveled against them. Their answer is unequivocal: Liberals want to get rid of the stumbling block of the message of Christ."[15]

A fourth element in Barthian thought is in respect of the Bible. Professor Brunner goes so far as to say: "Christian faith is faith in the Bible."[16] In his earlier writings Barth laid primary stress upon the *Crisis* of man. But his second edition of *Dogmatics* (1932) marks a significant shift, in which the Bible becomes the central subject matter of theology. It is in the Bible that Christ is revealed as God's Word. It follows that theology is first and last Biblical theology.

In turning their attention primarily to the Bible, Barth and his disciples make haste to distinguish between the Word of God and the Bible. Orthodoxy, they say, identified the two and thereby made of the Bible a fetish, a divine oracle equally infallible throughout. For Barthians, the Word of God is Christ, and the Bible is only a medium through which the Word is disclosed. The Bible is a human record and, as such, reflects all the errors to which human witnesses are subject. But just as a field contains gold, so the Scriptures, although an earthen vessel, contain a divine message, which is the Word of the Gospel. The Bible, as such, is not authoritative; but it witnesses to an authoritative Word.

How may one distinguish between the Bible and the Word? To the surprise of many, particularly to traditionalists, Barthians regard historical criticism as both inevitable and valuable. Let historical scholars dissect the strata of Biblical documents; let them freely distinguish between truth and error in Biblical history; let them destroy cosmological anachronisms, and the like. "What then," asks Brunner, "has been destroyed? We answer:nothing of importance . . . it is a matter of course that Biblical criticism and Bible-faith or Bible-authority not only are reconcilable, but necessarily together."[17] But when historical scholars have exhausted their researches, they have not, we are told, brought readers into contact with the Word. On the contrary, Brunner reminds us that "what I can know as rational is not God's Word, but general timeless impersonal truth."[18] He who would penetrate the Word within the Bible must do so by faith.

Barthians are sometimes accused of having no place in their system for religious education. On the contrary, "Its literature is alive with the question."[19] Dr. Edward Thurneysen, Barth's Timothy in the Faith, and others, are actively engaged in developing the "principles of an evangelical pedagogics." already the major directions are fairly clear.

First of all, teaching, like preaching, centers in the "ministry of the Word." The teacher's one objective is to bring the child into contact with the Word of God, which is Jesus Christ as revealed in the Bible. The norm of Christian education is Christ as witnessed to in the Bible. The Bible, not "life situations," constitutes the subject matter of the curriculum. Acting under the principle that "the Bible is its own best interpreter," the teacher will trust "to the power of the Word itself to carry its message home, rather than to his own expositions."

Barthian pedagogy, in the second place, rejects unreservedly the view that man is essentially, natively good. Instead it teaches that man is evil, basically wrong, and in need of salvation. The conversion of man cannot, Barthians claim, be brought about by polishing up the *old* man; nothing less than a *new* nature will lift him from the depths of creaturehood.

In the third place, Barthian educators reject the false principle of human autonomy. Deriving from Descartes, it is this principle that underlies the doctrines of "self-expression," the evil of which can easily be seen in certain forms of progressive education. It leads also to the sort of individualistic tendencies under which man ultimately rejects all authority. "A true Christian pedagogics," says McConnachie, "must start not from man and his values, but from God and his Word, in Jesus Christ."[20]

A fourth feature is that, although Barthians stress the necessity of Christian education, they nevertheless warn teachers that they cannot communicate the Christian revelation to their pupils. This truth, the truth that is God's Word, is not within their power to give. McConnachie goes even further and says: "The work of the teacher is not to give to the child views about God, or values, or religious ideas."[21] Yet in some unexplained way the teacher must be "the bridge" by which the child comes in contact with God.

Thus far we have south to set forth some of the characteristic phases of Barthianism. There is no doubt that it constitutes a direct challenge to the customary religious thought of Christian educators. How shall it be evaluated?

My own reaction is twofold. As a movement of protest Barthianism is rendering a long-needed service. That this is the best of all possible worlds; that man is the center, the measure, and the master of things; that evil is an antisocial appendix, from which man can be weaned by a little more progressive teaching and preaching; that it is not *what* people think but *how* they think; that Jesus was a good man who gave good advice; that the Bible is a problem-solver in "life situations"—against all such easy-going liberalisms may Barthians never cease to do battle.

It is at the point of construction, however, that Barthians find in me a doubting Thomas. In their stress upon God as the divine Other in religion, they offer a wholesome antidote to extreme doctrines of divine immanence which, in some instances, have confused the divine and the human and in others, have equated the divine in terms of the human. When, however, the objectivity of God is carried to the point of saying that whatever man, as man, can know is by this fact not God, then objectivity is purchased at the price of religious agnosticism. Although Barthians urge that in Christian education we should begin with God, not man, they make much of the fact that man, as man, can never know God. Their only way out of this extreme epistemological dualism is to resort to dogmatic supernaturalism. Although the "Word was made flesh," Jesus as a human personality, it is affirmed, discloses no revelation of God. A true revelation is accessible only to one who by faith can disengage Christ the Word from Jesus the man. This parallelism extends also to a distinction between what Jesus said and what he was, with the latter aspect being stressed to the extent that what he taught is of value, not for its inherent worth, but because it was Jesus who said it. A fear seems to grip Barthians, lest one become so immersed in the teaching message of Jesus that he will lose sight of the messenger.

This same conflict between relativism and absolutism, between natural and supernatural, is carried by Barthians into the Bible. Although the Bible is admitted to be the product of fallible men, and, as such, is subject to all the relativisms of Biblical history, it nevertheless contains buried within itself an absolute, inerrant, once-for-all-delivered Word. That God has revealed himself in the Word must in the final analysis be taken on faith. Moreover, the perception of the Word itslef is solely by faith.

To predict what will likely be the outcome of Barthian Biblicism in the experience of the common man, a glance at the early Reformation period is at least suggestive. Did not Luther make a heroic effort to distinguish the Word from the Bible? With what result? For himself this was more or less successful, especially in his earlier experience as a Reformer. For later generations, especially among the masses, the Word became identified with the Bible. Does it take much imagination to foresee that Barth's Biblicism will probably suffer the same consequences? Already disciples of orthodoxy, not to say of Fundamentalism, are looking with favor to Barth. But it is instructive to find that they say little or nothing about Barth's emphasis upon the historical errors of the Bible, of which Barth and Brunner make much, but much about Barth's Word of God. To the average layman the Word of God is simply the Scriptures of the Old and New Testament. Barthianism, then, can easily be a means of reviving Biblical authoritarianism under a new aspect.

The duality that runs through Barthian teachings in respect of Jesus and Christ is fraught with many possibilities of abuse. A resurgence of Christological traditionalism may easily result in the reduction of Jesus, the historical preacher and teacher, to the status of a mere ghostly appearance. Exactly this has happened in our historical past. In the age of Gnosticism, there was a battle royal, not to make people believe in the divine Christ, but in the real humanity of Jesus.

Our modern biographies of Jesus leave much to be desired. Their piecemeal, analytical, and often romantic presentations of Jesus are glaringly incomplete for some of us. But incomplete as they are, they nevertheless contain elements of solid worth. The earnest seeker after the truth of Jesus' teachings, or of the cultural patterns within which he labored with his disciples, will want to know more, not less, about the Jesus of history.

9. Christian Education as a Theological Discipline and Method

RANDOLPH CRUMP MILLER
Professor of Christian Education Divinity School
at Yale University
(Horace Bushnell Professor emeritus,
Yale Divinity School)

During the 40s confusion reigned. No one seemed sure of their identity, but theology had moved to the heart of the search. By the early 50s Protestants reached a consensus, Christian education was to be their name, and neo-orthodoxytheology was to frame their identity. Jews still referred to their concern as religious education, but always added from a Jewish perspective. Roman Catholics still used religious education, but understood it essentially as parochial schooling in Catholic tradition. On the Protestant side of the search for identity, few persons were as significant as Randolph Crump Miller. Since 1958 he has been the editor of Religious Education. *Through his labors the continuing quest for an identity has continued. Rightly, he has kept the focus of the REA on foundational issues. Indeed, he established Christian education as essentailly a theological discipline, moving it from a practical subject to a central place in departments of theology. He also defended the significance of Christian education for the whole ministry of the church and tried to establish Christian education as a discipline concerned for a comprehensive, educational program rather than only one aspect of ministry.*

Religious Education XLVIII (November-December 1953), pp. 409-414.

Christian education is coming of age as a theological discipline and method. It is asserting a new autonomy as a theory of learning the Christian faith. It is indicating new developments of Christian growth in the family. It is drawing upon the Christian revelation as well as upon the learning process as a source of a relevant theology. It is expressing itself through the dynamic Christian life of the local congregation.

In one sense, all of these so-called new developments are as old as the Christian religion and can be found in certain aspects of Hebrew religion. But in another sense, religious education began with the rise of the Sunday school in the early part of the nineteenth century and reached its highest level with the insights of Horace Bushnell who in 1846 wrote the epoch-making *Christian Nurture*. But Bushnell was not taken seriously for another fifty years and during this time most religious education was ungraded and Bible-centered, with little concern for the capacity or for the growing edge of the pupils. When finally Bushnell's insights were considered, they were for the most part misunderstood or divorced from the basic presupposition of the part that parents must play in the religious development of the child.

Progressive education began its influential career among the leaders of secular education after the turn of the twentieth century, and Church educators followed the lead of John Dewey and his cohorts. Mixed with sound educational theory was a secular metaphysics or a simple naturalism among the secularists, and a type of liberal Christianity among the Church leaders which lacked much of the profundity and depth of biblical Christianity. These leaders knew their educational theory, and they made use of all the findings of science in biblical study and theology as well as

in educational processes, but their system crashed against
the rocks of a resurgent orthodoxy.

It took a theological analysis to put Christian education
back on the right track. This was resented among some
educators who had not kept abreast of theological
developments or who were not theologians in any real
sense. A few of the most able among them were religious
naturalists who knew more about Henry Nelson Wieman
than about the classical theologians of the Church, and it
was hard for them to relate their teachings to any historic
theology. Many others were hard-working technicians who
were excited about developing new methods and techniques for stimulating interest in many areas of subject
matter. They saw education as a social process within the
context of a classroom situation, and often they saw clearly
the relation of religious attitudes to the community, but
they lacked precisely the insight upon which Christianity
insists: the social process of Christian education is provided
by the church which is the Body of Christ. A sociology of
education is not sufficient to provide a social theology of
Christian education.

I

With this background in mind, we need also to note
briefly three trends in Christian education before we look at
it as theological discipline and method.

The first trend is the rediscovery of the function of the
family as a primary agent of Christian education. From the
days of Deuteronomy to the organic unity of the family
stressed by Horace Bushnell to the experiments being
made today, there is recognition of the effective priesthood
of parents which has theological significance for the

interpretation of Baptism, Confirmation, and other equivalent rites in the various churches.

The second trend is the rediscovery of the function of the total parish in the comprehensive educational program. At first, this was a sociological discovery but it led to theological implications. If parish life is not a means of *redemption*, it is not truly Christian.

The third trend is the recognition that children are not little adults, but are developing organisms with growing edges which must be stimulated and directed. Graded vocabularies, projects adapted to age-levels, use of concepts within the capacities of growing minds, and other secular discoveries are important. But no one asked the $64 question: *What is the religious readiness of the child?* This is primarily a theological question, for it involves the relevance of the Gospel to a child's real concerns and needs.

II

These three trends indicate the significance of our basic problem, which is to find out how Christian education is to be a theological discipline and method. This means that Christian education must be defined theologically.

The purpose of Christian education is to place God at the center and to bring the individual into the right *relationship* with God and his fellows within the perspective of the fundamental truths about all of life. The major task of Christian education today is to discover and to impart the *relevance* of Christian truth. The key words here are *relationship* and *relevance*.

Theology is a description of relationships. It may be defined as "truth-about-God-in-relation-to-man." The whole of our Jewish-Christian tradition arises from man's experience of God's mighty acts in nature and in history. The Bible is the story of these relationships, in terms of covenants, judgments, and redemption. The focal point of such a theology is the coming of Jesus Christ, who through his life, death, and resurrection changed the relationship between man and God. "God was in Christ reconciling the world to himself." The developing theology of the Church, as for example in the doctrine of the Trinity, is always an attempt to describe experiences of relationship.

Ultimately this comes to the fore in our own experience in what Martin Buber calls the "I-Thou" relationship. This "divine-human encounter" takes place within the community, which is the church or fellowship of those seeking redemption. The relationship of the believer is not to an idea of God, important as concepts of God may be. A little child is not integrated in his home by his *idea* of his parents, but through his *relationship* with his parents in personal encounters. So it is with Christian faith; there is a personal relationship between the creature and his Creator who is the source of redemption.

There is a slogan to define this approach to Christian education: *Theology in the background: faith and grace in the foreground.* Christian nurture takes place when the believer trusts in God and in turn God's gracious favor comes to him, because that grace was there all the time awaiting the act of faith. Therefore, the application of theology to education leads to a dynamic personal relationship of faith and grace, and the ideas of theology arising from the relationships of men to God are the guides to a greater and deeper experience of God.

The theology which is in the background must always be *relevant*. Sometimes theology is so abstract as to be irrelevant. Yet redemptive experiences are going on around us at all times. The rhythm between rejection and acceptance in the home, the sense of frustration and the maturity of accepting oneself as he is, the conviction of sin and the assurance of God's forgiveness, the feelings of separation from God and then of being in communion with him— these occur in the lives of children and in the most mature adults. It is a matter of relationships, not of vocabulary or of abstract concepts.

The significance of this for Christian education is not always seen. It means that we may teach the glory of redemptive life on every level of communication and that theology is therefore relevant to every age-group. Religious readiness is developed far beyond technical theological capacity. But it means that the teacher of the younger Christians must have a theology relevant to his own capacities as well, and then be able to translate these insights into terms of the relationships of the younger.

Theology also contributes to our understanding of the learner. Theology gives us insights into the nature and destiny of man which are not part of the data or of the interpretation of the scientific view of man. Theology begins with the assertion that every man is the creature of God and becomes a child of God through Baptism (or its equivalent experience in communions without infant Baptism), and then grows in grace in the life and fellowship of the church. It says that man's destiny is to live in harmony with God and that after death there will be resurrection. But man is also a sinner. He is so disobedient, so selfish, so profoundly traitorous to the nature which God implanted, that he crucifies the best that God can do in sending his own Son. Thus man is capable of crucifying the best man that

God has made, and at the same time he is capable of being the Christ. One historic incident reveals to the full the glory and misery of man.

But Christian theology never stops with analysis. It turns to the cure immediately. The *reconciliation* which comes through Christ is the central issue. God has acted so that man will be saved if he turns in faith to the Father. It is the relationship of faith and grace which is the heart of Christian nurture.

Every learner fits into this pattern. Whether it is a child just entering church school, a person in the morning congregation, or an adult in the Bible class, the same fundamental understanding is there. The Gospel is good news for all people of all ages. It is the task of theology to provide self-understanding which is relevant to the particular age level. It is the task of Christian education to draw men into the redemptive life of the community of the faithful.

This leads to one more conclusion about the theological significance of Christian education. There is no education which is not also evangelism. Only as men are drawn by God's grace into the fellowship of the church do education and evangelism come together. To evangelize is to confront men with Jesus Christ, so that they will put their trust in God through him and by the power of the Holy Spirit live as Christ's disciples in the fellowship of the church.

It should be clear that Christian education is in itself a theological discipline. Because its teaching must build on the relationships which the learner actually has, and because its teaching must be relevant to the everyday life of the learner, much that is taught arises from experiences in the teaching situation. This is both necessary and desirable, for if education is to lead to nurture and evangelism it must

be in terms of meaningful experience. But it is also dangerous, as is demonstrated by the amount of bad and irrelevant
theology which has appeared; for unless education is the
impartation of Christian *truth* it is not Christian.

Theology is subject to the revelation found in Christ.
Only insofar as the educators are competent theologians
can there be success at this level of endeavor. Generally
speaking, the educators have not been competent theologians and the theologians have not provided a relevant
theology which provides meaning for the actual religious
relationships of growing persons. We will return to this
point when we examine the place of Christian education in
the curriculum of theological schools.

III

We turn now to another problem: that of method. We
have already indicated that theologians who provide a
basis for educational procedures must take account of the
relationships of religious living and of the relevance of
theology for the learners. It seems to me that a number of
current theologies, ranging all the way from neo-orthodoxy
to reconstructed liberalism, are capable of describing the
"I-Thou" relationship within the context of the redemptive
fellowship. My old professor, Douglas Macintosh, called it
"the right religious adjustment." Whenever a theology is
based on the mighty acts of God as found recorded primarily in the Bible and on man's response to God's acts,
there is the possibility of relevance for educational purposes. A barrier is placed before the development of Christian nurture when faith and grace are relegated to the
background and a fixed vocabulary of theology is placed in
the foreground.

The problem of method is technical. If we once develop a relationship theology which has the possibility of relevance at every level of human experience, the educational problem becomes that of finding methods which will make this relevance meaningful.

I will not take time to discuss the various battles between those who believe in content-centered and those who believe in life-centered teaching. It is pretty much a false antithesis. Any good teacher uses both, and it is in a proper balance between the two that we find relevance. But there is something deeper than this: *no education is religious unless it is God-centered*. We are to teach the relationship between man and God and man and man. The techniques will pretty much take care of themselves once we grasp the fundamental theological significance of what we are doing.

The trouble is, that we do not grasp the concept of relevance. There is too much taught even on the level of theological education which is not clearly relevant to the religious situation in which the student finds himself, or to the pastoral situation in which he expects to be. I believe that the documentary theory of the Pentateuch can be taught in terms of relationship and of relevance to seventh graders.

James Bradley Thayer writes: "While good teaching will differ widely in its methods, there is at least one thing in which all good teaching will be alike; no teaching is good which does not arouse and 'dephlegmatize' the students, which does not engage as allies their awakened, sympathetic, and cooperating faculties." (Quoted by Houston Peterson, *Great Teachers*, p. 341). Unless the students are aware of the relevance of what they are learning, we cannot expect this kind of response. Too often we can say of the students what Thomson said about the linnets, who

. . . sit
On the dead tree, a dull despondent flock.

The problem of relevance shows up at every level. The new Presbyterian (U.S.A.) lessons are shaded toward a neo-orthodox theology. On the kindergarten level, as one reads the teachers' and parents' manual, one discovers much help for adults which reflects the theology of neo-orthodoxy, some of it quite relevant; but one also discovers that the theological presuppositions lying behind the experiences of the children are those of modern child psychology and liberal theology. This is due, I think, to a failure to think through the theological understanding of children from a Christian point of view (Edith Hunter, "Neo-Orthodoxy Goes to Kindergarten," *Religion in Life*, Winter 1950-51.) The significance of neo-orthodoxy is that it cannot serve as a footnote to secular insights, although it may be able in its less extreme forms to use scientific data as footnotes for its Christian interpretation of man. This is no different from the problem of the theological student who cannot see anything relevant or redemptive in his class lectures in any of a dozen subjects, including sometimes Christian education itself.

John Wick Bowman describes Christian faith as *The Religion of Maturity*. The goal of Christian faith involves the putting away of childishness and immaturity. The marks of maturity are poise, originality, and disinterestedness, whereby we attain balance, power to bear fruit, and freedom from selfish motives. It is the full growth which is described in Ephesians: "reaching maturity, reaching the full measure of development which belongs to the fullness of Christ, instead of remaining immature, blown from our course by every passing wind of doctrine, by the adroitness of men who are dexterous in devising error; we are to hold by the truth, and by our love to grow up wholly unto him" (Eph. 4: 13b-15, Moffatt). Certainly this is a description of the goal of Christian education, showing the relevance of truth to the process of growing into the right relationship with God and with man.

Christian growth is a process of increased integration centered on the living God in our midst. But this process cannot be guaranteed by evangelism or education, or by the concepts of a relevant theology. The response of children and adults to the Gospel of Jesus Christ is in the last analysis a personal decision that rests in the mystery of God himself.

Our final question is the relation of Christian education to the curriculum of theological education. It is often an elective, or at best a few units are required for graduation. Being a late comer, it is often treated as a step-child. That is bad enough. But what is worse is that it is not considered a theological discipline at all. It is part of the practical courses, which means it is a study of techniques. The department of education is expected to provide tools, ladgets, and methods by which the Gospel may be taught. When it is just that, and nothing more, it has no independent existence as a theological discipline. It is something that can be learned outside the channels of the Christian religion, by borrowing from the secular educators who usually know more about techniques than we do. But this is to commit the heresy of making the Christian religion an adjunct to secular processes. It is this error which led to the excesses of the followers of John Dewey in both secular and religious education. Because no basic, Christian educational philosophy stood behind the process, the methods of Dewey led inevitably to Dewey's instrumentalism. It can be shown that Dewey's methods can be related to many other philosophies, but this is not generally accomplished. It is because of this separation of method and theology, that the religious educators went so far off the beam at the very time that new life was coming into the churches through the rediscovery of biblical realism and of the Reformation principles of theology.

The new trend in Christian education indicates that theology is basic and method is secondary. The Presbyterians saw this vaguely as they developed their new series of lessons, but they failed to get a complete integration of content and method. The Episcopalians see it in theory, but face the almost insuperable problem of solving it in practice. It involves, among other things, a complete theological training course for every editor along with a grasp of religious readiness of the various age-groups, and the mastery of methodology. This is the only kind of integrating program that will meet the requirements for an adequate curriculum.

Most of the theological schools have not seen this. If they continue to treat Christian education as a practical subject, they will be unable to train anyone to do the job. The experts they turn out will still be experts in new tricks of educational gadgets, and the pastors will fail to see the significance of their educational program.

I would not go so far as to suggest that Christian education belongs in the department of theology, but we must see it basically as a theological discipline, concerned with the whole ministry. Its problem is to describe adequately the existential situation, the religious predicament, to which the Christian Gospel has the answer. Its task is to make a theology which describes this relationship relevant to the learner of whatever age, and thus to bring the learner into a right relationship which God within the dynamic fellowship of the redemptive community. Methods need to be taught, and they are of the greatest importance, but the methods must be derived from the situation in which the individual finds himself and not from the secular world. The same methods are probably necessary, but because they are derivative they cannot dictate the results.

No one can be adequately trained for the pastoral ministry without an understanding of Christian education. It is against this background that the vows of those being ordained have meaning. The ordained is asked: "Are you persuaded that the Holy Scriptures contain all doctrine required as necessary for eternal salvation through faith in Jesus Christ? And are you determined, out of the said Scriptures to *instruct* the people committed to your charge; and to *teach* nothing, as necessary to eternal salvation, but that which you shall be persuaded may be concluded and proved by the Scripture?"

The Bible, then, is the source of Christian truth. But salvation does not rest on doctrine; it rests on faith in Jesus Christ. Doctrine stands behind faith, and salvation comes through God's grace.

The pastor is an instructor. It is his responsibility to teach. And he learns to teach through courses in Christian education. Therefore, everything he learns in seminary must be relevant, and biblical theology must describe God's mighty acts in history, whereby God acted to reconcile the world to himself. Every course, in so far as it is relevant, must teach Christian education; and Christian education, in so far as it is Christian, must be grounded in a relevant theology. Only in this way will the Gospel of Jesus Christ be taught to all people, of all ages, in all lands in terms of the relationship of redemptive living within the Christian community.

10. Catechetical Crossroads

GERALD S. SLOYAN
Department of Religious Education, Catholic University
of America
(Presently Professor of New Testament
at Temple University)

Regretfully, up until the 60s Roman Catholics had maintained a somewhat marginal role in the REA. Here and there a Roman Catholic voice could be heard, but it seemed as if Roman Catholics in the REA were not essentially involved in the quest for religious education, as understood by progressive liberal educators nor did they participate in the theological debate over Christian education engaged in by Protestants. In most cases, Roman Catholics, when they did write used the words religious education to refer to instruction in Catholic tradition within parochial schools. Other voices may have existed, but only this isolated schooling voice could be found within Religious Education. The REA, while desiring to be ecumenical, when it came to the nature and function of religious education, remained a Protestant affair. A major change occurred in the 60s when Gerald Sloyan brought an old and continuing debate among Roman Catholics into the REA. For the first time, we see a new word"catechetics" in the journal. We also are indirectly introduced to a debate between those who want to place emphasis on personal experience and those who believe that the content of the faith tradition is of greater importance. It is an issue somewhat similar to the Protestant religious-Christian education debate and Sloyan strives for a way out. Catechetics remained, however, theologically confessional, highly intellectual and concerned mostly with instruction.

Religious Education LIX (March-April 1964), pp. 145-161.

"Catechetical crossroads" are points where people meet whose work is the spread of the gospel, men whom the Lord has sent out without wallet or staff or sandals, who travel by two and two. "Catechetical crossroads" are also lines of convergence within the work of forming men in Christ. They are crossing points in the various forms of apostolic action, in the different aspects of the one message of new life in Jesus Christ, in the sources of revelation—"light and truth" as our Lord described it. All these matters can intersect, do intersect. At the crossroads we discover there is no one "but only Jesus."

It has been suggested that I open our deliberations by presenting a kind of position paper. Where are we, catechetically, in the United States and English-speaking Canada? Where do we hope to be? How can we get there? Does the child encounter Christ in our schools, our Confraternity classes? Does the adult meet him in the celebration of the mysteries in the parish church? Do we, in other words, speak with a single voice, and that the clear voice of the Master?

I

At Washington this summer, on the Catholic University of America campus, catechetics was a great popular success, and I am frightened. It never was a success before—until two or three years ago, say. You at least knew where you stood. All the best people were pretty thoroughly disinterested in the question. You could go about your lonesome business, and write letters to friends halfway across the country and all the way across the ocean, and in general get left severely alone. Catechetics was pin-men, flannelboards, methods. If you said, "No, I'm in the game at a theological level," or intimated that the celebration of the liturgy was the key to all, people chewed the remainder of the olive off their toothpick (or finished their ice-water float) and walked away. You had broken the rules. *They* knew what "cathechism-teaching, new style" was about. It was something you could see, like chemicals that changed color to show the difference between mortal sin and sanctifying grace. It was diagrams for the three levels of life: sentiment, rational (both natural, mind you), and *super*natural. O prefix triumphant, and all clear, clear, and *mea maxima* clear! It was Father Heeg's books, full of short words and big type. But now, as I say, everything's different.

People approach you nowadays with puckered brows and say, "I've read Father Hofinger's books and Jungmann's and (lamely) oh, of course, yours—and we've got this new approach going pretty strong in River City. I'm getting lots of resistance on it, but we're sailing right ahead. It's the older pastors, though; you can't sell them." Then they say "new approach," kerygmatic" and "new interpretations of Scripture" about six times in the next three minutes, and you're supposed to get the idea that they're *really* in the club. They're so advanced, in fact, that you feel kind of lucky you needn't bother to catch up.

If you should be fortunate enough to discuss their M.A. thesis with these people five or six summers later, the conversation is marvelously different. Usually, however, this kind doesn't come back a second time, let alone five more. They were sent to Washington (or Milwaukee, or South Bend) to check on the doctrine of the other prophets. Like jesting Pilate, they don't wait for many answers.

People are writing new courses in great numbers. They are dissatisfied with everything they have seen, so they sharpen their pencils and get blank sheets of paper and get right to it. This group is not nearly so numerous as the one that wants to know what textbook series to use. About three letters a week come to me regularly asking this question. My stock answer has become: "We don't have one yet, and that's undoubtedly a good thing. If we did the teachers wouldn't know in the first place why it was good, and in the second they would be discouraged by it, fight it, and then we'd be worse off than before."

II

The first important thing I should like to observe about the catechetical movement is that it is very widely thought to be a matter of "the pill." The doctor may be an eminently respectable one; some of the finest catechists in Europe, America, and Asia, none of them a quack, are cast in this role. Despite the sobriety of the doctors, the mentality prevails: find the pill, and dose liberally. There seems to be a genuine fear of long, hard study, of learning foreign languages, of doing research in what brought us to our present pass in catechetics, theology, and pastoral care, and what will bring us out of it. This leads me to say—and I speak to myself as much as to you—go sparingly in trying to make all things clear at a one-day institute, or three talks crammed into two days. Do nothing to confirm anyone in the wrong notion that the inner meaning of modern catechetics is available on easy terms or without tears. I am tempted to say: if you can't hold peoples' attention for at least two semesters, or six summers, or ten days of common residence and hard labor, or one night a week for all of three winters, then don't try. You'll confuse everybody, both the teachers and the taught, and even perhaps yourselves. Do all in your power to get solid training at a graduate level for some persons in numbers who can assume a leadership role in this central work of the church.

A second matter of great importance is the claim of "newness" that one hears on every side. This usually means "new to the practitioner" who was until recently blissfully unaware of the ancient treasure of faith in all its length and breadth and depth.

A Liguorian moralist finds the scheme of the virtues as developed by Aquinas "new." Both Thomist and Liguorian moralists together discover "new" teaching when they come to study in depth all that Sts. Paul and John had to say about life in Christ. It is shocking that the Catholic body should, on a wide scale, be describing as a "new approach" to teaching the faith of the church what has been in her inspired Scriptures from the beginning; what her fathers in the faith, both Eastern and Western, knew was the meaning of those Scriptures; what her service books of the East and the West have clearly said was the meaning of the words and deeds of the Savior, as prefigured by Abraham, Isaac, and Jacob, by Moses and all the prophets, as lived out in the lives of Peter and Paul, Andrew, James, and John, Cletus, Clement, Xystus, Cornelius, Cyprian. It has all been there, always. It is the ancient faith.

The problem is that the ancient faith has not been available to our people in its fullness. Child and adult alike, they have been served a distillation from which the most precious residue is absent and told it was "traditional." When they hear the church's *traditio*, her *paradosis*, her *kerygma*, for the first time it comes as an innovation, a change. The worst service we could do to the cause, I think, is to fall in with the erroneous assumption that a return to sources, a preaching of the gospel at full strength, is somewhat *new*. We may not tolerate this abuse in our hearing, least of all concur in it by declaring ourselves proponents of the "new theology" or the "new catechetics." We are the center party. Our glory is that, like the fathers of the first session of the Council in the only definitive vote they took, we think with the church. It is the novelties introduced in the twelfth century, or the fifteenth, or the nineteenth, that we cannot abide—the human traditions that our Lord Jesus identified as adulterating the pure Word of God, even while he upheld strongly a theory of the development of doctrine in Israel.

III

Is there, then, nothing new in modern catechetics? Of course there is. There is adaptation to cultures and mores, to the language patterns (a very important consideration) of the millions who are called to be Christian. There is the appeal to the findings of human psychology (both child and adult) that actually go back a hundred years but have been snowballing in the last four or five decades. The research findings in the sciences auxiliary in any way to the "knowledge of God and the blessed" that we share by faith— ancient languages, archaeology, patristic studies, especially those concerned with the second century—all these matters have a history in scholarship of no more than ninety or one hundred and twenty-five years. In this sense the findings of modern catechetics are new.

It is wrong, however, to label as a "new interpretation of Scripture" what the whole world of scholarship was agreed in 1900 was the only meaning of a particular passage or book. Much more important than that, the Catholic meaning, the Christ-meaning of an event, *cannot* be new, or else the Lord has deserted his church. It may be that men of the church have grown unclear on the message for a century, or five, or ten, through the mysterious processes of history; but the church does not forget, cannot forget. Much of what we come to know and hail as discovery Clement knew, Ignatius knew, Cyril of Jerusalem, Ambrose, Chrysostom knew. How shocked they would be to hear that the mystery of Christ's glorification was being hailed by any catechist anywhere before fellow Catholics as a "new dimension" of the mystery of our redemption!

And so I sum up: just because an insight is new to us through circumstances of our own bad catechizing in youth, or meaningless celebration (except for the little meaning yielded by private missal-use), or poor theological formation, we have not the right to lay this heritage at the door of the church of God. What is new to us is not new to the church or to Christ; and what is new humanly is not in any sense the substance of faith. Let us not involve either the Head or the whole Body in our default by labeling the ancient "new." This technique angers everyone, even though many cannot say why. The basic reason is that it is built on the false premise that there can be something absolutely new in the life of the church.

As a corollary to what we have just said we might mention that the only Scripture study worth doing in aid of catechetical improvement is that which looks into the religious meaning of the Bible. Critical questions are of importance. They are of great importance. They are not of supreme importance. One hears more and more nowadays of a certain childish faith placed in the notion that explaining the flood of Genesis in terms of the Gilgamesh Epic or the Adam story against its Babylonian background will somehow remove all difficulties believers have with the sacred narrative. Enkidu, Utnapishtim, and all the journeyers who go to sacred mountains or pluck from outlawed trees to unlock the secret of immortality have something to say to the Christian, it is true, but these teachers provide only the very beginning of wisdom. All exegesis that stops with such parallels poses the danger of rationalism of a new kind.

Read Origen on early Genesis, or Basil, or Theodore of Mopsuestia. They did not know the ancient near-Eastern texts but they did know Jesus Christ, and Paul's epistle to the Romans, and the fact of sin, and what the reality of poetry is, a concatenation of symbols. These men made much out of the ancient Scriptures, not little. Our modern advances will turn out less than half gain and more than half loss until we begin to come upon the ancient principles of biblical usage by the church in her preaching, her teaching, and her liturgical prayer, and use contemporary critical study in conjunction with those principles, not in disregard of them. Her chief ancient principle is not allegory, not paraenesis, not "spiritual sense," but typology, the idea that a great variety of things in men's lives stand for God, and of these Jesus Christ is the chief, and many persons and things in turn stand for him.

IV

I should like, finally, to mention one or two more hazards that seem to mark life on the new catechetical frontier.

One is the growing tendency to conceive all catechizing in simple, biblicist terms. We have discovered "salvation-history," which all too often means neither more nor less than Bible history on new and better terms. It is scholarly. It is enlightened. But it is mere Bible history which saves no one.

Children are invited to spend a whole year, frequently the first year of high school, proceeding earnestly from Adam to the Maccabees. Jesus in the gospels comes in the sophomore year; Christ in the early church (Acts and Epistles) in junior year; Christ in the church, the Holy Spirit at work in the Mystical Body in the senior year.

What is happening here? Well in the first place all sense

of immediacy is lost. Relevance, the Christ-life here and now, are matters that are being deferred because so much time is required to relate the Emmanuel prophecy to Jesus the Messiah or to reconstruct the postexilic situation. Relating Assyria to the monolithic threats of bigness in the young lives of students, making Syria and Ephraim meaningful in terms of all the "deals" they have witnessed by age fifteen in which canny men of little faith agree to sup with the devil—we are not finding time for that. Besides, it is mere accommodation. It departs from the primary literal sense. In other words, I find us retreating from the real work of catechetics because it is proving so satisfactory to teachers at the moment to give biblical lectures to young people. The reason? Well it is such a relief from the many years we spent giving them theological lectures. We have discovered the Bible lately, and we rush impetuously to share our treasure without taking time to do with it what the church has always done: teach Christ from it.

Finally: unless we celebrate, it will all come to nothing. The student has to meet Christ, really meet him. There are many places to do that: in one's neighbor, in one's enemy, in a thousand ways in daily life. But of all of these opportunities only the encounter in the Eucharist is the *summit* compared to which all other meetings are lower stages on the slope. Only the Eucharist is the *source* from which all other encounters derive their efficacy and meaning.

I find we are settling for verbalism on the catechetical frontier: better words, better chosen words, the Word of God even (which is our sole guarantee that the right things will get said), but words. We are making a partial reform, in other words, not a total reform. Because the movement is in such early stages in this country and Canada, this comprises a danger all its own.

We can't find the artists, we say. We can't sing. There is no good organist. So much *time* is taken by all that extra activity, when you only have them an hour a week. So we talk at them. We talk at them better, which is why this solution is probably worse.

Actually, of course, there is but a single problem: 'To do the truth in charity.' But we can't *do* unless we pray, and come forward singing, and eat. If there's time left over, then we can explain, with words. Christian formation is mostly doing.

11. The Strange History of Christian Paideia

EDWARD FARLEY
Associate Professor of Systematic Theology, Pittsburgh
Theological Seminary
(Presently Professor of Theology at The Divinity School at
Vanderbilt University)

Complete agreement has been rare in the history of the religious education movement. However, once the name Christian education had emerged and orthodox theology resurfaced to importance, differences increased. As might have been expected, a conflict between nurture and instruction also surfaced along with the Christian education debate. Sharing a commitment to neoorthodox theology and its implications for education, Edward Farley framed the issues which emerged in the late 1960s. Once again the issues of identity and purpose have surfaced. The quest is not ended, a new name has only made the identity issue more complex.

The present two-part essay aims to pursue one basic question. What is the relationship between the work of the Holy Spirit and that enterprise called, "Christian education"? The thesis presented here has both a negative and positive thrust. Negatively, it suggests that while the Spirit may be active in some sort of "nurturing" process going on in the church and family Christian education is not nurture, except in a very incidental way. Hence, most traditional ways of appealing to the Spirit to complete the nurturing process, to help and guide the sanctification process occurring in Christian education, are erroneous. In this sense the

Religious Education LX (September-October 1965), pp. 339-346.

Holy Spirit is simply superfluous in Christian education. Positively, the thesis attempts to describe the work of the Holy Spirit in Christian education the light of two particular clues. These clues concern the Spirit as the way God is contemporaneously present in the church, which means he is present in some way in connection with Jesus Christ. The second clue is provided by Paul's contrast between life "in the Spirit" and life "in the flesh." The positive thrust of this essay is to attempt to see what Christian education looks like when it is approached as education in the church of the Spirit, and when it is approached as education "in the Spirit" rather than "in the flesh."

However, we are not going to get very far unless we have something in mind by the term, Christian education. What is it we are talking about when we ask, Does Christian education need the Holy Spirit? Such a question is easier to answer when we observe something happening in a church school on Sunday morning than when we read the literature of Christian education, and hear people talk about Christian education. I must confess that as I read this literature, I grow more and more puzzled. It occurred to me only recently that a possible source of that puzzlement was the tendency to identify "education" and "nurture." This identification is responsible for a basic linguistic confusion in language about Christian education. This first part of the essay cannot claim that all confusion is dispersed. But at least one rather basic confusion may be located, and, insofar as that occurs, the basic thesis of this essay may in the long run be clearer. The reader may be aware that something is happening in the total argument beyond merely the question about the work of the Spirit in Christian education. In the final analysis a rather basic "philosophy" of Christian education is being presented here, or at least the seeds of one.

I

THE SUBLATION OF NURTURE AND INSTRUCTION

In this first part of the essay I would limit the inquiry to the linguistic confusion perpetrated by identifying nurture and instruction. I would like to do this by attempting to characterize some basic historical positions on the matter. This is not a "history of Christian education" or even a history of nurture. Rather I am attempting, through some historical samples (the most important ones, I think), to illustrate this confusion.

A. The Traditional View

First, the *traditional view*. Allow me vastly to oversimplify the traditional Protestant understanding of the way salvation occurs in the following summary. God through the sufferings of Jesus Christ grants to the elect his forgiveness, which sufferings and foregiveness are proclaimed in the preaching of the Gospel. The elected believer responds to this proclamation in faith through the interior workings of the Holy Spirit, and is thereby incorporated into Christ's body, the church. In this regenerated state the Christian grows under the continued operations of the Spirit as the Spirit works through the means of grace, namely the Word and the sacraments. The way this living Word is mediated is through preaching. The way the Word as it is fixed in Scripture is grasped, thereby clarifying the Christian life, Christian duties, Christian doctrines, is through teaching or instruction. And this can occur by catechising, or through instructions in schools founded for that purpose. As I understand it, there is no nurture here at all. Instead there is simply instruction in Christian duties and doctrines. Insofar as growth in the Christian life and sanctification occur, they happen through the means of grace as the Spirit illumines and applies the preached Word and the sacraments.

B. Bushnell's Family Nurture

Secondly, we have in the middle of the nineteenth century a book entitled *Christian Nurture* by one Horace Bushnell. Now you can imagine my surprise, when, after hearing Christian education spoken of in terms of nurture for over a decade, I found on reading this book that it was not about teaching at all, or even education in the usual sense of the term. This book turns out to be an extended commentary on Ephesians 6:4, "Fathers do not provoke your children to anger, but bring them up in the discipline (*paideia*) and instruction of the Lord."

This calls for a comment or two about this term, *paideia*, one of the most important and meaning-filled words in the Greek world. Its earliest meaning was simply, child-rearing. Its later and more typical meaning in Greek literature, becoming almost a technical philosophical term, was that which you did to produce the ideal man of hellenic times, which was the man of *areté* or virtue. *Paideia* therefore gathered together the whole Greek ideal of harmony between soul, body, mind, the ability of the mind to control the inferior aspects of the human being, resulting in both courage of the warrior and the nobility of mind of the philosopher.[1] *Paideia* was the instruction, the education, that produced this. But we cannot read the New Testament or Ephesians 6:4 through these lenses. In the New Testament and the Septuagint its typical meaning is simply discipline, the kind of instruction which occurs nonverbally, therefore instruction through correction and chastisement.

This is the way Jerome took it in translating it in the Vulgate, *disciplina*. And this is also the way the RSV translators see it in Eph. 6:4. But what is a *paideia* or discipline which is "of the Lord." Note that this part of the verse is in deliberate contrast with the first part of the verse. Fathers, do not provoke your children to anger, but bring them up in the discipline . . . *of the Lord*. This apparently means a discipline which does not merely not arouse anger. It is modeled on the way the Lord deals with his adopted children, which includes chastisement but a chastisement designed for good, permeated with love and forgiveness.

Note that in Eph. 6:4 and in Bushnell *paideia* is something going on between parents and children. Bushnell's book goes far beyong the intention of this text. His basic point is that there is no reason why we should not expect God to use the relations between parents and children as a means of grace, a way of appealing to, and even effecting children in and toward life in Christ. And as far as I am concerned, Bushnell's point is well taken. Furthermore, it is conceivable that such a process even be extended beyond the family to the church. That is, we should not be surprised if God uses the concrete human relations, the mutual forgiveness and love occurring in a church, as a way the Gospel is made known, responded to, and received. To appeal to a church congregation or a Christian family to exercise Christian *paideia* in this sense is merely to appeal to them exercise love toward one another, and to be Christian in their relations to each other, and not to forget those things when they relate themselves to the children.

C. Instructional Nurture

Thirdly, came the *religious education* movement. It came

after and alongside the Sunday School movement and after rather extensive instructional efforts were occurring in the churches. And while many of the spokesmen of this movement did not talk so much about nurture, nevertheless, this phenomenon of instruction which was occurring in the church began to be talked about as if it were Christian nurture. Or to reverse the matter, Christian nurture, while it still included what might go on in the family, came now to define instruction, and to be used interchangeably with religious education and Christian education. Christian education comes to mean Christian *paideia*, and vice versa. Now I would submit that something very peculiar has happened here. Does this mean Christian education or nurture stands for that which Eph. 6:4 or Bushnell had in mind, the concrete process according to which God used relationships between people as a way the Gospel might be heard and received? Apparently not. For that which is now called, nurture, is a deliberate, conscious, planned and instructional process taking place in a church at a definite time and place. What was it that happened at that time and place? Visibly it looked like what was occurring in public schools. There was a teacher, and pupils, and lesson materials and all that. Now it would make some sense to say that over and above this instructional process a nonverbal process is going on, a relationship between teacher and pupil which God can use for his saving purposes. And further this is the nurture of *paideia* aspect of this instructional situation. But what does it mean to call the instruction itself a *nurture*?

Now our first inclination might be to dismiss this whole discussion as just a matter of definitions of words. Yet something more important than definitions is at stake. It is one thing to say as Bushnell did that we should attempt to make our witness to children through the very fabric of our lives and our relations to them. Even then the nurture or *paideia* is the work of God. Something different is implied when we say that a conscious, planned instructional process *is* a nurturing, and furthermore what happens in that nurturing is the growth and sanctification of Christians. This is something Bushnell would not assume. He thought it worth hoping for, expecting. He thought it even natural. But his language is usually careful. He exhorts parents to beg "the spirit of their own heart in the children, *IF by the grace of God they may.*" The picture is that God can and will use the discipline which is of the Lord in his saving work. But in post-Bushnell religious education the picture changes. The English word, nurture, smacks of nourishing, hence refers to the actual process according to which life is maintained and growth occurs. When Christian education is seen *as* nurture, the picture is created of the denomination or the teacher effecting Christian growth through the educational or instructional process.

I do not know exactly when this conflation of nurture and education took place. If it began in the religious education movement, the fusion was a logical one. The neo-naturalistic spokesmen of this movement, disciples of Henry Nelson Wieman such as George A. Coe or Ernest J. Chave, could speak of Christian education as nurture in this sense quite consistently with their theological grounds. For Chave, religious education "is a systematic, planned procedure for making religion meaningful and operative in individual and collective living."[2] But, if religion is of God, how can there be a planned procedure that makes it operative for the individual? Chave had an answer. For he meant by religion "a persistent outreach on the part of man for meanings and values to inspire and to guide him in his restless search for a fuller and more satisfying life,"[3] and he meant by "God" the creative order in the cosmos. In short, religious education could itself *be* this nurturing process because the goals and means were all in the same continuum.[4] Now, given the naturalistic and humanistic orientation of such spokesmen, it is understandable why they talk about religious education this way. What is not understandable is why educators who apparently do not share this theological framework talk about Christian education in the very same way. Thus the International Council on Religious Education in a report in 1930 formulated by Paul Vieth takes over this same language of efficient cause in which Christian education is simply nurturing. The verbs of this report in which the aims of education are described are, to develop, to lead, to effect, and to foster. And in the list, goals which are eminently human goals, like character development, are "fostered" and "developed" in the same way as goals which are not eminently human goals, such as "a sense of personal relationship with God," or "consciousness of God as a reality in human experience."[5]

Now when we read histories of Christian education, we find that the religious education movement received almost a definitive refutation in H. Shelton Smith's *Faith and Nurture* in 1940. Here the shaky optimism and naturalism of the religious education movement was supposedly exposed, and thereafter the new Reformation theologies of Niebuhr, Brunner, and Barth began to create a different theological undergirding for Christian education. Perhaps so. Yet the new undergirding does not seem to effect very much the confusion of talk. The causal language is still there although slightly weakened. In the report of the Special Committee on Christian Education Objectives of the Commission on General Christian Education in 1958, the verbs that describe what we do in Christian education are not fostering and developing . . . rather we are assisting, helping, aiding, and enabling. And we are still doing these things in such a way that make it sound as if the goals were on the same continuum as the means. Hence (to cite the report)[6] Christian education is aimed "to enable persons to become aware of the seeking love of God," and to enable them "to respond in faith to this love." "To help persons be aware of God's self disclosure." Now the verb "enable" means "give power to," or "give a capacity for. . . ." And Christian education seems to mean the present complex institutional enterprise which embraces curricula, teachers, class meetings, learning theory, denominational planning, etc. How is it that such an enterprise enables someone to "respond in faith to God's love"? This is still to talk about Christian education as a nurturing, something Bushnell never did, nor as far as I know does the New Testament.

Further examples of the confusion are found in Wyckoff and Cully. In one place Wyckoff says that "the aim of Christian education is to nurture the Christian life."[7] In this statement nurture is not a noun as in Ephesians 6:4 but a verb, and as a verb an expression of what Christian education does to the Christian life. The picture is that of Christian education effecting the Christian life in human beings. Yet Wyckoff also says that "Christian education is best carried on *as nurture* . . . " thus suggesting that Christian education and nurturing simply mean the same things. Here the teacher is the prime mover, "constantly trying to help the individual to become receptive to the reality of God. To lead and guide the pupil to the place where he may experience the reality of God." The theological assumptions needed for such a statement are the same as those of Coe and Chave. For a teacher can produce capacities or conditions of experience of an object only if that object is within the same continuum as the pupil and teacher. Thus a teacher can do this for a pupil in relation to mathematical, historical and scientific realities. Wyckoff does add that all this happens "only through the Holy Spirit." But if this is so, what does he mean by nurturing the Christian life?

Cully is confusing because, in one place, she speaks of Christian nurture so broadly that it seems to cover everything that happens in and out of the church through which God works his redemption. Yet in other passages she clearly speaks about the church school as "a way through which children are nurtured in the Lord."[8] And she means by this that the child "is brought into the possibility of a relationship with God who loves him and saves him."[9] Whatever this "possibility" is which is created in the church school, it does not mean learning concepts or moral lessons. What then does church education do that makes it "possible" for God to relate himself to the child, when prior to that effort there was no such "possibility?" The point of this illustration is to show that modern writers who seem to reflect the criticisms of Shelton Smith against the religious education movement and who *seem* to be working in the new world of theological revolution, still perpetuate the same confusion which occurred when Bushnell's nurture and institutional instruction were identified.

The confusion is perpetuated because a crucial element is omitted. There has been and is in the church a phenomenon akin to instruction in the public schools. Whatever else that instruction might effect, its specific and immediate task concerns the intellect, and such ordinary matters as information, understanding, insight, and perhaps even skills. To speak of Christian education as fostering, developing, helping, enabling, or nurturing the Christian life is so broad a description that whatever distinctive place it has in the church is lost. Actually it (what happens in the church education with the teacher, pupils, materials, etc.) does not directly "foster" Christian sanctity. What it does foster, develop, enable, etc., is (we hope) some sort of clarity, understanding, or skill. In other words the identification of nurture or nurturing with Christian education identifies an ultimate goal (the Christian life), which is the goal in some sense of all activities in the church, with a penultimate goal, the specific concerns of education. In biblical language this identification erases the legitimate distinction between *paideia* and *didache*. Or to put it in the language of 1 Cor. 12, *paideia* as an ultimate goal is pursued by all the organs of the church which are distinguished by the *gifts* of the Spirit: teachers, prophets, administrators, etc., but as Paul says, "Are all teachers . . .?" The second confusion is that by retaining the causal language of the religious education movement, recent writers make Christian education sound like something which simply produces or effects the Christian life.

II

NEO-NURTURE AND NEO-TRADITIONALISM: A DILEMMA

So far in this attempt to set forth the problem, I have mentioned two historical views of Christian education, the traditional Protestant view and the nurture view as found in the religious education movement and in subsequent writers, who still speak the same language. Now let me go a step beyond this by speaking briefly about two more views, and I would use these two to clarify more specifically the dilemma before us. The two are what I would call the view of existential or neo-nurture and neo-traditionalism. Admittedly, it is difficult to characterize them. For they have not crystallized into distinct movements nor do they yet have outstanding spokesmen such as the religious education movement had.

As I said previously, accompanying the criticisms of the religious education movement came a new era in theology and a new vocabulary. In the 1930s the term summarizing this new era was the now useless term, neo-orthodoxy. Since that time the new era has split into two basic theological streams, one associated very closely with existentialist philosophy whose spokesmen are Tillich and Bultmann and their disciples, the other finding in Karl Barth its chief inspiration. As I see it, two views of Christian education are emerging out of these lines. I am calling the one which follows Bultmann and Tillich, neo-nurture. The other, which follows Barth, neo-traditionalist.

A. Existential or Neo-Nurture

The tendency of American Christian educators to think of Christian education as nurture has never really abated. Perhaps this explains why the dominant mood today is what I am calling neo-nurture, which is simply the attempt to characterize Christian education as nurutre, but in the categories of existentialist theology. The two books that most quickly come to mind are David J. Ernsberger's *A Philosophy of Adult Christian Education*, 1959, and David R. Hunter's *Christian Education as Engagement*, 1963. The language of both books is the language popularized by Reuel Howe and others. A key word for both books is relevance. Beyond that we hear about man's predicament, man's condition, man's needs, estrangement, engagement, encounter, and revelation always occurs between God and the specific situation of specific man. At the most general level I guess this means that when God discloses himself to the twentieth century he adapts himself to the problems of the twentieth century. Therefore God's Word in the present is not merely a repetition of his Word to the Middle Ages. God aims the arrow of his revelation at you and at me. Christian education comes in as that which makes sure the arrow really hits the target. It helps God focus on the target. What is the target? Concrete human needs, our predicament, "where are we." Our predicament according to whom? Mr. Ernsberger has some difficulty making up his mind on this point. He describes Bible study as aiming to "bring man's need and God's action together in a creative, redemptive . . . dialogue,"[10] which sounds like without the study in small groups God's action wouldn't quite make it. It also appears that the needs are to be determined by the group itself, which Ernsberger calls "an important medium through which God confronts Christians." Yet Mr. Ernsberger recognizes that certain adult groups just might not have real insight into their needs. They might come up with practical demands of the Norman Vincent Peale type, or with a shallow version of their needs. So it remains for the teacher himself to elicit from them their "real needs," and with this end in view he introduces the appropriate material. How is it that the teacher knows when the poor unenlightened laymen in the small group fail to come up with their real needs? Apparently because the teacher knows their Real Needs. This makes the teacher a kind of inside dopester who has the inside dope about the needs of his group. On that basis he knows what material to use and how God's action and human needs can be brought together. God himself seems to be either passively helpless in the situation or else a very poor marksman. For God waits for Christian education to present a good target for him so he can hit it with his self-disclosing arrow. What controls the situation of revelation here? Obviously the group's or the teacher's analysis of their needs.

Mr. Hunter is more interested in what he calls engagement or encounter. And I guess we have Martin Buber and Emil Brunner to thank for that. He wants Christian education focused on "immediate encounter with God" rather than instruction or truth. He wants educators to have a strong conviction that the educational program "must find its focus on what God is doing," thus "*enabling* man to respond to what God is doing."[11] The organizing principle of the program is what he calls a "religious issue," which he defines as any issue arising out of an engagement or encounter. Our suspicions, already aroused by such language, became confirmed when we read his examples of "religious issues." These issues that supposedly are consequences of engagement all sound straight from a text book on child psychology or on the psychological development of the teen-ager. Examples of these issues that come into being where God has acted and man has responded are 1) appreciation of animals and life, 3) the clash between freedom and authority, 3) decision making. Now how does a teacher recognize when an engagement with God has produced a religious issue? By consulting the teacher's guide.[12] And if the teacher plays his cards right he will "enable people to respond now to what God is now doing in their lives." Now how does the teacher know when God is doing something in the lives of the pupil, and what it is he is doing? And what precisely does the teacher do to "enable him to respond"? And how does he know when they are responding correctly or what the correct response is? Perhaps all that is in the teacher's manual also. He doesn't, as he says, want to teach people *about* religion, but *in* religion, and to do this he proposes "engagement training." Now if he is following the definition of engagement laid down at the beginning, this apparently means making people proficient in encountering God as well as each other.

All this is neo-*nurture* in that it sees Christian education as a means through which salvation takes place. But what makes it *neo* is that the Christian teacher actually mediates revelation by spotting the correct needs. Or he sets up an encounter with God by "enabling" it. I realize that we cannot always take words at their face value, and that these men may not be saying what they mean. Yet in contrast to the naturalism and humanism of Coe and Chave, I find this sort of thing more akin to magic. When we consider what Coe and Chave meant by God, by religion, then at least their view of education and its possibilities was cogent. But the neo-nurture people apparently mean by God the transcendent God who acts out of himself in freedom. If so, how could they turn church education into a needs-meeting and encounter-producing phenomenon mediated by educators turned mystagogues? At least traditional nurture had merely the problem of talking loosely and crudely about fostering this or that goal in the Christian man. The neo-nurture people seem to say they are fostering experiences of God himself. Such literature does not of course exhaust or even accurately reflect the possible contributions of Kierkegaard or Heidegger for Christian education. This yet remains to be done, if it is done at all.

B. Neo-traditionalism

Histories of Christian education are usually quick to point out the change in theological climate in the 1930s and

1940s, and quickened interest of Christian educators in theology and theological foundations that accord with the basic content of the Christian Gospel. Such foundations and motifs would be the helplessness of man in radical evil, the centrality of revelation in Jesus Christ, the transcendence and freedom of God, the absolute priority of God's grace. Given such themes it is not surprising that dissatisfaction would arise not only about the religious education movement but about the very concept of nurturing into sanctity. As far as I can tell, however, most Christian educators who have actually adopted these fundamental motifs, reflect them mostly by qualification. That is, to the usual formulae about fostering, enabling, helping, etc., is added a phrase, "under the guidance of the Holy Spirit," or "by God's grace."

Yet there are those who have rebelled against nurture more radically. Sensing the immanentism involved in the language of developing Christian character, enabling encounters and all that, this group wants frankly to set forth Christian education merely in terms of its human possibilities. Christian education becomes in fact theological education . . . the education of the Christian according to which children and adults are given instruction and also skills in the knowledge and interpretation of the content of Christian Gospel. Such as I understand it was the view behind the *Faith and Life Curriculum*.

A version of it is found in James Smart, and also in John Fry's *A Hard Look at Adult Christian Education*. What makes this view "neo" is the desire actually to give the layman a theological education, a training in theology. And yet such a view must face some difficult questions. For we remember that the context of this education is the church. And we also remember that the subject matter of this education concerns in some way the Gospel. Is it possible simply to adopt some notion of education from the public schools or the surrounding culture and assume that this will not be effected when put in this peculiar subject matter? This is simply the question whether or not education in the church is for the reason "strange," "unique," or "peculiar." It would be perilous merely to ignore such a question. Secondly, what has God constituted as the means through which his saving work occurs? Are we to acknowledge preaching and sacraments as such means, but reject church education as totally irrelevant to that saving work? Hence we have something of a dilemma in this history of nurture and its opponents. Nurturing seems to pass over the distinctive features of educating and suggests causal relationships between human efforts and divine effects. Mere theological education suggests that church education has no relation at all to the ways the church is called to witness to the Gospel and to grow in grace.

Paideia has therefore traveled a long way from the time of Ephesians 6:4 and Bushnell. From a Christian way to discipline the children so as not invoke their anger, to a way parents should make their testimony to their children, namely through their lives, examples, and relationships, to something done by an instructional and institutional enterprise which fosters sanctity, to something which mediates revelation to human needs and enables man to encounter God. Such it seems to me is the strange history of *paideia*.

12. Christian Education: Instruction or Nurture

IRIS V. CULLY
Associate Professor of Christian Education Yale Divinity
School
(Presently Professor of Christian Education,
Lexington Theological Seminary)

Theory in religious education has been dominated by white, male academics while the practice has been left to white women. Iris Cully along with Sarah Little and Rachel Hendrelite are important exceptions in the modern period. Each has made an important contribution to theoretical issues in Christian education as well as led in the formation of a new professional group–Directors of Christian Education. In this particular case, while Cully argues for nurture as the means in Christian education, a common agreement that the primary context for Christian education is the church school surfaces. By 1967 the early emphasis on Christian education as a total ministry of the church had died, or at least become hidden. Identity had focused on the nature of schooling, but the quest goes on.

New stirrings in religious education form a protest concerning the breadth covered by the field. With specific reference to the word of the church school and the curriculum through which its work is accomplished with thoroughness. It is good to have this statement made, and to analyze what is meant by the terms we use. It can be helpful to ask what we think we want to accomplish and what it is necessary to accomplish. It is important to look at

Religious Education LXII (May-June 1967), pp. 225-261.

the work of the church school in relation to the teaching function of the church.

Three terms will be the focus of our present attention: instruction, education, and nurture. Finally the use of the term "work of the Holy Spirit" will be explored with reference to religious education. Whatever is said will be only a beginning. Others must continue the discussion.

INSTRUCTION

Instruction comes from the Latin *instruere*, meaning "to build," "establish." The word "structure," a building, comes from the same root. Instruction deals with facts and meanings in order to give the learner information and understanding. It is a way of teaching the what and the how. Instruction in this sense has always been found somewhere in the church's teaching function.

Religious instruction would consist in giving the learner a knowledge of the material in the Bible, the history of the church, and basic Christian doctrine. This is a task which the weekly period of religious instruction should be well-fitted to accomplish, limited in time, in space, and often in the preparation done by its teachers.

No teacher with a concern for learning would equate memorization with instruction. "Imparting knowledge" must include more than this. First there must be meaning. Who determines the meaning? Is it the teacher, the writer of the material (through the editor), the parish clergyman? How simply is meaning to be conveyed? As the learner advances in years, there are two needs before the curriculum planner: to add material, and to deepen its meaning.

This is more complicated than giving knowledge or

information. It requires that the teacher see a pattern in knowledge, the movement in history, and the reason for doctrine. He must have understanding, and see meaning. These are not memorized; they must be grasped inwardly. Even an agreed-upon interpretation can be meaningless to both teacher and learner. Anyone who has tried to "teach" the Christian understanding of God as Trinity, or who has struggled to show how the crucifixion of Christ could be involved in the redemption of the world knows this. Simply telling a class that the Jews are God's *chosen* people will not make the learner accept this fact. *Chosen* for suffering is not the way the American learner would understand this word.

Instructional material is mediated to the pupils through the teacher, so the material must first teach him. His perception of the information and its interpretation are prior to his teaching. He will omit what is unclear to him, gloss over what he does not agree with, and bring in auxiliary ideas which occur to him as pertinent. He will do all this, unless he is provided with a lecture to be read verbatim. Even curriculum materials which provide questions with answers cannot succeed in guaranteeing that the pupils will give the answers expected. The teacher has to correct them by reading from the book. How can one get past the teacher's own enthusiasms? He feels awkward about the grossness of Old Testament history, so he expurgates it. He is enthusiastic about the Ten Commandments, so these are discussed and memorized. This teacher is conscientiously doing what seems best to him. The American educational system does not produce the kind of teacher who will obey teaching instructions without modification, nor learners who will accept instruction without question.

If the curriculum maker cannot be sure that the teacher perceives the material as written, neither can the teacher assume that the pupil perceives as he is taught. Perception is a factor in learning. No matter how glorious the heritage of the first century church may seem to the teacher, pupils who have been studying during the week the glories of imperial Rome may have learned that this was just one sect among many. Sunday is not the only instruction time and perceptions are built in many encounters. Pupils listen politely to instructions about "love one another"; "do not bear false witness." They politely refrain from shattering the Sunday school teacher's illusions or challenging him to confess the truth: that these are statements which require soul searching rather than lip service. To avoid inquiry into the way instructional material is perceived by the learner, is to show indifference to the seriousness of the instructional task.

Instruction requires *skills*. These are the methods and the techniques through which teaching takes place. The teacher tries to structure the perceptual field of the learner in order that the latter may understand and so receive the instruction. The small child learns through stories which need to be well-written and artfully told. When he can enter into the biblical story, he can both remember the facts and grasp the meaning. Older learners need to use the tools of research, and to explore through discussion. Further skills are required to elicit from the pupil what he has learned. It may be comforting to some teachers to assume that teaching and learning are one, but this is not the fact. Instruction is tested through the learner's ability to communicate. This may be done in graphic forms by young learners, and in various writing forms by learners who have progressed to such skills. It can be done verbally through questions and discussion.

Instruction thus far has been concerned with the intellectual aspects of learning. This is not the whole of religious learning, although some may wish to confine the work of the Sunday church school to this area. The understanding of the symbolism of a religion is not necessarily instruction, for symbols arouse emotional response and elicit actions. The cultivation of habits pertains to the way a person conducts himself during congregational worship, or in other areas of group life.

The development of attitudes grows out of instruction in its fullest sense. If religious instruction does not help the learner to understand how one should feel and act toward others in particular situations, it is sterile. Attitudes go far beyond the intellectual understanding: they involve the whole self. The opportunity for action must somewhere be provided for: the teaching and encouragement of witness in daily life. Finally, there is a need for the development of appreciations, the apprehension of forms into which religious insights are expressed where the sensitivity required is not first of all intellectual.

EDUCATION

The word "education" goes beyond instruction. The dictionary finds its rootage in *educare*—"to rear, bring up, education"—but also lists the possibility of *e-ducere*—"to lead."[1] The words "develop" and "growth" enter into this definition. Education is a more inclusive process than instruction. It would seem to involve the whole person. This is a broader basis for curriculum, providing for the enrichment of instructional material as well as the expression and testing of instruction. Knowledge and skills would be put to use in areas related to the basic learning.

The question is whether or to what extent the church

school has educational responsibility, and where it does not, who is to perform this function. Let us keep in mind that education, like instruction, is intellectually oriented. The educated person has more than knowledge, and the religiously educated person is one who understands his faith. He has faced doubts and questions, tested his affirmations with those who disagree, and drawn conclusions, while keeping openness to revision. He has convictions and not simply answers. He holds some things to be true, not because the teacher or the book told him, or because he made one hundred percent on a quiz, but because these things have become clothed with meaning. However true they may have been in essence, he has now become aware of their truth. This happens when facts become related in a pattern which mights for insight. Wholeness is grasped.

To achieve this kind of learning, the teacher must himself be free enough in his attitudes and full enough in his knowledge both to "bring up" and to "lead out." He needs to understand how learning takes place. A subject has come alive for some people because of a teacher's enthusiasm. The religious faith has become real for others because a teacher reached out in warmth and love. The human factor cannot be avoided in the educative process.

Education assumes a knowledge of methods for teaching, an awareness of the teacher himself as a factor in the learning process and the involvement of the learner. It further includes areas previously mentioned under instruction but not enlarged upon because they are broad enough to come under "education."

Such is the development of *habits*. In its simplest form, a habit is a pattern of action which one uses automatically, but for which, hopefully, one understands the reason. The simplest religious habit is the matter of behavior in a church service. To walk and not run, to sit quietly (if only for the sake of others), to know how and what to pray upon entering the service, to know when and why to stand and sit, to learn the skill of entering into a responsive reading, and how to follow the hymnal—these are skills and habits to be learned. When children sit among adults at the service, an example is provided by those who through long practice have learned to use the forms of worship with ease. Pupils also need to learn habit patterns with respect to their interaction in the class, including the behavior expected by the teacher. Cues may be picked up without verbalizing, but habits form a distinct area of learning.

The development of *attitudes* grows out of instruction. If religious instruction does not help the learner to understand how one should feel and act toward others in particular situations, it is sterile. Attitudes go beyond intellectual understanding: they involve the whole self. If the pupils in a class avoid a new member because they are already a closely-knit group, he may leave in discomfit, unaware that he might have found Christian fellowship. What attitudes is the learner to take in the situations which face him during the week? There may be little enough time, but one can think of no other occasion where these can be dealt with.

Attitudes find expression in *action*. A class dare not be so confined in its task that it has no room to point toward action, to consider the varieties of possible action, and to discuss the results of action. The present emphasis on the church in the world makes this a serious concern. "Action" cannot be construed entirely as the work of singing in the choir, assisting in the women's group, or teaching a church school class. Action concerns the infiltration of Christian people into the world, expressing their learning about Law, Grace, Covenant, Gospel Redemption. Learning *about* these must also involve some direction toward living as if they were true.

The realm of *appreciations* or *aesthetics* is more a part of education than of instruction, because the intellectual understanding may enhance knowledge but cannot be its primary focus. Apprehension and awareness enter into the process. This is why small children can enjoy modern art where some adults reject it, or why young people have the "feel" of some music which older adults insist do not fit the categories labelled music. There is a great wealth of aesthetic forms in religion, some meant for liturgical use (hymns, altar appointments), others for religious expression (oratorios, paintings). The church school may refuse this educational role for lack of time, personnel or resources, but if it does so, the aesthetic response to religious faith will be minimal and will find its expression through inadequate forms. Art forms express theological understandings. Aesthetics can provide methods for instruction when the resources of the hymnal and other religious music, art and poetry are used to enrich and reinforce instruction.

Symbolics includes the vocabulary of religion, the picture symbols used in the building, the symbolic behavior and gestures used in worship, customs, rituals, religious objects.[2] Some traditions make more use of symbolics than do others. Symbolism may become empty because it was taken for granted that the worshipers knew why to sit, stand or kneel at specific points, and symbolic objects became decorations. Knowledge needs to be accompanied by a feeling for the symbolism involved. Appreciation might be a usable word, but appreciation is an attitude engendered in response to the symbol. At this point it becomes more than instruction.

This educational task might be left for the Confirmation

class, already burdened with everything which it is thought
only a clergyman can effectively impress upon the young. It
might be accomplished by the parents who are supposed to
be accompanied by their children in church. Perhaps if the
parents are instructed they can educate their young. Sometimes, however the young prefer to accept knowledge from
anyone other than their parents. Sometimes parents are
tongue-tied when the occasion seems to require religious
instruction. This is particularly the case when the words
"appreciation" and "attitude" are introduced. Adults know
how to act at a service of worship, but their response to a
child's inappropriate action reflects the anxious defensive-
ness of a parent: he ignores the behavior or summarily
rebukes the child. A less-involved person might be more
helpful in the religious education of the child. Teachers
and parents are co-workers. The child from the non-reli-
gious family is completely ignored in any system which
categorically insists that some areas of learning are materials for instruction in the church school and others are hte
province of the whole church or of the family. The teacher
and family become parents-in-the-faith to such a child until
or unless his family also become concerned enought to
attend worship.

Education goes beyond instruction in that it develops
attitudes, habits, actions and appreciations. While these
cannot be fully developed without the influence of the
family and participation in the worshipping community,
the church school has a responsibility for initiating, culti-
vating and enriching these areas as methodology for instruction and the application of learning. Education involves the teacher himself, relationships between teacher
and class, relationships among the members of the class and
the methods used for instruction.

NURTURE

Nurture is derived from the Latin verb, *nutrire*, to suckle, nourish. Perhaps it could be said that "nurture" includes and goes beyond the previously delineated terms. It is training, development and nourishment. *Nutrire* shares shades of meaning with *educare*, but is more elemental. Without nourishment, the infant would die. Without direct feeding, the growing child might find some way to eke out a minimal existence.

Nurture goes beyond the meaning of development, because it introduces a factor apart from the natural tendency of the organism itself to mature. It implies a person through whom this process can be implemented. The image of the nursing mother is there. A person could be self-educated but he could not be self-nurtured. The religious person who worships God in the beauty of field and mountain has an educated form of devotion but devotion is only nurtured fully through worship within a religious community.

The nurture of the individual human begins with the mother, but does not continue or end there. Nurture given in the religious home does not differ in most respects from the love and nourishment given in any family where mutual affection exists. Nurture in the religious family would differ not in the results, but in the motivation: namely, the assurance by the parents that God's love for them is the ground of their nurturing love. Further, it would include religious reflection on the experiences of family life—in joy and sorrow, wrong-doing and reconciliation. As the child grows, he becomes part of ever-larger social groups, and there are moments when parents are dismayed to see the degree to which a child can absorb the language, gesture, dress or other characteristics of the group with which he is associated at the moment.

Imitation as a learning factor is a matter of nurture, picked up from individuals and groups, of which the family is but one. Cues come from the family. The small child goes to church because his family goes. He may even refuse to go on the same basis (Dad stays home; why can't I?). In adolescence, however, he may avoid church and disclaim all interest in religion for the same reason. He has a need to establish personal identity before he can accept interdependence. Reaction to persons also occurs in the church school class. No teacher can avoid the role of significant adult whom the learner imitates. Better for him if he acts human! To stay away from church as well as to attend; to forget the answers as well as to know them; to be resentful as well as accepting.

The development of habits, attitudes and actions are intellectually comprehended through instruction, and worked out in the educative process, but their implementation derives partly from nurture: from being among people who practice certain habits, hold particular attitudes, and participate in various actions. One is also nurtured in appreciations: living in the midst of fine art, hearing great music and being taught from literature.

The climate of the parish nurtures. Some parishes exude exclusiveness: a self-contained group, indifferent to some newcomers and hostile to others. Other parishes are inclusive groups, eager to increase their numbers, or to make the stranger feel "at home." The cultural setting of the parish also nurtures, affecting a particular educational-aesthetic "level" which influences all comers.

The church school class is part of the climate, lives within it and is affected by it. While particular classes differ, being the reflection of specific teachers, the total atmosphere of the church school will usually be similar to that of the parish. Here the learner is fed simply by the kind of presence provided by the surroundings. He is affected by the orderliness and attractiveness of the classroom, the kind of setting provided through its resources, the climate the teacher effects between himself and the learners, the relationships of the learners with one another.

The nurture process cannot be compartmentalized. The church school class looks at the ethical situations which the learner brings from home, school or work in the light of the biblical instruction. However brief the time may be, this is one way in which the living quality of the Bible as the written word of God is made clear. A problem in religious living, looked at away from its immediate context, can be seen in a new focus.

With each broadening contact of life, the process of nurture is enlarged. The church school nourishes; the service of worship does also. Church school teachers and ministers nurture when they talk about God's love, tell about it in biblical stories, and show it in their relationships to other people. A congregation filled with the joy of the Lord nourishes all who come into the midst.

This nourishment cannot be arbitrarily separated from instruction in the church school. The teacher may instruct the learner in the biblical background of worship and help him to understand its meaning, but he "instructs" most profoundly when the learner sees the teacher participating in worship. He is nourished by the teacher's witness and this could lead him into similar commitment.

One purpose of religious nurture is *commitment*. Knowledge, and even understanding, does not evoke commitment, for commitment involves the whole self. Commitment cannot be confined to the evangelistic meeting, as some in American life have supposed, or to the witness in liturgy or sermon, as others might hope. It has also come about because of a process begun within the church school class. Commitment begins in encounter with the living God who calls men into love, obedience, faithfulness. It requires decisions and decision. These are actions of the whole self, for neither intellectual conviction nor emotional attachment alone is sufficient.

GOD IN THE EDUCATIVE PROCESS

What then is the work of the Holy Spirit in instruction, education, and/or nurture? Bonhoeffer has taught us not to expect God to do what we can do for ourselves and for one another. After all honest effort has been made by the teacher, what is left for God to do?

Instruction is a human enterprise through which learning is communicated to the pupil. Aptitude, motivation, and concentration enter into the process as they would in any intellectual discipline. Learning religion is not basically different from learning history, mathematics, or philosophy.

Education is also a human enterprise, realized as teachers help develop in the learner habits, attitudes, actions, appreciations and integration of subject matter. The teacher, sensing the seriousness of his work may indeed pray for himself and for those whom he teaches. This is different from asserting that the process of edication is accomplished by God. People can be well educated and not be religious. Religion is one area of total development.

Nurture arises from creation and continues the work of creation. The believer in God sees the divine work in the growth of persons from infancy through adulthood. As persons are made in the image of God, so they participate in the love of God and in his righteousness. Those persons with whom the learner comes in contact may inhibit or distort the work of God and this is why teachers feel a sense of responsibility for the kind of persons they are and the ways in which they teach. God the Holy Spirit is at work wherever growth, development and transformation are taking place, whether or not he is recognized and invoked. We may not blame our mistakes on him (although every teacher marvels at results which occur in spite of personal ineptitude), but there are times when we see some change in learners, influenced doubtless by the instructional, educational process, but with a new slant. This is insight, integration, even transformation, decision, commitment, conversion. These flow from the nurture process but are not necessarily in a direction the teacher might have predicted—or even wished.

One reason for the widespread dictum that *we teach but the Holy Spirit brings response* is the remembrance that in the recent past, responsible persons in religious education had a tendency to assume that the making of a Christian was a human task. The illusion gave way to reality when the fact was faced that many factors in the learning process are beyond the control of the teacher. Some people have an excellent intellectual understanding of religious faith, but completely lack the ability to surrender the depth of the self to God's grace. The control of life through knowledge makes the uncertain freedom of commitment difficult. Others, secure in an ability to keep the rules, grow into people of honor and virtue, but are never able to view with the acceptance of their Lord, those people who fall into more obvious sinfulness. Some have left the church in adolescence, and return years later with a vigorous faith. Why are such varying responses made by people regardless of religious instruction? There is a factor here which has not yielded answers to the methods of orderly inquiry.

Affirming the work of the Holy Spirit in teacher and learner points both to the serious responsibility of teaching and the impossibility of predicting commitment. The God-given freedom of each person enables him to make a choice among responses. The teacher may point toward what seems to him appropriate ways of religious response. Intellectual instruction is one way; breadth of educational experience and opportunity within church, school, society and home are other lays. Nourishment through worship and through human responses in relationships is another way. The outcome will be in God's time.

13. Religious Education as a Discipline

D. CAMPBELL WYCKOFF
Professor of Christian Education, Princeton Theological
Seminary

As we approach the present decade the question is still unre-solved: Is our name to be Religious Education or Christian Educa-tion? Nevertheless, a new question surfaces: Is whatever we are an academic discipline? Wyckoff, known for having established an exemplary department of Christian education, shaped the MRE degree and the profession of Christian Educators suggests that Christian education is a special case of religious education, a practical discipline within the field of practical theology. Clarity and the possibility of an identity emerge, but it remains a Protestant perspective. More significant is the continuing confusion between religious education and Christian education. While they share in common an inquiry into teaching and learning modes, they divert on the issue of education's response to revelation and tradition. If content has anything to do with method, then the identity question is open again.

Our topic is intended primarily as an invitation to in-quiry, and not primarily as an assumption. We are not assuming that Christian education is, or meets the require-ments for, an academic discipline. Rather, we are inquiring into the meaning and function of an academic discipline, hoping that we may be able to weigh our intentions and efforts against the results of such an inquiry, in order to discover what it would mean if religious education were developed as a discipline. We might then be able to decide

Religious Education LXII (September-October 1967), pp. 387-394.

whether or not to move in such a direction, and what conditions and commitments would be implied if we did decide to try to develop our field in a disciplinary way.

We are dealing with no easy question. Currently there is a series of studies being published centering on the analysis and assessment of humanistic scholarship in America. Richard Schlatter, the general editor of the series, reports:

> In the course of our discussions . . . about the volume having to do with scholarly work in the field of religion, we came upon a peculiar difficulty—peculiar that is to the field of religious scholarship. A number of American scholars maintain that religion is not a scholarly discipline like art history or musicology or classical studies because religion demands of its students creedal commitments incompatible with free scholarly inquiry. In the end we decided to have two volumes on the study of religion. . . .[1]

The two books turned out to be Clyde A. Holbrook's *Religion, A Humanistic Field*,[2] which analyzes quite directly the possibilities for the development of religion as a field of scholarly inquiry within the university context, and the book edited by Paul Ramsey, cited above, which consists of straight reviews of the state of research in the fields of the history of religions, Old Testament studies, the study of early Christianity, the history of Christianity, theology, Christian ethics, and the philosophy of religion.

Further, there was held at John Hopkins University, in May, 1961, a conference on education as a discipline. Papers were presented by an illustrious array of international figures in the field of education. These papers, together with discussion by respondents, were published under the editorship of John Walton and James L. Kuethe as *The Discipline of Education*.[3] The reader is left with the impression that there are a number of differing opinions on the meaning and function of a discipline, the status of existing disciplines, and the possibility and desirability of developing education as a discipline. Walton, for instance, defined a discipline as "a body of subject matter made up of concepts, facts, and theories, so ordered that it can be deliverately and systematically taught."[4] He proposed two general categories for the classification of the subject matter of education: The school as an institution, and the process of education (pp. 7-11). Yet his respondent R. S. Peters, immediately shot back, "I just cannot grasp the thesis that education could ever be *a* discipline in any ordinary sense; it is rather a focus or meeting place of disciplines" (p. 17).

In our own field, J. Gordon Chamberlin has raised the question, assessed the situation (gloomily), and, incidentally, helped to define what might be meant by a discipline of Christian education:

> . . . Is there a "field" or "discipline" of Christian education? The religious education movement made a significant contribution toward "bringing education back into the church." Under its influence denominational boards of education were developed and departments of religious education became a fixture in seminaries and in a few universities. Philosophical and theological principles were expressed in particular methods and organizational structures, so that the discipline included both a philosophy and a set of appropriate skills which, if employed competently, would produce intended results. Following the lead of general education that was being established as a scientific discipline, religious education sought similar status. However, many of the aspects of church work that were included in "religious education" twenty-five years ago have since become independent disciplines—such as counseling, recreation, and church-and-community studies. And in the light of new theological questions being raised about the church's mission, it has become more and more difficult to distinguish teaching from other aspects of the church's life. How

is teaching different from preaching, or from pastoral
work, or from administration?

. . . The current approaches to church education, growing from the work of such writers as Miller, Sherrill, and
Smart, can hardly be called a discrete discipline. No effort
has been made to work out common principles of formulation, methodology of study, or scope of content . . . With
no live debate within the field, no consistent effort to work
out a common set of principles or processes, it is obvious that
there is now no discrete discipline of Christian education. . . .[5]

Chamberlin's own book, needless to say, is a contribution to
the development of such a discipline, as are a few other
works that will be reviewed later in this paper.

The definition of religious education as a discipline is,
then no easy matter. The attempt is surrounded with
theological difficulties, educational hesitancies, boundary
problems with other presently established disciplines, and a
certain lack of experience and sophistication on the part of
those of us who currently occupy positions of influence in
the field. But, easy or not, whether or not we are prepared
or inclined to the task, we have set ourselves at least to
investigate the possibility.

The Uses of a Discipline

A very practical approach would be to ask, under the
circumstances, what the development of our field as a discipline could do for us as teachers and researchers. The fact
is that, discipline or no discipline, we are held together by a
common enterprise, an enterprise consisting of a host of
activities and programs: church schools, meeting on Sun-
days, weekdays and during vacations; weekday church nur-
sery schools and kindergartens; camping and conference
programs; a youth ministry; the teaching of religion in

schools, colleges, and universities; and all the other activities and programs that an enumeration like this suggests. Our particular job is to teach about this enterprise, to train people to conduct the enterprise, and to inquire into its various aspects through research.

This is, of course, entirely too simple a statement of our job. To teach Christian education in a seminary, for instance, means dealing with pre-ministerial students, pre-professional Christian educators, lay people who will volunteer their services but who want seminary training in their background and professional people who are after advanced degrees or short-term continuing education. It means keeping up with one's colleagues in the theological, behavioral, and educational fields. It means working with people in the field in programs of leadership education, evaluation, and improvement. It means to engage in Christian education, teach about it, and to rethink and rebuild it, all at the same time. Add to this the tasks and views of those who do college work in the field, those who do advanced graduate work, and those who do research, and something of the complexity of the task, looked at even from the practical point of view of servicing the enterprise, emerges.

If they are even to be good service men for the enterprise, Christian educators have some decisions to make about their approach, when it comes to teaching and doing research. These decisions involve four options. The *first* option is to find and pass on what Peter Berger calls "recipe knowledge" about the field. There are ways of stating objectives, handling groups, and patterning organizations that are useful and effective. They can be explained to people who can then go out and use them. We teach one course that is pure "recipe knowledge." It is an attempt to tell seminary seniors who have taken positions as ministers of

170   *Who Are We?*

education exactly what they will be up against the first day on the job, and what to do about it.

The *second* option is to throw students right into the enterprise, so that they may, by trial-and-error and also by creative involvement, become practiced Christian educatiors. Let them jump right in and find out at first hand what the problems and questions are. Then the teacher and researcher can act as resource people for helping them to solve their problems and answer their questions. In the process they will learn through "action research" and through instruction that is focused in the most practical way.

The *third* option is to locate in a related field, and to concentrate the academic training of the Christian educator there. Become a real psychologist, or a real social psychologist, or a theologian, or a New Testament scholar, or a Christian ethics man. Then move into Christian education leadership, bringing the insights and training gathered in an established discipline to bear upon the enterprise.

The *fourth* option is to become conversant with the enterprise, widely read in the related fields, and well-versed in the history and theory of religious education itself, bringing all these to bear upon the construction and reconstruction of a body of principles that will serve to set, guide, and correct the practice of the enterprise.

None of these options is unrealistic or far-fetched. Those of us who came into teaching or research from successful parish practice are likely to incline toward "recipe knowledge." Those who see the task as professional training in the most practical sense will choose thoroughgoing involvement. Most of the really brilliant young leaders in our field have come from solid training in other disciplines, primarily theological and behavioral. But there is something to be said for the fourth option, centering upon the construction and reconstruction of Christian education theory.

Choosing the fourth option would force us to work at the development of a discipline of Christian education. The construction and reconstruction of theory is first of all a matter of establishing basic categories for inquiry, and hammering those categories into a framework for thought about the field. Once the framework is established (subject, of course, to refinement and reworking), the Christian educator will know where to go in the related disciplines, and what to ask of them. With these resources gathered and organized, principles may be formulated, fleshing out the skeletal framework of the discipline. These principles are to be used in setting up, guiding, and correcting the enterprise, and in the process tested, experimented with, and subjected to research.

The establishment of religious education as a discipline, through the selection of this fourth approach to our task, would not in any sense imply divorce from the practicalities of the enterprise. I see religious education as a practical discipline, deriving its categories from the questions that inevitably arise in the process of trying to carry on the enterprise effectively and intelligently. I see the derivation and substantiation of theory as undergirding an informed and valid practice in religious education.

What, then, would be the uses of such a discipline? A discipline of religious education, developed as a body of principles or theory, built on a framework of practical categories would provide us with a common basis for teaching, doing research, and effecting conceptual and practical advance for our field. It would do so primarily by providing us with a useable and shared language, a vocabulary and grammar for the field.

One of the major results of the development of religious education as a discipline would be the encouragement of research, which is possible only when some common language base has been set. Our experience, problems, and findings could then be communicated easily and understandably. Mutual criticism would be facilitated.

Furthermore, the language of our discipline, thus established, would become known to the other older disciplines and their practitioners, thus enabling interdisciplinary conversation and inquiry. To envision what might happen in this regard, look at what has happened to the discipline of sociology of religion since it established in categories and language. Sociology of religion has become the one interdisciplinary and international field of discourse involving religion. As an example of what happens to a field when it fails to establish itself as a discipline, look at psychology of religion, where nothing really new has crystallized since 1902, and where discussion has to be carried on in dialects that are almost mutually unintelligible.

IS IT RELIGIOUS EDUCATION OR CHRISTIAN EDUCATION?

Perhaps one of the first steps in developing a language would be to figure out what to call the discipline—religious education, or Christian education? I have used the terms almost interchangeably thus far in this paper, but have now come to the point where I am going to define my terms and resolve to use them precisely henceforth.

There is a level of education at which we teach people how to do things; this is the level of technical (or in its nontheological meaning, "vocational") education. There is a level of education in which we help persons to engage in critical inquiry and in the discovery and testing of values against the richest possible historical, cultural, and experimental background; this is the level of liberal and scientific education. Then there is a level of education at which views and appreciations of what is highest, best, and most valuable permeate thought and feeling and guide and motivate human behavior, this is the level of religious education. To study religious education in this sense is to study it as an aspect of education, that aspect of education that culminates in commitment.

Christian education is to be seen as a theological discipline, a branch of practical theology. Theology, in my view, springs from the astonishing fact of revelation, what we in Christian education have come to refer to as "God's self-disclosure and seeking love in Jesus Christ." The various theological disciplines are ways of trying to come to grips with the face of revelation. Biblical studies attempt to identify, analyze, and interpret the sources of the knowledge of revelation. History, studied theologically, traces the modes and means of response to revelation through the years. Theology defined as what goes on in a seminary department of theology discusses and interprets the meaning of revelation. Practical theology's task is to suggest appropriate modes and means of response to revelation, such modes and means as worship, preaching, teaching, pastoral care, and social action. *Christian education as a discipline is then an inquiry into teaching and learning as modes and means of response to revelation.*

Let us juxtapose these two. Religious education as a discipline is an inquiry into teaching and learning as modes and means of response to revelation. What may be said

about these two in relation to each other? In a statement
that we have used for several years with students just coming from the college or university into our M.R.E. program
at Princeton Theological Seminary, we have said:

> The concept of revelation can bring into focus for the Chris-
> tian educator the disciplines in which he has been trained in
> college or university. The liberal arts and the sciences are
> the most advanced and useful ways we know of grasping our
> world, organizing our experience, and mining for meaning
> and new truth. Revelation—the self-disclosure of God and
> his seeking love in Jesus Christ—provides a new setting for
> understanding and using the liberal arts and the sciences.
> This new setting is both liberating and corrective; liberating,
> in that it provides a perspective from which one may
> evaluate these studies; and corrective, in that it will not
> permit these studies to be exhaustive. Understood in this
> way, the central concept of revelation allows Christian edu-
> cators to pursue, weigh, and use the behavioral and edu-
> cational disciplines with integrity.

Christian education partakes of religious education; religious education is sharpened and corrected when it becomes Christian education. The generic processes of helping persons to commitment to value, processes which the
Christian educator in fact shares with every other educator
who is attempting to bring the educational process itself to
fulfillment, are religious education. In this sense the Christian educator is a religious educator, and needs to know and
understand himself as such.

Self-recognition of the Christian educator as religious
educator provides two significant relationships that otherwise might be missed. The first is to persons engaged in
"secular" education. The second is to persons engaged in
education within other faith communities. One has only to
engage in the discussions and studies of the Religious Education Association to know how significant (I personally

would say essential) these relationships are. The alternative is a kind of in-group indoctrination and socialization carried on in increasingly sectarian isolation.

The broad discipline, then, in which we are located is that of religious education, the inquiry into teaching and learning as modes and means of commitment to value. Within this broad framework, some of us are concerned with the inquiry into teaching and learning as modes and means of response to revelation, which contributes a particular theological perspective to the total inquiry, and makes us Christian educators.

DISCIPLINARY REDUCTION

The question is often raised of the possibility of reducing religious or Christian education to some other established discipline. Aspects of the study of religious education do in fact reduce to other disciplines. The study of the philosophy of religious education is philosophical, and should be inquired into and taught by philosophers. The study of the history of religious education is history, and should be inquired into and taught by historians. The same is true of psychology, and the other behavioral sciences in relation to religious education. This is true also of ethics and asesthetics.

There would seem to be two solutions to the problem. One would be to solicit the services of philosophers, historians, behavioral scientists, and the rest, to perform the required services on behalf of religious education. This would be legitimate, and ought to be encouraged. It would bring about the possibility of a most fruitful interchange between the religious educator and the other disciplines. The need for such an interchange is *mutual*. We are, I believe, well aware of our need for the specialists in the other disciplines. They are perhaps not so keenly aware of their need for us.

The second solution to the problem is for the religious educator to become sufficiently a philosopher, historian, behavioral scientist, to be able to bring the insights of these disciplines to bear upon religious education with honesty and integrity. This would seem to be a requirement for the religious educator in such areas as philosophy of religion, history of religions, and psychology and sociology of religion. The Christian educator cannot escape being in addition, a theologian.

But this does not "reduce" either religious education or Christian education; it merely locates them and shows their disciplinary relationships. Religious education is still the inquiry into teaching and learning as modes and means of commitment to value; no other discipline is so defined as to deal fully with the constellations of phenomena involved in this inquiry. Christian education is still the inquiry into teaching and learning as modes and means of response to revelation; no other theological discipline pretends to undertake this inquiry.

Two comments ought to be added on this matter of disciplinary reduction. The first is that there are disciplines related to religious and Christian education that badly need development. We are seriously hampered, for instance, by the lack of serious and sustained inquiry into the history of religious and Christian education. We are also handicapped by the deplorable condition of psychology of religion. Without deserting our own posts or violating our own responsibilities, how might we help to set processes in motion to deal with such deficiencies?

The second comment is that we probably ought to attempt at every point to reduce our discipline to some other.

This is the only way in which to keep it sharp, vital, and related. The incalculable values of interdisciplinary and multidisciplinary inquiry in the behavioral sciences have been the direct result of trying to give up discrete disciplines and to reorganize the field of inquiry more effectively.

A PROPOSAL FOR A DISCIPLINE

There appears to be a basis for the definition and development of a discipline, and a need to do so. Furthermore, we do not go into the enterprise unequipped—just inexperienced in this particular kind of thing, and short on maps.

A discipline of religious education and Christian education can, and needs to be, developed that will essentially consist in a set of categories in which to organize our queries and our findings. Such a set of categories will serve as a framework for the construction and reconstruction of religious and Christian education theory. It will serve as a framework for research and development. It will serve as a framework for inquiry and communication with other members of the discipline, with members of other disciplines, with those engaged in the field operations of the enterprise, and with students of religious and Christian education.

As such it will also provide a recognized and defensible location and function for religious education in higher education and for Christian education in theological education, so that members of the disciplines of religious and Christian education will know who they are and with whom they are in working conversation.

Religious education belongs in the context of a total education—early childhood education, elementary education, secondary education, higher education, professional education, and adult education. In all of these, distillation of and commitment to meaning and value are the culmination and fulfillment of every other activity and inquiry. Thus there is, for every participant in the educational enterprise, a concern with and responsibility for religious processes, qualities, and outcomes. To understand the dynamics involved and to teach people to guide and participate in them is the work of the person who teaches religious education. There is then no subject matter to which he is not in some way related; there is no human process of discovery and fulfillment in which he is not interested; and there is no period in the life span in which he is not involved. Furthermore, there are no emergent social and cultural events, whether they be agonies or achievements, that the religious educator does not see as occasions for inquiry and action leading to the discovery of meaning and value and commitment to the implications of such a discovery.

That the locus of the religious education enterprise is in both church and world should surprise no one, considering its roots and relationships. That it is conducted mainly by lay people in secular settings is only to be expected. To inquire into it and teach about it is, then, chiefly a responsibility of the college and university. But if that responsibility is to be taken on and fulfilled, religious education must be defined and developed as a discipline amenable to research and teaching. Part of our proposal is that this task of definition and development of the discipline of religious education be undertaken, and on the basis of as broad participation by the humanities, sciences, arts, and professions as possible.

The discipline of Christian education, on the other hand, is a discipline of practical theology, focusing on the educational ministry of the church. I have elsewhere spent

considerable effort in trying to establish that the basic categories for the discipline of Christian education are: objective, scope, context, process, personnel, and timing. In
other words, a theory encompassing our purpose, the essential content and experience involved in our educational
enterprise, the setting in which it can most integrally take
place, the procedures and methods to be used, the partners
to the enterprise and their various roles, and the sequence
anticipated and planned for, will provide the conceptual
guidance required for the planning, conducting, and
evaluation of the practical enterprise. The functions per-
formed by the enterprise, and informed by the discipline
are method (the basic educating relationships), curriculum
(the plan for implementing the objectives using the most
integral methods), and administration (the elements of
planning, organization, management, and supervision required to undergird the curriculum plan).

But the questions of objective, scope, context, process,
personnel and timing, I am convinced, are theological questions! They are answered for Christian education only
when biblical studies, history, theology, and ethics are taken
into account. This does not mean that Christian education
is subsumed under these categories. What it does mean is
that the Christian educator, responsible for an enterprise of
the living church, constructs his theory and practice in
relation to the most penetrating inquiry possible into the
nature and meaning of that church.

The two disciplines, religious education and Christian
education, meet and to a great extent fuse at the point of
inquiry into teaching and learning as modes and means of
commitment to value. Christian education is thus to be seen
as a special case (albeit a very special case) of religious
education.

If religious education (with Christian education as a special case) were to become a discipline within the spectrum of higher education and theological education, two other matters would have to be explored, matters which must wait at this moment for further definition and clarification: (1) Its specific place in the education of the professional religious or Christian educator. If professional education were interpreted as orientation to action as a professional, engagement in professional action, and reflective re-orientation, the discipline would probably function centrally at the first and third stages. (2) Its specific relationship to the research process: establishment of categories and problems; gathering, analysis and interpretation of data; and the formulation and refinement of principles.

14. Religion In Education: A Jewish Perspective

ALVIN I. SCHIFF
Associate Professor of Education Department of Religious Education Yeshiva University
(Presently Executive Vice-President on Board of Jewish Education of Metropolitan New York)

The theoretical issues of the nature and purpose of religious education as a concern of Jewish participants never focused in Religious Education. *Typically they avoided the debate by reporting on Jewish education. In this particular article what they share with the other members of the REA is clear: the REA has become essentially a community of school persons who, while differing in many essential ways, maintain a common concern for schooling and instruction. When Protestants talk about Christian education their usual point of reference is the church school—a specialized form of ministry within a local congregation; when Roman Catholics talk about religious education they most often refer to instruction in parochial schools; Jewish educators similarly talk about Jewish education in schooling-instructional terms. Regretfully, Jewish concerns for informal education through ritual and family life rarely surface. Yet Jewish educators, like Roman Catholics and Protestants search for common understandings and a sense of identity.*

Judaism is a multirooted way of life. When we speak of Judaism we are, in essence, considering a postbiblical reality. While the Jewish faith is derived, in the first instance, from the Bible, it received its life style—its form and

Religious Education LXIV (November-December 1969), pp. 485-490.

method—from an era that begins with the canonization of the Old Testament. Essentially, contemporary Judaism—in its traditional and deviant forms—is the result of a millenium of Rabbinic effort to explain, rationalize, organize, and classify the various dimensions of the biblical encounter with God. The original sources for the Jewish view of education are the discussions and discourses of the Tannaim and Amoraim—the Rabbis and Sages of Talmudic period that stretches from the second century B.C.E. to the beginning of the sixth century of the Common Era.

Using these sources as a frame of reference, I would like to dwell upon the first of two fundamental concepts, without which, I believe, religion in education has little real value. These basic ideas are: 1) the uniqueness of education in Jewish religious life, and 2) the synthesis of the religious and the secular in education.

I

Jewish education occupies a unique position in Jewish life. The study of Torah (which includes the Pentateuch, the Prophets, the Sacred Writings, the Talmud, the Rabbinic commentaries and other religious writings) is a cardinal principle of the Jewish faith. Knowledge and study in Judaism are not only a means to religious and ethical behavior but are in themselves a mode of worship. Indeed, Jewish liturgy reflects the fact that worship finds expression on the intellectual as well as the esthetic and the emotional planes as it combines the moment of prayer and study.

The study of a Biblical passage (or passages) or a Talmudic tract is integral to every traditional Jewish worship service. In fact, reading from the Bible in its original Hebraic form with cantillation—the accepted sing-song mode of intonation used in public recital to help convey the structure and meaning of the Holy Scriptures—is the most important part of the Sabbath service and other services as well.[1]

The uniqueness of education in Judaism is noted on four levels:

1) importance of schooling;
2) responsibility for education;
3) attitude toward teachers; and
4) status of the learner.

In the Talmud there is a proliferation of statements emphasizing the cruciality and significance of educating the young. For example, one dictum clearly warns: "It is prohibited to live in a city in which there is no *melamed tinokot* (teacher of the young)."[2] There are numerous other similar utterances to the effect.

Nothing, save matters of life and death, are important enough to postpone the learning of Torah.[3] So crucial was Torah study deemed for the survival of the Jewish people, that one of the causes enumerated in the Talmud for the destruction of Jerusalem was "the neglect of the education of children."[4] Schooling was not to be interrupted, even for the rebuilding of the Temple.[5] During the post Bar-Kokhba years, in face of the interdiction of Torah study by the Romans, the highest Rabbinic authority of the times ruled that Torah learning must go on regardless of the consequence, including the threat of capital punishment.[6]

The esteem and power ascribed to Torah study by the Talmud is underscored by the first century episode in which the founder of the famed Yavneh Academy, Rabbi Yohanan ben Zakkai, attempted to remove the curse of premature deaths that afflicted a family in Jerusalem by recommending, "go and study the Torah and you will live."[7] Indeed, learning has been a cornerstone of Jewish faith and survival. In the hierarchy of Judaic values, education is considered equal to all the other commandments put together.[8]

Historically, a balance was struck between *individual* responsibility and *communal* responsibility for educating the young. Throughout Jewish religious literature there are exhortations to the *individual*, never to cease his self-education,[9] and to the *parent* to honor, meticulously, his responsibility for the schooling of his children.[10] On the other hand, the *community* was directed to supply instruction to children, particularly to those children without parents or whose parents could not provide them with an adequate education.[11]

Concerning the attitude toward the pedagog, it should be noted that in Rabbinic writings there is no higher distinction than that of being a scholar and teacher.[12] In actual practice, there has often been a wide gap between the respect paid to the teacher and the tangible remuneration for his instructional efforts. This is due, in large measure, to two unrelated factors. The first is a Talmudic tenet that maintains that since the instruction of the young is a holy duty it cannot be reduced to the ordinary status of an income-producing job.[13] The second is the depressed socio-economic condition of the Jewish communities in medieval and early contemporary times.

Notwithstanding their generally grave material and social disadvantage, Jewish communities in the diaspora and Israel always equated respect for teachers with respect for God. *Umora rabcha kemora Shamayim*, "And let the reverence for your teacher be like the reverence for Heaven," says the sage in *Ethics of the Fathers*.[14] According to another source, honoring one's teacher takes precedence over the honor one owes to his parents.[15]

In Judaism, moreover, respect for the learner is legion.[16] Parents' greatest personal aspiration has been, traditionally, to have a son who is a *talmid hacham* (a person who excels in the study of Torah), or at least a son-in-law who fits this description.

In Eastern European Jewish communities a *yeshivah bohur* (a young man trained in a school for Jewish studies) was expected to be a life-long student of the Torah. There were no excuses for not studying the Torah as much as possible. Neither poverty, nor the pursuit of a livelihood, nor the raising of a family could free a Jew from the obligation of *Talmud Torah*, daily Torah learning.

I recall in my college days at Yeshiva University that elderly Jewish women would come to the study hall with bowls of fruit, cakes and cookies for the students. For them it was a *mitzvah*, a holy deed of the highest form (as it had been for their mothers before them, and their grandmothers before them), to serve students engaged in the study of Torah.

Many of the Jewish immigrants who came from the ghettos and shtetls of Eastern Europe to the blessed shores of America during the last decades of the nineteenth century and the beginning of the twentieth century brought with them the ideal of "learning for learning's sake" and the zeal for establishing the primacy of Torah study in Jewish life.

It is this attitude to Torah study that has motivated the characteristic Jewish reverence (notwithstanding social, political, or economic status), for ALL learning (religious and secular), for ALL learners and for ALL imparters of learning.

The principle of reverence for study (and for the human resources and the processes involved in achieving it) have serious implications for our modern age; especially, when one considers the growing disregard in our materialistic society for intellectual values and intellectual achievements. "Intellectuals are . . . seen, at best, as impractical, and, at worst, as schemingly subversive; . . . excellent students are thought of distastefully as 'grinds,' and far more status is won by the distinguished athlete than by the distinguished schoolar."[17] The findings of a recent Columbia University study, entitled *Adolescents' Attitude Towards Academic Brilliance*, vividly underscore the stark truth of this statement.[18] Counteracting the tendency to depreciate the value of the intellect, the intellectual and intellectual accomplishment is an educational task of gigantic proportions.

II

Unlike the universally accepted, almost uniform posture in Judaism concerning education, there is considerable divergence of opinion regarding the second concept I would like to discuss: *synthesis*.

On the right, the strongly ritualistic, isolationist school of thought maintains that the *religious* and the secular are two separate, distinct and noninterrelatable domains, and that the twain must never meet. Secular values, accordingly, may be tolerated only to the extent that they are absolutely necessary for life in modern society. Followers of this approach advocate day schools (i.e., parochial schools) in which there is clear and absolute division between religious studies and general studies.

On the left, is the liberal, universalist philosophy that stresses, almost to the exclusion of ritual, the universal-social values of Judaism. This posture views the public school as the only appropriate educational institution for American children and opposes the introduction, into the system, of any religious values or influences. It suggests that religious instruction belongs solely in the supplementary week-end or week-day congregational school. According to this philosophy, it is the business of religion and religious education to be concerned with the values and problems of the larger secular environment.

In between these two poles of thinking lie the ideologies favoring synthesis of the religious and the secular. The pro-synthesis adherents generally support the idea of the Jewish all-day school, in which pupils receive their total formal educational experience. The Jewish Day School, like the Catholic parochial school, unfettered by the problems and legalities of church-state separation, can be particularly effective in synthesizing the religious and secular disciplines.

The classic definition of synthesis in education posits that it is "the harmonious blending of religious teaching concerning God, man and nature, with the knowledge of the ages, with the other currents of creative culture and with contemporary humanizing forces, into a living . . . reality in the hearts and minds of children."[19] Within the framework of this definition, I would like to consider two schools of thought.

One approach postulates that synthesis is the conscious intellectual integration of religious and secular values. This view, which I like to call the *one-world* concept, is achieved via the direct interaction of instruction in religious and secular studies, and the influence of each discipline upon the other. Propounded by German-Jewish rationale theologists, this philosophy maintains that each discipline is the indispensible helpmate of the other. It is most aptly described by Dr. Immanuel Jakobovitz, Chief Rabbi of the British Empire.

> Synthesis means that there must be an interplay and interrelationship between all learning and thinking. In

more concrete terms, it would mean that . . . religious
studies will enable students to get a different grasp and
insight into secular understanding. It means that one's view
of science, or attitude towards the place of man within the
universe, or analysis of nature, and each individual's role
within it, is radically different, and crucially colored by his
religious convictions. It means that whether one studies so
absolute a subject as mathematics, or any of the physical
sciences, or even more so the behavioral sciences, or enters
into the realm of metaphysics, or philosophy, or ethics, or
any area of scientific or literary human interest, embracing
even the arts, he will do so in a different capacity as a . . .
[religionist].

Synthesis also means that whether one will practice later
on as a physician, or a physicist, or as a lawyer, he will do so
differently; he will have different motivations for his work,
let alone different ethical rules, governing his professional
conduct as a result of being . . . [religionist].[20]

Following this thought through to its logical conclusion,
we might say that via religious learning and outlook, a
person acquires a different and distinctly religious attitude
to his patient, or client, or scientific research. He will be
guided primarily by rigid moral rules and motives, and not
by the pursuit of expediency, self-interest, or mere lucre,
and is objectives will be the quest for truth and service,
rather than just success or acclaim.

At the same time [that religious education will influence the
secular], such a synthesis will relate the truths revealed by
science to the purpose, origin, and destiny of life revealed by
religion, thus securing an orderly harmony in human
personality, which only a religious perspective can provide . . . .[21]

In reverse, synthesis means that scientific training and
skills and the methods of analysis and research (the tools
supplied by scientific reasoning), which students have ac-

quired, will enable them to benefit in their religious studies and insights. By applying these methods of thinking, whether empirical or deductive, and by utilizing the literary and historical data which they absorb, they can advance their religious work and penetrate deeper into an understanding of religious teachings and their literary sources.

According to the *one-world* philosophy as presented above, synthesis fructifies both elements in the religio-secular partnership. Maimonides (1135-1204), the famous Jewish medieval philosopher, talmudist, astronomer and physician was the finest exemplar of this kind of integration.

So much for the *one-world* approach to synthesis. Its implications for education are clearly evident.

III

The second view of synthesis claims that there is no real conflict between the religious and the secular or scientific, but recognizes the significant divergence between the *mood* of the religionist and the *mood* of the scientist. This position holds that beneficial interaction in the classroom between the worlds of religion and secularism is neither desirable or realistically obtainable. It says that synthesis is entirely an individual matter, and is best achieved by exposure to both worlds in an educative atmosphere conducive to harmonization. Synthesis, it suggests, is *ad personum*; it is the psychological internalization of the varying elements in both worlds.

According to Dr. Samuel Belkin, president of Yeshiva University, the outstanding proponent of this approach, the religio-secular synthesis is not one of truths or hypotheses; it is a synthesis in the personality of the religionist of the best of sundry disciplines.[22] This school of thought, which I refer to as the *two worlds* approach, suggests educational combination rather than instructional integration.

The theoretical basis for this view is established by Dr. Emanuel Rackman, a leading exponent of the *two-worlds* philosophy, in the following rationale.

From a philosophical point of view there can be no conflict between religion and science. The scientist makes no claim to truth—absolute truth. He offers only hypotheses. His judgments are purely quantitative—never qualitative. He makes no pronouncements on values. Chemicals are never good or bad. Atomic energy is never beautiful or ugly.

The religionist, on the other hand, has an altogether different manner of discourse and what he has to say pertains to aspects of existence with regard to which the methods and conclusions of the scientist must forever be neutral. For this reason it is possible to live in both worlds and suffer no conflict of premises or conclusions.[23]

Concerning the differences in method, the author of this statement posits that

> natural science, social science, and democratic experience, have in common a readiness ever to question, ever to explore, ever to experiment. No truth, no absolute is ever so sacred that it cannot be challenged. Even its antithesis may be tried. The open mind and the open society respect nothing as ultimate. The religionist, however, is bound by dogma, and absolute, ultimate truths. Furthermore, the natural and social scientist, and the democrat always seek to manipulate and change nature and society while the religionist pleads for awe and humility in one's encounter with both. Thus, the real conflict today is between those who believe that man's last best hope is a sustained skepticism with regard to everything, and those who seek salvation in truths revealed by a transcendent source . . . .[24]

According to this analysis, the challenge to religious education is how to train a student to live with commitment to an established tradition and to God, the Creator and Lawgiver, and at the same time, to delight in constant experimentation, with a high regard for philosophical positivism and ethical relativism.

The basic difference between the two views I have just described, is, I believe, one of method and not of purpose; the differentiation is procedural and not substantive. The *one-world* philosophy favors direct, integrative classroom instruction, while the *two-worlds* view suggests a non-integrative approach in a school atmosphere which will ultimately aid the synthesizing process.

There is no disagreement, however, concerning the desired behavioral end product of religious and secular learning. That *diseratum* is a religious, ethical, goal-oriented, and cultured personality sensitive to changing environmental conditions and able to meet changing personal-social needs. Achieving this purpose has been, historically, the greatest challenge to Jews in Israel and the diaspora, and it remains the profound challenge of Jews and non-Jews in modern society.

Religion and religious education must be concerned with the problems of poverty and wealth, with the ways and needs of modern man, with social justice and social injustice, with civil liberties and civil disorder, with the hopes of labor and the plight of unemployment. Religion and the religious school must speak to the problems of health and housing, of play and rest, of education and rehabilitation and of war and peace.

The religious school—whether it be of the all-day or parochial variety or of the supplementary type—cannot afford ostrich-like concern for the ritualistic aspects of a pupil's behavior. The philosophies of synthesis imply that social problems are indeed religious concerns, and that the most significant challenges to the religious school are the vital economic, social and international problems of modern society. In helping resolve these questions, the religious educator will find his greatest reward. "Charity," says the Midrash, "blesses the person who *gives* even more than he who takes."[25]

The challenges to religious education speak out to the lay community, as well. According to Judaism, one can have a meaningful life only if he is an active member of society, is concerned for the welfare of others and works for the benefit of the community. It is the view of Judaism that by performing acts of *Tzedakah*—deeds of righteousness, justice and kindliness—we not only imitate God, but we also become his partners in the process of perfecting an imperfect world.

15. Is Church Education Something Particular?

C. ELLIS NELSON
Professor of Practical Theology, Union Theological
Seminary
(President, Louisville Presbyterian Theological Seminary)

In this seminal essay, C. Ellis Nelson marks a significant turning point in the history of REA. A new Protestant voice, a new stance, a new name, and just possible, at last, an identity. Nelson framed an understanding of church education which comes close to what European Roman Catholics have called catechesis and Jews informal education. Christian education is intentional socialization, or an induction of persons into the life and ministry of the community of faith, an understanding broader in perspective than the church school, but still having particularity. While broadening the context of education to include every aspect of the church's life, Nelson insists that education in a community of faith must be deliberate, systematic, and sustained; or better, intentional efforts leading towards a Christian mentality. At last a clear call to identity was given, but the time wasn't ripe. Roman Catholics and Jews didn't accept it and soon church education became understood as Protestant church schooling.

Since World War II education has enjoyed a flourishing life within the church. There have been differences of opinion between professional leaders about the relationship between theology and education, and there have been leaders who thought group methods were much better than the classroom for religious education. But these differences

Religious Education LXVII (January-February 1972), pp. 5-15.

only added zest to a movement that was expanding and experimenting with new curricula and new media of communication. During the latter part of the 1960s, things began to change. Public interest in religion began to wane, social problems became more acute and demanded attention of church leaders, and financial support of all church enterprises began to decline.

Today, as we enter the decade of the 1970s, we find education from the local church to the National Board in a demoralized state. Congregations are having to release their directors of education and National Boards are cutting back on personnel in a desperate effort to keep their budgets in balance. If the problem were only financial, we could grin and bear it; but the signs of the times reveal a steady decline in church school enrollment, a youth generation that is almost completely alienated from the church, and professors of religious education who have given up the Sunday school as a means of education.

What then can we say about the near future for which we must make plans? We could analyze trends in our society and then attempt to plan church education to meet those trends. But futureology is a risky business; we might just as logically plan for a new period of Puritanism in revolt against the present permissiveness as we could assume the permissive mood will become commonly accepted. Do you remember how much breast-beating and editorial moaning there was in the mid-1950s when the Purdue study revealed how conforming young people were.? No one predicted that the youth generation of the mid-sixties, with its new-found strategy of confrontation and its determination to do something about racial justice, would produce such devotion to social causes and such alienation from legally-constituted authority. Who can say what the youth generation of the 1970s will be like?

Rather than attempting to describe the future about which we might plan an educational program, I want to propose that we accept the present situation for what it is—a time of uncertainty and a time when we have to examine very carefully what we are doing in order to husband our resources. In short, we can no longer solve our problems in church education by merely adding professional workers to explore new ideas and interesting proposals. We must now think through our problems in church education by a vigorous examination of what church education is about and work within those limits as efficiently as possible.

DIFFICULTIES WITH THE PROBLEM

Many—perhaps most—people when asked to state what church education is about would reply teaching in Sunday school or leading a youth group. So at the outset we have the confusion of *education* with a particular *agent* of education—the Sunday school. This confusion is of long standing and is deeply rooted in our history. Fortunately, Robert Lynn and Elliott Wright in their new book *The Big Little School* (Harper) have told the story of the Sunday school so we might understand its presence and significance today. It is Lynn's thesis that the Sunday school is intimately related to nineteenth-century evangelical Protestantism. Where that evangelical spirit is alive today with its support system of a close-knit congregation, the Sunday school is prospering as illustrated by its growth in the Church of the Nazarene and Assembly of God denominations. Where that evangelical spirit is in decline, as it is in many mainline denominations today, the Sunday school is losing enrollment.

His thesis is given added support by tracing the relationship of the professional religious educator to the Sunday school in the twentieth century. The first generation of professionals (as illustrated by George Albert Coe) attempted to formulate a sound educational philosophy. The second generation of professionals after World War I attempted to turn the Sunday school into a good educational agency by means of teacher-training courses and "educationally sound" curricula. Both these efforts failed to make much change in the Sunday school because the Sunday school is tied to the evangelical spirit. It is a school of the heart rather than of the mind.

The most comprehensive and careful recent study of the Sunday school, sponsored by the United Presbyterian Church, shows that Sunday school teachers generally placed high on their list nurture-type goals such as "the imparting of knowledge and faith to immature minds." The more educational type of goals, such as "learning is experimental" or the teacher is responsible "for providing an environment in which . . . growth can evolve freely," were the ideas with which they disagreed. A good Sunday school teacher, this survey showed, "should primarily be sincere."[1]

This study supports the Lynn thesis that the evangelical spirit is still the power supporting the Sunday school. Professional leaders of church education must now realize that the Sunday school is not so much an agency of education as it is an agency of a particular form of Protestantism and that we cannot easily or quickly turn it into an educational agency. This situation requires that we face more realistically the role of various agencies of education in the church and the relation of actual, lived theology (in contrast to official creeds) to educational possibilities. We will come back to this matter after we have attempted to clarify the meaning of education in the church.

A second major source of confusion about the role of education in the church is the nature and function of the church. Here we must not detain ourselves with a precise definition of the church. Whether we say the church is to nurture faith in God as revealed in Christ or is the place where the word of God is preached and the sacraments rightly administered or that it is to continue the ministries of Christ in the world today, we are saying that the church has a concern for the whole person in terms of faith or spiritual life. There is good reason for this imprecision as anyone knows who has worked closely with people who have been led by the Spirit of God. The Spirit has a will and a way of its own and is not subject to human control.

Because of our theological belief about the importance and freedom of the Holy Spirit to convert and guide individuals, we rightly see that *all life experiences* have an educational potential. Holding to this belief in the spirit we say that *any person*, teacher, minister, parent, friend can be the person through whom the Spirit works, or that *anything* such as a work of art can be the trigger that sets an individual on the way to faith in God. Because we prize faith in God above all else, we have generally assumed that the educational world of the church should have the same goal and that all of a person's experiences may be channels for the Spirit to bring about change and dedication.

I think we should assume that the general goal of church education is the same as that of the church, but education is a particular human process that should not be confused with the work of the Spirit. At the practical level a lot of sloppy, ill-defined educational work, poor teacher preparation, and inadequate curriculum materials are excused because we say or think that the Holy Spirit is the real force. I hope to show that we are not forced to choose between the work of the Spirit and the work of the educator.

The third cluster of confusing notions grows out of the second. If you take the position that education is related to *all experiences* a person is having, then you are open to the notion that the educator should be concerned about everything that comes along. In the congregation, the minister of education may become the jack-of-all-trades because he often is the soldier where "the buck stops"; however, it is more likely that this happens because his understanding of education includes the idea that everything is education. Thus, he finds himself involved in everything from church night suppers through Boy Scouts to building repairs because all of these things can be educational. In the church at large the "everything is educational" philosophy has such wide acceptance that boards of Christian Education are often a depository of any cause or program that does not fit in or is not wanted by other boards and agencies.

The "everything" philosophy is not wrong; indeed a person *can* use almost anything for education. But we should make a distinction between what an individual *may use* for educational purposes out of his total experience and the *deliberate activities* of the educator who is attempting to help students learn how to think or how to decide important issues. Therefore, if we can clarify the role of education in the church, we could more clearly decide what is central and what is peripheral for educational purposes. We would be able to decide not what may be done but what ought to be done, not what is good for the general cause of the church but what—if left undone—will not be done or would be done poorly by someone who does not understand educational processes.

THE ROLE OF EDUCATION IN THE CHURCH

Definitions are always hazardous because they attempt to confine human experience in neat categories and we know that human life is never simple or easily contained. But my purpose at this point is not so much an effort to define church education as it is an effort to separate the role of education in the church sufficiently to see it with greater clarity. Therefore, the following definition should be read as a tentative statement.

The general purpose of education is the same as the purpose of the church, but the particular role of education is to foster deliberate efforts to help persons in the church develop a Christian mentality.

A few comments are in order. I have already indicated that insofar as education has a purpose, it should be the same as that of the church. This means that the educator is concerned with good music, well-planned worship, helpful sermons, dedicated lives, mission to the community and other elements of the church's life. All of these things make the church a living community of memory, service, and hope. From these elements, individuals may at their point of personal need appropriate knowledge, insight, and devotion. In this sense, anything could be appropriated by a person to change his life or make him a better Christian. Because the educator shares this purpose of the church, he—like the angels in heaven—rejoices when a sinner is converted (Luke 15:10).

This does not mean that all of the life of the congregation except the classroom is devoid of education. Rather, it means that experience can cause a person to change but also that experience is not education unless the person reflects on his experience. So a crucial aspect of this definition is that, as the human mind works on what it experiences, such activity can be participated in by others in order to shape it into meaningful ideas and images.

The central part of the definition is "to foster deliberate efforts to help persons in the church develop a Christian mentality." *Deliberate* is the key word. Anyone can be an educator in the church if he has (1) a deliberate purpose in his work that he can express, (2) methods which can be examined and (3) results which can be appraised. Thus, the choir director can be an educator when he deliberately engages in teaching the way a hymn should be sung and explains why. A minister may in sermons and counselling situations help a person develop a Christian mentality and, in these moments, be an educator.

The most difficult part of the definition is "Christian mentality." These words could hang us up forever, so let's just get the main meaning for our purpose. "Christian," shall we say, means what the church says in its official creeds. "Mental" means both the mind at work and a state of mind. At work the mind reasons, broods, remembers, classifies, describes, lurches into generalizations, solve problems and at night dreams (daytime, too!). A state of mind consists of values, attitudes, fears, hopes, ambitions, and patterns of behavior. Normally, we understand the mind and we work with the mind through language although visual art and music are also avenues to the mind. We must point out that the mind is a phenomenon by itself. Not all its operations are open to education. It is only when we deliberately attempt to develop a mind by procedures which stimulate thought, supply information, analyze experience, formulate human events into patterns of meaning, and so on, that we can claim to be educators. A more general way of stating the same thing would be as follows: the role of education is to help people make sense out of their experience in the perspective of the Christian faith.

FIRST TEST: AGENCY

This definition of the role of education in the church has little value unless it helps us make decisions about our work.

Through such discussion we'll also discover a better idea of what the definition means. Let us test the definition with the three major areas of confusion I mentioned at the first of this article and see what difference the definition will make in our understanding of those particular problem areas.

What does this definition have to say about the Sunday school as an agency of education?

(1) Schooling and education can be thought of as separate matters, although they can also overlap. For example, a Sunday school that trains children by indoctrination and emotional conditioning to act in certain ways would not be educational by our definition because it did not develop Christian mentality, although a stereotyped "Christian behavior" might result. On the other hand, education can take place in Sunday school if the leaders develop the pupil's ability to reflect on, and decide about, the Christian faith.

We must not forget Lynn's analysis that professional religious educators have had little effect on the Sunday school, even though they tried to give it a sound educational philosophy and curriculum. The trouble was that teachers and local church educators continue to see the Sunday school as an agency of Protestant piety. An educational approach to the Sunday school would attempt to help teachers and leaders become educators and that is what newer forms of teacher training can do. *Instrotech* and other diagnostic methods of examining a teacher's work assume teaching to be a human enterprise which can be improved by analysis and practice. Adding more time to the Sunday school or meeting during the week or paying teachers will not necessarily make the activity more educational, according to this definition.

(2) The idea that education can be a part of, or apart from, schools opens up some new opportunities. As already

indicated, many church leaders can be educators. We could greatly increase the educational work of the church if we looked for occasions other than Sunday school settings for deliberate efforts to help people think through the meaning of Christianity. Officers' meetings, choir practice, parent groups, adults grouped by vocational interest, and other natural gatherings in the church could set aside a portion of their time for educational activity related to their interest or their leadership role in the church. Ministers have often used congregational worship as a place where they help the congregation to think about a hymn by a brief comment before its use or to learn more from Scripture through a brief discussion concerning the passage before or during its reading. It is the intentionality of these acts that makes them educational.

SECOND TEST: RELATION OF EDUCATION TO THEOLOGY AND MORALS

1. Theology

Education is not, and should not be, separate from the currents of thought that shape and are shaped by theology. But the way we connect it with theology has been an issue since the inception of religious education as a field of study; and I am coming to believe that the way we have attempted to work with this matter is unsatisfactory for the future.

At the beginning of the twentieth century religious education became a critical field of inquiry. This came about because psychology led the way for the social scientist to break away from philosophy and to form a separate field of inquiry based on rational methods of research. When this happened, church educators began to stand on their own: they had ground they shared with psychologists, which resulted in a view of man not totally dependent on traditional theology. It is possible that the first generation of religious educators overreacted to late nineteenth century revival theology. It is possible they were too much influenced by the optimistic mood of the social gospel prior to World War I. For whatever reason, the leading religious educators before 1930 interpreted their role *as that of theologian*; and the "liberal" theology they retailed held an optimistic view of man that was intrigued with building the Kingdom of God on earth. Religious education to these leaders was both *the means* and *the message* for reforming the church and society.

In the 1930s the American brand of neo-Orthodoxy came into being with an emphasis on the sinfulness of man and the ambiguities of the social situation created by man's pride and pretentiousness. This movement of thought, born in Europe when World War I signaled the collapse of idealism, was strengthened by the rise of Nazism and World War II. It dominated the theological landscape in America until the 1960s. Church educators who adopted the neo-Orthodox position interpreted their role as *teachers of theology*, and educational knowledge was used to give clues as to how people of different age levels could learn theology and absorb the "strange" world of the Bible.

Today we do not have a major pattern of theology. About the only system of thought that presents itself with some vigor in theology is existentialism; but that stance is by no means widely accepted. It is countered by a resurgence of rationalism in the form of linguistic analysis, a resurgence of humanism in the form of theologies of revolution, and a resurgence of native nineteenth century American pietism that is concerned about an immanent God dealing with private matters.

If this description of the general theological situation is fairly accurate, how is the church educator to respond?

The educator is a theologian in the sense that he has some thought-out system of belief, and he certainly will explain those beliefs if he is true to himself. But the emphasis I think should go to the suggestion that the church educator, at least for the immediate future, should think of himself primarily as one who fosters a theological inquiry. This stance applies to high-school students and above, for children are not capable of this kind of thinking, nor have they had the experience necessary for theological inquiry. In practical terms it meens adult groups must learn how to bring their beliefs to a conscious level and then to examine those beliefs in the light of our knowledge of the world and society. Such a process would also require a diligent study of the Bible and a comparison of beliefs in different eras of Christian tradition. I will admit that this is a large order, but is it not the work of the educator as distinct from other church leaders?

2. Morals

Sunday school is indelibly associated in people's minds with morals. Indeed, morals are the substance of most Sunday school lessons if the teaching is done by a person whose religious life has been formed by popular Protestant piety. The exodus of teenagers from the Sunday school is occasioned, I believe, not so much because the Sunday school is boring or inadequate but because the teenagers are in reaction against the morals that were taught them in Sunday school when they were children.

Many parents also perceive the Sunday school as the place their child will learn to be good. Rejecting or resisting the role of the moral teacher, parents often assume the

Sunday school will do that for them. One minister in a town near New York saw this condition in his Sunday school so clearly he closed the Sunday school. Soon his congregation dwindled in size, for parents saw little practical use for the church if it did not provide a school to teach the children how to be good. This minister then reinstated the Sunday school to get the parents back in church—a strange twist in which the Sunday school justified the church!

Given this powerful connection between morals and the Sunday school, should we expect the educator to teach morals or to help people understand and form moral standards?

This question may be impossible to answer. Yet the fact of cultural and moral changes in our society is so clear that we must be aware of its power and significance. Erik Erikson has said that just as people can have a sense of who they are and take satisfaction from acting out their self-image, people can also experience identity confusion, feeling that they are losing their grip on themselves. Erikson believes that we are going through a period now which is comparable to the Protestant reformation. This alienation consists of "*fears* aroused by discoveries and inventions (including weapons) radically expanding and changing the space-time quality of the world image; inner *anxieties* aggravated by the decay of existing institutions which have provided the historical anchor of an elite's identity; and the *dread* of an existential vacuum."[2]

There seems to be little question that we are going through a period of identity confusion for the reasons Erikson mentions, and the result is a crisis in moral standards.

The basic story we know rather well. Science and technology have produced new ways of solving problems, extending the power of man and giving him the ability to predict and control more areas of his life. The automobile and airplane extended man's ability to move rapidly and this changed patterns of living. Communication has become instant and remote events are now factored into daily thought. New birth control devices separate sex from marriage. Computers and new electronic devices makes surveillance and record-keeping fairly simple. The way we use these developments constitutes one set of moral problems. The car can bring pleasure or allow a person to get away from a bank robbery. Improved communication can enhance our knowledge and appreciation of the world or can be used to "sell" an unscrupulous politician to the electorate. Computers can make airplane reservations at the blink of an eye or store false information about individuals without their knowledge.

But the story of how technology is changing the child-rearing situation is not well known and may be a more serious moral dilemma. Rapid change in our culture erodes the position of an established group, such as the church, which normally supplies stability and community in a culture. The present generation of older children and adolescents gets the feeling that they will be in a different world from that of their parents, so parents lose their position of authority and respect. As life becomes more "instant" through TV and the parents are out of the home doing things their children cannot understand, children are cut loose from family restraints sooner. The openness of society and the multiplicity of opportunities to do all kinds of things—many of them good and desirable—emphasize *experience* as the mode of self-discovery. This mode is in contrast to the older way of finding one's self through or against authority figures such as ministers, teachers, or parents, or through reason and imagination as when children read and played to fill their expendable time.

Technology does two other things that affect our children and youth. It makes human labor less and less important so that it becomes more difficult for adolescents to find meaningful jobs, thus closing off one of the most important processes of maturation. At the same time, many jobs require high competence and that means a long period of training. So our youth are side-tracked for eight to twelve years during which time they have no socially-approved role other than getting ready to be adults. It is no wonder that they continue their mode of self-realization primarily through experience and that they feel depressed by a system that will not take them seriously.

So we have two areas of ethical conflict on our hands that come rather directly from our technical society. We have the area of personal morals, where we see our experience-centered youth using drugs, sex, music, and money in ways that scandalize the average Presbyterian adult. Then we have social ethics, where in matters of race relations, social equality, distribution of wealth, and treatment of minority groups, this youth generation is the most morally sensitive we've had in a long time. At this point the adult church generation finds itself on the defensive because the young can truthfully say that the Christian faith supports their social ethic. Indeed, we face the same irony with many of our youth that we face with black Americans. For many black Americans Christianity has no appeal or power, not because it is untrue but because the only form of it they know is associated with inhuman racial attitudes. For many of our youth, American Protestant Christianity is so as-

sociated with social ethics justifying our exploitation of
less-privileged classes and races that they are searching for
meaning elsewhere.

What does all this mean for the educator of the church?
The easiest thing to do is to grow long hair, rap with youth,
jump on a motorcycle and go charging off on a mission. I
don't want to fault this formula too much, for length of hair
is unimportant, rapping is good, and the mission may be
important. But what is the *distinctive* approach of the church
educator?

First, we need to understand what is happening to us and
this is just plain, hard, intellectual work. The few comments
that opened up this question do not begin to get at the
complications in the matter. Unless we get some understanding of what is happening in our society, how can we
ever hope to transcend and perhaps modify the conditions
that shape us? Granted Americans value action above
thought, should educators accept that priority?

Second, we need to sort out the relation of our religion to
morals. This is by no means easy, but we have the Bible as a
case book. The Ten Commandments, for example, were
originally ten simple statements of words. As recorded in
Exodus, they have been elaborated to serve a stable community. As expanded in the Talmud over a thousand years,
they require eight volumes! Polygamy, usury, war, slavery,
and a host of other current ethical conditions have a history
of codes in the Bible. The church educator should be able to
help people sort out the way religious beliefs and social
conditions relate to morals and help them use the same
formula for understanding conditions and morality today.

Third, we need to work with the congregation because
social conditions affect everyone. If identity confusion gives
people "the feeling that they are losing their grip on them-

selves," then the church educator is just as obliged to help the middle-aged businessman in his situation as he is to help the teenager cope with his problems.

At this point I believe the church has an advantage over all other institutions in the community. We have a voluntary association dedicated to, or predisposed toward, finding the meaning of God in their lives. The history of the church gives us a tradition heavily weighted toward ethics and a hall of heroes who fought for human rights and dignity. Our problem as educators is how to use these assets in order to help church people bring their religious beliefs into a meaningful interaction with social conditions. This is a mental task including an adjustment in one's values.

Where does the older child or teenager get any help in moral decision-making? Adults in authority deal with events, usually under pressure, in haphazard order to remedy a condition often going out of control or when sanctions have to be applied. Is it any wonder our children's moral immaturity extends well into their twenties or that they find the freedom of college such an emotional crisis? Moral decision-making needs practice. What institution in the community is better equipped than the church to foster such practice sessions?

TEST THREE: SOCIAL JUSTICE

Today there is considerable interest in social action as the model of church education. This comes about because of the tremendous social problems that America has never properly faced nor adequately factored into the politcal and economic domain. One has only to mention race relations, rights of minority groups, the almost uncontrolled exploitation of natural resources, along with our careless pollution of earth, water and air to get a sense of our unfinished national agenda. Some of these agenda items have reached a crisis stage. Our national mentality of high energy focused sharply on problem solving puts a lot of pressure on leaders in all institutions to work directly with the crises in the nation.

The hard, disagreeable facts of our social life have created a renewed interest in the strategy of social action. We need only to be reminded that the intransigent white racial attitudes toward black Americans created a situation which caused black youth to invent the "sit in" in the early 1960s as a tactic for getting some of their basic human rights. This tactic, widely used in racial matters, was picked up by students in the late 1960 for confrontation with college authorities. For the past decade young people have been thinking about and experimenting with ways to change society. This preoccupation with strategy has been reinforced by professors and other leaders who have rationalized force as a normal or even natural part of social change. This thinking ranges all the way from those who have a socialist state in mind as the desirable end of social action to those who want merely to remedy specific griev-ances in order to make our actual political and social life reasonably equal to the Bill of Rights and the Constitution. Learning, all of these groups would say, does not come about fully until one has committed himself to a course of action. Then—and only then—will experience interact with thoughts, each influencing the other, and new understand-ing of reality emerge.

That social action is an appropriate work of the church is not questioned. However, the leadership of social action projects should be in the hands of people who are skillful in politics and have time for the negotiations and compromises that are required. That social action can provide learning which is more powerful than, and different from, that which comes from textbooks or classrooms is not questioned. Social action is a more intense and dramatic form of the "everything" approach to learning. But what is learned? One person learns the stupidity of bureaucracy and retreats to a commune; another learns that working class people have a different life-style and will not change it just because he expects them to do so. These learnings could be educational if the person having the experience reflected on them and developed a concept of how bureaucracy functions or how class values determine conduct. Having experience and knowing things is not education. It is what we do with experience to shape it into meaning that can be examined and communicated which makes it educational.

Therefore, the problem for us as educators is to help church members develop a mentality for social justice. To do this we will need to work along two lines.

1. A Concern for Individuals, Their Attitudes and Values

Individuals are the building blocks of any human enterprise and they are the central concern of the educator. I know that this person-centeredness can be easily overdone, and I certainly do not mean that a person's self is formed by his own will-power, separate from others. The peer groups with which the person is associated are powerful influences, and group activity belongs in the general plan and strategies of the educator. The exact nature of this person-group interaction is not well known and need not delay us at this point except to note that it should not be overlooked.

More important, perhaps, is the idea of what a person gives himself to or what values he develops for his life. By "values" here I mean those attitudes toward himself and others that he voluntarily incorporates within himself and that he believes are desirable for all people. It is at the point of a person's values that social goals are important. The major concern of the church educator would be to help develop the kind of person who would normally want and expect people of all races to have equal justice in America. If we must have a paradigm, then I would suggest that the educator is a coach preparing people for corporate life and helping them understand life's situations while they are living in them. This is not a passive role. The coach is deeply involved, but he can't play the game for the players, and the players know it. That is why I think coaches are normally so popular in high school and college. The relationship of the coach to the person (pupil) is one in which the pupil knows that the coach is helping him develop his skill and self-confidence to perform in the game that he and his friends deem important.

Somewhere in the many articles I have read on youth alienation, I recall the story of a professor who was talking to a student about his academic work. The student grew more and more restless during the conversation saying he was disenchanted with studying and was going to drop out of school to work directly with social problems. Then he turned to the professor and berated him for studying while the world las in such a mess. The student ended the conversation with this challenge: "How high do the flames have to rise outside your window before you go outside to extinguish them?" The professor stunned by the criticism and sympathetic to the student's social concerns did not know how to react. He told the story to Erik Erikson and asked what he should have said. Erikson replied, "You could have said, . . . 'and what will we do when we get outside?' " That comment shows the role of an educator and the limits of his work. As a citizen, the professor could be involved in social action and he could learn a lot from the experience, but social action is not designed to educate; it is designed to bring about social change.

2. A Concern for the Church as a Training Ground

Institutions are the agents of change in our society because they have corporate power and are capable of staying with problems over a long period of time. Institutions are, in short, the human way to express and conserve the attitudes and values of a group of individuals. What, then, is the distinctive work of the educator who is concerned about the institutional mission of the church?

A good place to start such an inquiry is with Kenneth Underwood. Trained to be a minister, he was a professor of social ethics and editor of *Social Action*. Moreover, he is one of the few scholars who has ever made a case study of exactly what happens in churches when a particular social and political problem has to be faced in a community. That study, *Protestant and Catholic*, is a realistic assessment of what churches will actually do in social affairs and a cataloguing of their political ineptness. The Danforth Foundation turned to Underwood to make a long and comprehensive study of campus ministries which he placed in the context of the American church situation. In his report he faces directly the problem of the church in relation to social action because the campus ministry is so identified with protest and the reform movement. A careful reading of this report is absolutely essential for anyone who attempts to lead the church in social action.[3]

Underwood, who is as devoted to effective participation

of the church in social change as anyone could be, deliberately avoids the term social action and what he calls the "vague terms" used in ecumenical literature (also national boards?) such as "servant role" or "mission of the church to society." He used the term "social policy."

> To talk of social policy is to talk of projecting oneself and others into the future, of being able to achieve goals with others, of being effective organizationally. To teach, to lead worship, to preach in such a way as to enhance the powers of others to participate in the formation of social policy, is seen as one of the most important aspects of being human and being Christian. To claim to be a Christian who loves God and neighbor and not to attempt to be an effective person in the formation of just social policies is to talk nonsense in the modern world. The purpose of education in the church and university, or better, the best test of its quality, is that it enhances the capacity of laymen to achieve just social policies.[4]

Underwood, you see, has a rather clearcut idea of what education in the church should be and he gives it in more detail in these words.

> At issue is not whether elite, policy-making, professional groups are to be the only recipients of Christian ministry or whether the lonely, depressed, poverty-stricken, and forgotten of the inner city are to be the focus of the church's leadership. At issue is whether the actions of the former are being critically and constructively reflected on in the church for their effects on the latter and vice versa. The issue is not whether the church's best-educated, most professionally minded clergy are now in suburban churches rather than in the big cities, but what provisions are being made in the university and church for new literature, leadership training, and educational settings that open up the realities of social influence of these suburban constituencies on the body politic, on professional services, on new careers for the poor, and in turn bring the needs and experiences of the

poor and forgotten in all areas of the church to the attention of those who can act to help them.[5]

Notice that when Underwood makes social justice the proving ground of the Christian faith, education becomes:

(1) A way of enhancing "the capacity of laymen to achieve just social policies."

(2) A learning how to participate in the formation of social policy.

(3) A critical analysis of how one social class and its way of life affects another social class.

(4) The provision of literature, training, and educational settings that "open up the realities of social influence of . . . suburban (churches) . . . on the body politic."

Thus Underwood saw education as something particular and definable, when social justice was the goal. Apparently all through his study he searched for a principle that would mark the limits of what the church could do educationally before it passed into the politics of social action. In the preface he stated it in these words:

> The policy researcher stops short of telling leaders of an institution what they are to do, what alternatives are to be chosen, and the time and place of the choice. He knows he cannot envision the concrete circumstances of decision. But he can as part of his responsibilities engage in illustrative speculation about the possible influence of certain choices.[6]

What larger charge do we educators want than these four educational tasks Underwood proposes as essential if social justice is the proving ground of church activity?

In addition to Underwood's suggestion about the role of education in creating a mentality for social justice, we should remember that the church in its own life as an institution provides a laboratory for helping people learn how institutions operate. Young people and others need training in how to work with and through conflict situations.

The Presbyterian Church is excellent for this purpose. We believe in governance so much we named our church after our system of goverance! We (as do other denominations!) brag about the government of the United States being a copy of our church government. If so, why should we not train politicians for the state in the church? For this type of training we need only the actual conditions of congregation and community.

There is nothing in Presbyterian polity that prevents young people or others from talking to the representatives they elected to the Session about their concerns. Church members could insist that Session meetings be open, that members be given opportunity to speak. And why should not the Session's agenda be posted and minutes be made available? There is no rule that prevents open hearings on the congregational budget prior to its formulation for congregational approval.

The educator can help church members or church school classes do research on ethical affairs and then present them to the proper church court for consideration. Matters such as the church's investment policy, its employment policy, or its use of purchasing power in relation to the companies that supply goods and services are open (or should be open) for review. If we did something like this well, we would be turning out young people into society who would have a procedure for making change and enough savvy about institutional lethargy not to get discouraged with institutional bureaucracy in society or government.

REMADE MINDS

If we need a biblical reference to support the contentions of this paper, I would suggest these words from Paul.

> Therefore, my brothers, I implore you by God's mercy to offer your very selves to him: a living sacrifice, dedicated and fit for his acceptance, the worship offered by mind and heart. Adapt yourselves no longer to the pattern of this present world, but let your minds be remade and your whole nature thus transformed. Then you will be able to discern the will of God, and to know what is good, acceptable, and perfect (Romans 12:1-2, N.E.B.).

Paul at this point in his letter to the Romans has just finished his major theological work and is turning to illustrations of what this theology will mean in practice. These two verses are a summary of all that went before. Because of what God has done for us in Christ, we are to dedicate our whole life to God. To do this, we need a new orientation which can come about by the *remaking of our mind*, resulting in the ability *to discern* the will of God and *to know* how to live.

16. Education in the Black Church: Design For Change

OLIVIA PEARL STOKES
Associate Professor Herbert Lamin College, Bronx, New York
(Presently Educational Consultant)

Few blacks have contributed to Religious Education, *though a concern for racial justice was occasionally voiced. Indeed, many of the articles have been racist, and not until the present has a distinctive black voice been heard. Recently, black religious educators have joined in the question, what is religious education? With the emergence of black consciousness, black theology and black church studies, a new search for religious education from a black perspective has emerged. Olivia Pearl Stokes has made a significant contribution to this concern in terms of church education for black peoples. Still the issue of an identity for religious education remains, and the voices of ethnic and racial minorities are understandably yet to make this issue their primary concern.*

This essay attempts to address two difficult questions: (1) What are some of the implications of the new black theology for educational programs of the black churches? (2) What educational guidelines are suggested by the emerging black theologies that enable black church educators to equip their leadership with new Christian values for the black perspective?

WHY CHANGE? SOME MAJOR REASONS

(1) *A Social-Racial Revolution.* The United States shook

Religious Education LXIX (July-August 1974), pp. 443-445.

with a different kind of revolution in the 1960s. The new black awareness was born with its demands. Its effect on black America has been exhilarating and exciting. The black awareness and its implications for expanding American democracy will probably never end. It's growing!

The black social and racial revolution of the 60s, led by black college youth, unsettled unjust social traditions and practice. Youth used dramatic attention-getting methods. Sit-ins, demonstrations, marches, mass jail sit-ins, all said to America that its Judeo-Christian proclamations were not its practices. The country was practicing racism on blacks.

Starting on the campuses, the movement for social justice and human dignity was supported strongly by the black church, the Southern Christian Leadership Conference, and the total black community mobilized for action. The black people had walked out into "psychological space" in an age when white people were walking on "moon space."

American blacks joined spirits with African ancestral kin: those youthful giants among Africa's emerging national independence leaders, in the 1960's. Blacks, world-wide, were turning from an oppressive past towards a full future of unity and nationhood. The task undertaken would not be easy, but it had to be achieved for the good of all mankind. The winds of freedom buffeted Africa and America at gale force.

(2) *The New Black Movement.* The new American "BM" factor, black movement, black migration and black psychological mobility, was awakening the national character. Black persons had a reversal of feelings about themselves—from little self-esteen to feelings of genuine self-pride, from self denigration to expansive superiority. Freed of the burden of feeling "black is bad," black spirits were lifted. Responding to the "great Society" national in-

itiatives and the newly funded "war on poverty" programs, blacks began to value their creative capacties, special talents and gifts. Study and reflection on the black experience led some persons to value their life experiences as "expert" knowledge. Poverty projects were, by law, beginning to involve those affected by decisions; and many poor blacks demanded roles as paid consultants. "There arises sometimes the notion that one need only be black, unlettered and poor, and by these credentials be identified as men and women of great wisdom."

The militants, supported by aware youth, began to be shocked as they unraveled the fact that unknowingly blacks had been living lives by the restrictions whites had dictated and imposed. Black movement leaders and people were painfully aware of the failure of white leadership, both national and local; as blacks experienced the widening of the gap between the "haves" and the "have-nots." Blacks felt the absence of moral and ethical responsibility and integrity of national government leaders, as Dr. Martin Luther King, Jr., led this nation into an agonizing appraisal of its racist and oppressive behavior.

"SOUL" became the mystique of the movement. "SOUL" was "the graceful survival under impossible circumstances."[1] "SOUL" became the black password because it unified brothers and sisters who had suffered the same mistreatment, and unified them in their determination to build a just America, ridding it of racism as well as economic, educational, and political oppression against blacks.

Blackness, like "SOUL," was molded into a political-cultural concept. However, blackness is more than a political-cultural category. Blackness is an ontological-philosophical-theological category. It is ontological in the sense that it affirms the existence of the black man as a legitimate and significant part of a God-given humanity to which all other races belong. Blackness is a philosophical concept in the sense that it requires a critical examination of fundamental ideas about God, world, man and good and evil which have arisen out of the black Christian experience. Blackness is a theological concept in that it affirms with the Hebraic-Christian tradition that all of God's creation is good and may be used by God for the revelation of his will, mind, purpose, and love in the world. Blackness represents a person's commitments, his beliefs, his ideologies.

(3) *The Black Religious Experience.* The black youth lit the fires of social revolution, and the black clergy picked up the torch and marshaled the black church and community forces for the struggle. Religion is inherent in black African and Afro-American life.

Young theological scholars and students began to reflect on racism as expressed in classical theology and the religious practices in American churches. Black theology, inspired by Dr. James Cone, was the result. Today there is a healthy diversity of theological thought among black theological scholars. Their conceptual contributions have stirred the general theological field and may become the saving grace for an America founded on the Judeo-Christian faith.

(4) *The Urban Context of Black Life.* America is an urban civilization. Black children born in urban cities in the 50s became the first group of youth to experience the critical revolutionary period of the 60s and the fundamental social change that was rocketing America. They were inspired by the various civil rights campaigns which eventuated in unexpected national, state and local legislation. They carried the banners for the spokesman of Black Power that frightened White Power.

Their grandparents and often their parents had come from the rural South and were unaccustomed to thinking in terms of positive political strategies and radical "system" change on major social issues. Often there was a grave mistrust of each other's thoughts and feelings. Parents and grandparents had been conditioned by their past situation of racial injustice and survival needs. Black fellowship sustained them, and the attitude that "trouble don't last always" helped them to endure injustices.

(5) *The Media "Spotlight" on the Black Wretched.* White America was barely aware of the wretched plight of its benighted inner cities until TV focused on every self-proclaimed black leader of the masses. Marshall McLuhan says it took the invention of print to tear man from his tribes and plant the dream of isolation in his brain. It took riots and the civil rights struggle to focus the consciousness of white America on the immensity of three hundred and fifty years of historical oppression and the devastating effect of racism on a minority people.

The horror of continued oppression became a reality to America through the eyes and ears of the media. The result was fear and panic in whites. The deadly rage of blacks was fed as the TV pictured national and international oppression. The media all presented blacks as "The Problem." The implied question was why blacks had not lifted themselves up by "Operation Bootstrap" as other immigrants had done. White Americans failed to realize that black Americans were brought as slaves against their will to this country, while white immigrants came in search of the "good life."

THE EDUCATIONAL MISSION OF
BLACK CHURCHES: PRESENT AND FUTURE

The black church, holding Christian values and standards, sees itself as a servant of social change—by which education functions to help build an informed and critical citizenry that is able to function politically, economically, socially, and educationally in the institutions that are the fabric of the society.

This educational mission of the black church is informed by the following theological rationale.

> The church is mission when it participates in God's mission. We become instruments of God's mission as we participate in his reconciling ministry. The goal of mission . . . is God's purpose that alienated man be reconciled to God and to his fellow men.
>
> If mission prevails, men should be fully liberated and would then be free to worship his Creator and serve the needs of his fellows. Only the man who has experienced psychological and spiritual freedom can stand for sociological, political, economic, and educational freedom. A Christian man becomes responsible for justice among men because he believes in a just and righteous God, who wills the abundant life for all of his creatures. Therefore, anything that dehumanizes, desocializes, and depersonalizes a person, in any way, is contrary to the will of God.
>
> Christian mission today requires radical change in our present structures, practices, and ideologies. This means revolt against many religious, educational, social, political, and economic structures. Thus it is the educational task of the black church to join theological reflection with those processes which expose the structures which enslave; to develop techniques for freedom, and to give structures to those values of the black experience for building community for God's people.[2]

Allied to this perspective on mission are other theological affirmations that guide education in the black church.

(1) The church of Jesus Christ is concerned with the

whole of man and all persons and their conditions in society—moral and spiritual, political and cultural.

(2) Christ's church is present in the social order as one of God's instruments of social change.

(3) God's creation of black persons is good and they are persons of worth and dignity.

(4) The Gospel of Christ can be brought to bear upon the individual and corporate life of persons of the black experience.

(5) The black community is the first setting for developing a "community of Faith" to forward God's mission in the world.

(6) Jesus Christ is Liberator.

(7) Jesus Christ gave his life to increase the love of God and neighbor.

With this understanding of the black church's mission, the suggested objectives for Christian education in the black church are:

(1) To study the dialogue in black theology, in the context of the Christian faith, in order to help persons become aware of God as revealed in Jesus Christ, the Liberator.

(2) To understand other religious faiths of black people—Islam (faith of Muslims), African traditional religions, humanism, and secularism.

(3) To help black people know why they are and what their human situation is in the American society.

(4) To enable persons to investigate and evaluate the historical black religious experience, beginning with Africa, through slavery, into the contemporary urban society, and to seek its relevance for life today.

(5) To help blacks fulfill their liberating role as disciples of Christ in the world.

(6) To share with white Americans, and all God's people, the God-given black perspective of the Christian faith.

(7) To enable and equip black children, black youth and black adults to discover their divinely created human potential.

(8) To utilize religious education as a major tool for liberation, freedom, and justice in the American society.

(9) To design a broad-based educational program that aims at helping blacks remedy the past deficiencies in American society and the church and become a dynamic part of the process that directs the forces of change toward just and humane ends.

(10) To stimulate blacks to engage in sharing, from the black experience and perspective, meanings, values, and purposes and power, with ourselves and others in a world where constructive sharing is the only alternative to mutual destruction.

(11) To equip blacks with those skills and strategies that influence those responsible for today's critical decisions and choices, thereby controlling the present and creating the future that black Americans want.

Thus, education in the black church, with insights from black theology, must become a part of that indispensable structure for survival and transformation that ameliorates those societal ills Christian faith is committed to remedy. Education in the black church must also give its members an opportunity for the self-understanding of blackness, a sense of black personhood as well as assistance in the development of black community goals and programs. Likewise, education in the black church must aid black Americans to function more efficiently in their roles as citizens, students, parents, neighbors, change agents, opinion- and decision-makers; and, through these respective roles, to improve the quality of their daily lives and that of their nation.

With this understanding of the black church's mission, it is imperative to design education to teach the Bible in the context of a problem-centered and this-world approach. Instead of expecting the world to come to the church, Christian education in black churches must address the problems of the real world faced by black people. For the black church, education must be concerned with living this life, to the fullest. Uncertainty is the constant of our time.

THE ETHNIC SCHOOL: A SUGGESTED MODEL FOR BLACK RELIGIOUS EDUCATION

The new demand on Christian education in the black church is that education must contribute to self-understanding and fulfillment. Black youth are demanding of their elders to know more about their actual situation in America, and the heritage of the motherland, Africa.

In the past the central function of the black church School was to acquire knowledge of the Bible on the assumption that one would therefore be a good Christian. Previously, the central purpose of the black church was to meet the spiritual needs of persons and secondly to nurture the oppressed. Today, to these concerns must be added the formal education for liberation in face of pandemic struggles for full freedom and justice as defined by Christian faith and as seen from the black religious perspective. To address these new concerns and needs, the ethnic church school is now emerging as a promising pattern for black religious education in the future.

At any given time there are three different curricula interacting in a school setting.

Curriculum I is the formal course offerings complemented by those supportive activities growing out of the study program. In the past, the Sunday School was built around Curriculum I with its emphasis upon teaching the Bible and the history of Christianity.

Curriculum II deals in the main with social development, especially with the nature and function of authority and decision-making. When a group determines the rules that governs its operation of that of the larger community, it is dealing with Curriculum II. If the students work in committees or plan cooperatively on a project or when the responsibility for the life within the learning setting is in the hand of the students, Curriculum II is operating.

With the new black mood, the demand is for full voice and a co-equal vote in the structures and decisions that affect blacks. This mood is also having its impact upon the black church. The pattern for decision-making in the black church has been to rely very heavily on "what the preacher wants" or decides. *Change is needed*. Black church people need to make their voices, wills and votes count in the decision-making process in their church, civic groups and community life. Democratic governance is one way to help a person to self-fullment. God created persons with minds, will, and spirits—to be free. Curriculum II deals with the socio-psycho-religious components of what it means to be a black human being, who is free by virtue of his humanity, both in the black church and the wider white society.

The focus of *Curriculum III* is black self-awareness and self-development. Curriculum II deals with the "inner-space" feelings of being a black human being. The content of Curriculum II is a variety of experiences. The aim is to help each person to discover himself as a person within the larger black experience, to develop psycho-religious grounds for self-respect and to develop an understanding about a question of "who am I?" as a child of God, as an American and a world black citizen.

Though the concerns of Curricula I and II can be accommodated in the ethnic church school, it is uniquely equipped to address the needs of Curriculum III. Indeed, this has been its specific value throughout its history.

The ethnic church school, as a part of the religious life of a community, is an ancient concept and institution. The synagogue school is probably one of the earliest institutions of the religious community. In America, its main purpose has been to teach the Jewish culture, language, traditions, and family life practices to the Jewish child and youth. In short, it has instructed young Jews in the faith and practices of their community.

A comparable institution is present in the Greek Orthodox community in America. Its religious schools seek to help both adults and children understand the liturgy, tradition, and language of their ancestors. Both of these religious minorities have sought to retain their own values and traditions through the medium of the ethnic church school.

The purpose, program, and content of the ethnic church school in the black church would be similar. Its curriculum would be black history, black church history and contemporary issues viewed from the black perspective. It would celebrate the genius of the black experience, as expressed in the life of the individual, the black family and the black Christian community. It would aim to develop creativity within its members, to express their religious insights through drama, music, dance, painting, poetry, and creative writing.

The black church has always been in the forefront of liberation and quasi-black religious nationalism among black people. The ethnic school can be seen as the modern expression of this movement. In the black church, the freest, largest, and most economically secure institution in the black community, the ethnic school could become the black resource center and the transmitter of African culture and the Afro-American heritage for black Americans. Within a Christian faith grounded in the indigenous black community, the growth of black pride, self-esteem, and self-development could take place in a loving rather than a hostile climate.

The ethnic church school can help black folk recognize that in Richmond, Virginia, in 1800, Gabriel Prosser, a slave, initiated a revolt and supported it with the biblical injunction that slaves could assume the role of the Israelites and discharge the bonds of slavery with the aid and comfort of God; that Denmark Vesy, in 1822, headed a group of members from the Negro Methodist Church in an uprising in Charleston, South Carolina; that Nat Turner, a Baptist exhorter and mystic, after spending months in prayer and Bible study, planned an insurrection that bloodied Southampton County, Virginia, in 1831. These prophetic insights, found in these black heroes, are evidence that the spirit of black people was free to revolt against their white master's oppression. God, for the black church, and the black worshiper, is authentic. He has always been the God of liberation, the God who set captives free.

The black ethnic school will highlight, for black and white Americans alike, that most movements among black people owe a large degree of their success to black leaders who were prominent in the life of the church, or to pastors who led their congregations in the struggle for freedom, equality, justice, and liberation. This fresh portrayal of the role of the black church and its fighting saints would, thus, give moral support to the present liberation struggle of black people.

THE TEACHING-LEARNING PROCESS
IN THE ETHNIC CHURCH SCHOOL

It has been acknowledged that the black Church School has traditionally adopted what Paulo Freire, in *The Pedagogy of the Oppressed,* calls the "banking concept of education":

> Knowledge is a gift bestowed by those (teachers) who consider themselves knowledgeable upon those (students) whom they consider to know nothing. . . . Education becomes an act of depositing, in which the students are the depositories, and the teacher is the depositor. Instead of communicating, the teacher issues communiques and makes deposits which the students patiently receive, memorize, and repeat.[3]

Another characteristic of "the banking concept of education" is the view that persons are manageable human beings, adaptable to the authority structure of the teacher.

> The more students work at storing the deposits entrusted to them, the less they develop the critical consciousness which would result from their intervention in the world as "transformers" of the world. The more completely (students) accept the passive role imposed on them, the more they tend simply to adapt to the world as it is and to the fragmented view of reality deposited in them.[4]

The teaching-learning process is quite different in an educational system which has the elimination of social, political, and economic oppression as its goal. Liberation education gravitates towards a learning situation in which the teacher is a communicator and not a banker, where the teacher is a partner in dialogue, rather than a narrator.

Liberation education seeks to transform structures so that persons become beings for themselves, not instruments manageable by others and by structures to which they have to conform. Liberation education for the black church engages its participants in critical thinking and in the quest for mutual humanization to realize the fullest potential of the divinely-created person. The teacher who holds this philosophy views each person in profound trust, with a God-given potential and creative power. In this framework, the teacher becomes a partner with the student and a teacher-student learning situation develops. Liberation education requires that teachers see themselves as persons living with others around common goals. The search for solidarity requires dialogue, community, and interaction for the discovery of meaning.

Because "the banking concept of education" begins with a false understanding of persons as objects, it does not promote the development of liberation and creative thinking about the reality of one's own life situation. By contrast, liberation education forces individuals to look authentically at their world and to engage in action-reflection with a view to transforming their life situations. Liberation leaders and teachers work from a philosophy which says that persons are conscious beings, purposefully intent upon transforming the world to what God intended; as they best understand his will.

Liberation education is the process of helping persons deal with the problems of individuals in their relationships with the world. Liberation education is a cognitive process in which teachers and pupils together are responsible for growth and understanding. Students, in this process, are not just absorbers or docile listeners, but rather become critical coinvestigators in dialogue with the teachers and the parents.

Liberation education is informed by a problem-solving
and problem-posing process.

> Problem-posing education bases itself on creativity and
> stimulates true reflection and action upon reality, thereby
> responding to the vocation of men as beings who are au-
> thentic only when engaged in inquiry and creative trans-
> formation. . . . Problem-posing education affirms men as
> beings in and with a likewise unfinished reality. Indeed, in
> contrast to other animals who are unfinished, but not his-
> torical, men know themselves to be unfinished; they are
> aware of their incompletion. . . . The unfinished character
> of men and the transformational character of reality neces-
> sitate that education is thus constantly remade. . . . In order
> to be, it must become. . . . Any situation in which some men
> prevent others from engaging in the process of inquiry is
> one of violence.[5]

Thus, the role of the educator in the problem-solving and
problem-posing process is to create, with the student, authentic conditions under which knowledge, at the level of
opinion, is superceded by authentic knowledge at the level
of reality.

One example of the ethnic church school became flesh
and blood when a cluster of eight churches, in Los Angeles,
established EGO (*Educational Growth Organization, Ethnic
Growth Organization, Economic Growth Organization*) which
operates a Saturday ethnic school in the facilities of their
eight church buildings. The findings of this project are
instructive for appraising the impact and the future of the
ethnic church school.[6]

Findings during the first year of the Los Angeles ethnic
church school demonstrate that:

(1) The program had a tremendous impact on adults.
They learned about themselves, their responsibilites and
they gained real satisfaction from action-reflection service
projects.

(2) The reading level of children (low to begin with because of the need for remedial help) increased because the resources used reflected their own background.

(3) There is a need for religious celebration. The EGO school, therefore, created "an act of celebration and commitment" for youth who completed the EGO program. It is a service celebrating manhood and womanhood and was developed as part of the workshop experience for boys and girls when they reach their fifteenth year of life.

(4) Children cannot learn very effectively on empty stomachs. The school found it necessary to provide a twenty-minute breakfast period. This is a problem resident in many of the nation's public schools and it was acknowledged in the ethnic school. Breakfast provides stimulation for learning.

(5) Limited resources, especially reading and library facilities, exist in the home as well as in the public and educational sectors of the community. Accordingly, it was necessary to develop an African and Afro-American library to provide relevant background resources.

(6) The ethnic school provides experiences which build a strong self-image, self-respect, and self-understanding. It supplements the Hebrew-Christian traditions with Afro-American culture and traditions. The ethnic school is a valuable vehicle for understanding and appropriating the role of the black church in the black community, past, present, and future.

(7) The learning experiences in the ethnic school enrich the teacher as well as the participants.

(8) A merger of the traditional Sunday church school and the Saturday ethnic church school is required. These two modes of religious education must coalesce into a single Christian education thrust to interpret the emerging theology of the black experience in America.

(9) The ethnic church school must become an advocate for such concerns as community health, public education, economic development, consumer affairs, citizen and the law, and community development and organizations. These are vital areas affecting the lives of the black community; as well as areas which are a vital part of the issue-oriented and problem-posing process of education that informs the ethnic school.

CONCLUSION

Change is uncomfortable and rarely welcomed. Usually it is resisted overtly or covertly. Therefore, it must be planned for if it is to occur. To institute a formal and planned system of education in the black church calls for putting into motion a definite set of strategies by which desired changes are likely to be brought about. The educational design for change in the black church in concept, in mission, and in strategy, represents a faith and hope for meeting today's needs in complex urban cities and in traditional black churches.

Effective change of the American society is a potential that the black churches can have a significant part in influencing. The risk is high, but the goal is worth the sacrificial cost. Our faith, our black people and all God's created ones, require and demand that change come, and that this oppressive and unjust society become the kingdom of God on earth.

17. The Intersection of Religion and Education

GABRIEL MORAN

Interim Director, Boston College Institute for the Study of Religious Education

(Presently Adjunct Professor at New York Theological Seminary and Boston College)

As we come into the present, our identity confusion continues. What is in a word? What is a religious education? What ought we to call what we do? Roman Catholics, Jews, and Protestants alike are in search of a vocabulary or, perhaps better, an understanding. Agreement does not exist. Indeed, confusion seems to reign in greater proportions than ever before. There are those who defend each of the various understandings present during the seventy-five year history of the REA. Roman Catholicism is simply symptomatic of the rest: James Michael Lee prefers religious instruction or the modification of behavior along desired religious lines, Berard Marthaler prefers catechesis or intentional socialization within the total life of a community of faith, and Gabriel Moran prefers religious education giving an interpretation which comes close to that held during the earliest years of the REA. A full circle for some, new polarities for others. The quest for identity has become more troublesome than ever.

My title, the intersection of religion and education, is an intentionally clumsy one. There is no direct and unawkward way to state the issue. For the past dozen years, I now realize, I have been working with others to invent a field for

Religious Education LXIX (September-October 1974), pp. 531-541.

which a language does not exist. For five of those years, I
have consciously worked at the language itself trying to free
a couple of words from their institutional domestication.
My concern with certain precisions of language may strike
some of you as obsessive or at least impractical. But we
cannot find practical answers if there is no way to ask the
right questions, and we cannot ask the right questions if we
do not hone out the language so that it will get us somewhere. E. E. Cummings once said: "Like the burlesque
comedian, I am abnormally fond of that precision which
creates movement."

Cummings is a good person to cite in this context because
he is someone who uses ordinary speech with that peculiar
kind of precision that reveals the unordinary in the ordinary. Our task is not to invent a new language or to negate
ordinary speech but to rediscover religious meaning that is
still sedimented in ordinary speech. A woman in Brooklyn
said to me the other day: "I want to stop all the discussion
and just say my prayers in peace. Let theologians discuss
their problems until they come to conclusions and then I
will listen to them." At first sight her statement may seem to
be a logical and novel suggestion. Actually, however, I think
we have already had too much of what she asks for. War is
too important to be left to the generals, and religion is too
important to be given to theologians. The religious difficulties which are confronting us today call into question the
premises that gave rise to theology and theologians.

The task is not, as was only recently claimed, to translate
our problems from religious to secular terms. Rather, it is to
rediscover a religious language that Christianity can contribute to but which Christianity does not own. A secularizing
movement sounds radical but it turns out to be intramural;
theologians become secular theologians. A movement to

invent or rediscover a religious language threatens the existence of theology because theologians would no longer be in charge of the words.

Ten years ago I was interested in theology and catechetics, and in building a bridge between the two fields. For a brief moment I thought I could be a bridge but my footing was unsteady from the start. By 1968 my hold in catechetics was gone and by 1970 my other foot was out of theology. What surprised me, however, was that I was more interested than ever in the issue that first attracted me. I found myself having come full circle to what I can only call the intersection of religion and education.

This intersection of religion and education should logically be called religious education. Unfortunately, the operative meaning of that term in contexts affected by the Christian church is one that I and many others cannot accept. Despite valiant efforts by teachers, the still functioning meaning of religious education is one that connotes ecclesiastical thought control for children.

The problem has now been compounded by the rise of religious study which in reaction to the churches pretends to total neutrality and scientific objectivity. Religion can no doubt be studied that way and perhaps at times it should be. But that kind of study is not the only possibility for the meeting of religion and education.

There is a third thing which has legitimate claim to the term religious education, an activity which is neither proselytization nor antiseptic observation. I mean a religious education which from the side of education would challenge the quality and purpose of all education; and from the side of religion would challenge existing religious institutions with the test of education. Neither the contemporary Christian church nor the contemporary educational establishment is very comfortable with this principle. From the point at which I raise the question of religious education, I am less interested in what the church says of religious education than what religious education says about a church.

This position is neither anti-church, anti-institution, nor anti-authority. I am simply saying that religious education should determine the specific form of religious authority and not vice versa. That is a position for which it is difficult to get a hearing in the contemporary church. On the right there is constant denunciation, but on the left there is thundering silence; I find the latter more disconcerting. Toward the right one must admit that this kind of religious education is a threat, but we shall see who in the long run is truly conservative of the best in the Christian past. To the left one must say that they had better get on with the job of greater organizational change that follows from religious education. There are millions of people in this country who combine a loyalty to their religious traditions and a resistance to the inadequacy of church form. Albert Camus wrote in the 1950s: "What we need today is groupings of people who will speak out clearly and pay up personally."

II

To speak further on this kind of religious education I will first pursue the religious part of it and then draw some educational conclusions. My concern is with the religious as distinct from the theological, a distinction not easily admitted into church discussion. I use as my key term the word revelation. As a starting point for religious discussion I first have to distinguish the word revelation from any Christian expressions. I wish to fill out a broader based meaning of the word. While Christian theology stands paralyzed with a language of the reformation period, an enormous cultural, social, religious movement is all around us.

It does seem to me that there is a movement which has various aspects but is a single movement in which a search for religious regeneration is integral. During the 1960s some people began talking about the Movement with a Capital M. They weren't entirely wrong, but their vision was narrowed down mainly to a youth movement against the war. What has to be kept in mind is a larger struggle in the world, one that cannot be prematurely generalized into human liberation but which does in fact include all human groups and one must add: nonhuman groups. The first part of my book on revelation leads to the women's movement and the ecological movement as the most comprehensive basis on which to build a religious understanding.

A crucial element in this movement which I failed to develop adequately is the struggle of older adults and little children. I would insist on these two being kept together. The very young and the very old have a natural alliance if the people in the middle don't interfere. Religious conceptions and human freedom are tested by birth and death, most cultures recognizing that death is a kind of birth and birth is a kind of death. This publishing season's fad is children's liberation, but it will take more than a season's fad to redesign society so that it would be a nice place to be a child or to be old. We like to call ourselves a child-oriented society but we flatter ourselves. We are not oriented to children so much as to an adult need to dominate which is allowed expression in reference to children. We have long run our world on this principle of domination and exploitation, but the women, children, and animals are calling a halt to the whole business.

My search for a religious language arises from this

movement which is at once ecological, feminist, and generational. If our religious notions do not test out well in
that light then we are on the wrong track. We need a word
and image that can synthesize all of the complex interrela-
tions of our lives. Of course, one person's synthesis is
another person's dichotomy. A common way to go after a
synthesis is by balance, caution, and juxtaposition of all the
elements. That is the one way I am sure will not work. The
workable human synthesis we urgently need requires a
careful but daring choice of metaphor.

When one tries to express the totality in a word that can
comprehend all divisions one is forced to resort to metaphor. One must take an image from ordinary speech and
stretch it beyond ordinary meaning. If someone charges
that my metaphor ultimately fails, he or she is certainly
right. But if someone doesn't like my metaphor, I want to
know what his or her metaphor is. A fruitful metaphor is
one that is a unity including distinctions and one that can be
enriched by a circular argument heightening the tension of
unity and diversity.

The purifying of the metaphor takes place through a
negation of all that limits it. At the very end one must negate
the very meaning of limit so that the last word if one demands words is a double negative. Beyond that is silence.
After writing forty volumes of theology, Thomas Aquinas
could only conclude that God is not being. It may not sound
like a very fruitful conclusion, but it summed up his books.
He instructed that his books be burned, but the command
was fortunately not carried out. All of that work before the
last step is not useless. The way of double negation and
silence is associated more with the East than the West, but
this religious path is what is emerging among the sons and
daughters of America.

The journey is a perilous one, but for many of us it seems to be a necessary one. We are trying to find something in other cultures, in our forgotten past and deep inside ourselves. I find myself driven as it were against my will to a meaning of religion that takes leave of ordinary reality and disappears behind the double negative. My somewhat tenuous connection to reality is through the twin bases of community and education. By locating the word religious as an adjective describing education, I am able to keep the negating element within a positive context.

The danger in mysticism whether eastern or western is that the holy man looking for his soul is liable to become messianic and/or I suspect that if the holy and solitary monk stays sane it is because he finds his soul as a kind of sister and they, that is, he and his soul, form a kind of community. "I know not of your soul," wrote Victor Hugo, "but as for mine I know that she is eternal." I think that if I stayed in my room all day studying religion I would go out of my head (or worse into my head). If the religious is experienced at the limits of education and community, then I learn of the sacred or holy in working to extend those limits.

III

About twelve years ago I chose the word revelation to work with as my comprehensive word to found religious inquiry. I consider it to have been an extraordinarily lucky choice. I do not really know why I chose it. What I do know is that each year it becomes a more fruitful metaphor. It has provided me with a way to step out of Christian theology without attacking it. There may be a better metaphor than revelation, but I know of few strong competitors. I want a word that will not prematurely exclude anything before the silence and can itself end in silence. For filling out the meaning of the word I am more interested these days in R. D. Laing and Norman O. Brown than Rahner or Schillebeeckx, though I do not hesitate to use material from Christian tradition. I am conscious of appropriating a word with a checkered history within Christian tradition. That is where I started, and that is what I do not wish to deny. I wish to place that past in a context that will make sense of the past. Thus, my primary meaning for revelation cannot be its usage in Christian theology but its meaning indicated in Norman O. Brown's thesis that the aim of the revolution is revelation.

Why is the word revelation a good metaphor? The reason is that it has some chance to comprehend the main divisions in the world. Starting from within Christianity, the obvious division is between Christian and not Christian. In some ways that division is a minor one, but it is the first big religious division that must be surmounted. There is, second, the division between religious and nonreligious. Despite differences among the world's religions, there is something identifiable as religion which distinguishes religious groups and those that are not. The word religious also refers to part of my own self as opposed to another part of my life that is not religious. Third, there is division among the humans in ways that are racial, national, and generational. There is especially the division of women and men. Sex and religion have always been on intimate terms, and the writing on religion today which is oblivious to a worldwide women's movement is staggeringly obtuse. Fourth, there is the division between the humans and the nonhumans. No one protests against the phrase human liberation, but the dogs and the trees are worried. If one does not get to the ecological problem, then each liberation victory is like winning the poker hands on the Lusitania.

Revelation is a category which can bear sexual communal, social, political, institutional, and ecological meaning. The word is a verbal noun which refers to active relationships. The word implies a personal element but does not exclude the nonpersonal. Especially important is the fact that the word carries the sense of surprise, a little seductive intrigue, and the not quite rational. We all have the temptation to settle down and fit the world into our plans. Of course, it never does quite fit, and to save ourselves from ourselves we have to find a way to live with change, diversity, and novelty. What we need is maneuverability and a tolerable level of diversity and unexpectedness. If we are working with the wrong tools, we are liable to feel tossed from one side to the other.

These are puzzling times for all of us. I was brought up to believe that the world had progressed from polytheism to monotheism. I was told that a few people wanted to get rid of the one remaining God, but there seemed no reason to do that, God being a pretty reasonable fellow like you and me. I learned that there were a few embarrassing things in the church's past, like witches, devils, and the Galileo case. However, we had explanations for all that. In addition, we were adjusting our religion to enlightened and secular America. The people who were confused in the 1960s were little old ladies who couldn't swing with the new enlightened church. The news media had a field day reporting that upheaval. I think that during the last few years there has been a much greater upheaval, but it has not been as well covered in the news media. I suspect that it is because this upheaval comes straight at the religion reporter who in most cases is about forty years old, white, male, and liberally educated. Pity us poor middle-aged, white, western males; it's not our decade.

A half dozen current phenomena selected almost at random:

1) Michael Kaufman's new book, *In Their Own Good Time*, has one amazing chapter after another. Among them is a chapter describing a businessman getting off the train and going home to celebrate his regular witchcraft meeting. Witches have returned to America.

2) A neighbor of mine in the advertising business has one hundred people to his apartment every morning to chant a Buddhist hymn. Thousands of religious communes are springing up in the country.

3) The most popular movie of all time is a story of demonic possession and Catholic exorcism. Interest in the devil is growing.

4) Richard Goodwin, speechwriter for liberal presidents, has a book called *The American Condition*. He begins by saying that in the case of Galileo vs. the Roman church the church was right and Galileo was wrong insofar as the church was concerned about the inherent limits of human life while Galileo and his heirs were afflicted with a rationalistic and destructive hybris.

5) A historian of science, William Irwin Thompson, abandoned his university post to work at preserving education. His solution: A school in Southhampton, Long Island, modeled on the medieval monastery and named Lindisfarne.

6) A notable book of this publishing season is *The New Polytheism: The Return of the Gods and Goddesses*. The author, David Miller, discovered that his students were interested in Greek mythology to help them sort out their religious lives.

With reference to the last cited book, *Time* magazine made an important comment, namely, that Miller does not acknowledge that popular Roman Catholic piety has preserved much of what he is looking for among the Greeks.

Not by accident some of the most imaginative religious writing is coming from Catholics or former Catholics. Several of them might even have more to offer if they could sift through their Catholic upbringing instead of rejecting it. Rather than replacing one god with many gods, a Christian god with Greek gods, western god with eastern god, we need ways of speaking and imagining that allow us to accept the diversity of our experience.

If we do not have a way to handle this diversity we are still at the mercy of contrived apologetics, as exemplified by the movie *The Exorcist* which Pauline Kael called the greatest vocation poster for the Catholic church since *Going My Way*. Despite the resistance of movie critics, *The Exorcist* obviously touches something real in the lives of millions of people. I still think that the invention of the devil in the Christian middle ages was a cruel and unconscionable hoax, a scandal second only to the invention of hell. On the other hand, the supposition that enlightened men with their minds and machines were going to eliminate the terrifying irrationalities of life was a pretty bad hoax too.

So now we are back to ground zero and our age resembles the fourteenth and fifteenth centuries which so desperately needed a way to cope with the exploding forces of the universe. Martin Luther produced a best selling catechism and it was followed by the Catholic version of the catechism, a book which H. A. Reinhold called "K rations for the field." This is not the sixteenth century and neither a Luther nor a catechism can save us. We are faced with the possibility of greater chaos than anything imaginable in the sixteenth century. We also have the chance, perhaps for the first time in human history, to situate religion in an educational setting that would ameliorate the negative effects of religion while enabling religion to be central to life.

In summary, there is a religious upheaval which cannot

be contained within the existing Christian church, Christian theology, or the Christian conception of religious education. What is needed is the rediscovery of imagination, metaphor, and symbolism in our daily lives as the basis of a religious language. That is my reason for using the word revelation and for claiming that we need a new field whose appropriate name is religious education.

IV

In a concluding section I would like to draw out a few principles of what this meaning of religious education is. First, religious education pertains to all of life and to all of education. When one says that, there is danger that the statement might be taken as a banal generality. If one simply says that religious education is education, education is life, life is everything, one has said nothing. I have tried to suggest that education is a very specific structuring of the environment to go in one direction rather than in another, and there are very specific obstacles against which specific protests must be raised. Religious education in the short term is that protest against the closure of our life, education, and imagination. At the very least, it is a protest that no finite thing is god.

Gabriel Marcel wrote: "We must perseveringly say no to the awful power to withhold ourselves from the Absolute Thou." That is still putting it in properly negative form, but the effect is the positive unleashing of what goes beyond our powers to speak or imagine. Paradoxically, we recognize the greatness as we recognize the finiteness of our lives and that we are bound to the earth in a cycle of life and death. One of the scandals of Christian theology, exacerbated in recent times, was the claim that space and place are not important because we have a god of time. One must love the earth and have a personal turf where one can discover one's own limits. Devotion to one's people at the center of the earth remains the enduring character of religion. That is not primitive romanticism but advanced ecology.

The second principle is closely related: religious education at its best is accomplished through the artistic and cultic. Roman Catholicism to its credit retained a strongly cultic or sacramental character at least until recently. While the rest of the world is discovering sacramentality, the Catholic church seems to be losing its sacraments. I don't mean just the seven major sacraments designated by the Council of Trent but the seventy or seven hundred little sacraments that held people's lives together. Rituals, symbols, and gestures give abiding calm in a chaotic world. The unspoken framework which gives intimation of eternity is the most powerful religious education.

In this regard, school has never been a very good place for religious education. If the danger of education is to settle down complacently with the rational and discursive world as the end, then school is too limited a platform from which to launch the protest of religious education. Schooling is a useful and probably a necessary contribution to being an intelligently religious person today, but it can only be an element within a larger pattern of religious education. One could help religious education by seeing that school is not aggressively anti-aesthetic.

Religious and sacramental activity that challenges rationality is reemerging at the end of a period called the enlightenment. The new period is not one of darkness but of admitting that there is a dark side to life and that an uncontrolled use of reason is the worst kind of insanity. A religious education for our time must take its cue from elements that are not current fads but are perennially religious material: the dynamics of fairy tales, the harmony of the ecological system, sexuality, the tribal rites of North American natives, and the Buddhist *koan*.

This brings me to my third principle: religious education in the Christian church ought to be not a study of faith but a way of knowledge. I realize in saying this that I run counter to most of what is said in the church about religious education. I think that religious education is Christianity ought to be what it is in other religions, namely, a carefully structured set of experiences which can issue in a path of knowledge and techniques to direct one's body. Most of us who are teachers probably shy away from words that sound directive, but there is a way to demonstrate skills that is not coercive. I do think that a guru with his followers is dangerous. But if the talent of master, teacher, or prophet were situated in the give and take of a community of women and men then we might finally have a religious education that would be effective.

No other religious group has the answer for Christianity. Religious education is everywhere deficient, and Christianity could make an important contribution to improve it. But Christianity's contribution is knowledge and practice, not faith. To the extent that faith connotes a positive human attitude it underlies all religious education but is not in the special possession of any group. Knowledge and practice do differ from one group to another and are also capable of being shared.

People are leaving the church in search of sacraments, mystical prayer, and religious community. If church theology and history were presented as something other than victory communiques, people might find that there was more to their religion than what is subsumed under the term Christian faith. Perhaps many of us have to go around the world to come home again, but the journey would be less traumatic if there were a linguistic and communal setting in which we might experience a human way of living, dying, and going beyond dying.

18. Does The Church Really Want Religious Education?

CHARLES F. MELCHERT
Associate Professor of Education, Colgate Rochester
Divinity School/Bexley Hall/Crozer
(Presently Dean and Professor of Religion and
Education, Presbyterian School of Christian Education)

We have returned to our beginnings, and once again everyone is asking who are we and why we exist. Clarity and shared understandings of the words we use seems called for, and Charles Melchert, now on the faculty of the Presbyterian School of Christian Education, makes a significant attempt to once again define religious education. But he does more than that, he asks perhaps the most significant question of all: Does the church (or synagogue) really want religious education? It may have been meant as a rhetorical question, but it is the question; it has been the question all along. The differences in names may be more ideological than definitional. What's really behind each name; will it be religious education, Christian-Jewish education, church-temple education, or catechesis? Perhaps our identity needs to include them all.

Education is something intentional, valuable, understandable, long lasting, interpersonal, and moving toward wholeness.
Do we need it?

It has become a cliché to suggest that we are in the midst of a crisis in religious education. The signs of crisis are all around. Sunday school enrollment down sharply; parochial schools closing; religious leaving their orders and teaching; reduced denominational staffs; and so on.

Religious Education LXIX (January-February 1974), pp. 12-22.

Clearly these are signs of a more fundamental crisis which strikes at the heart of the self-understanding of the churches of our time. There is genuine need for the quest for renewed understanding of what the church is, has been, ought to be, and could become. But within that context there is also need for a renewed understanding of what religious education is, and what it is for in the church.

That there is some uncertainty about what religious education is, or about education in the church is not hard to demonstrate. A philosopher from Temple says that religious education must be indoctrination,[1] while a philosopher at Oxford affirms that religious education cannot be, under any circumstances, indoctrination.[2] James Michael Lee says that a person is always being educated at every moment, all of one's experiences are educational,[3] while Marc Belth identifies the phrase "all experiences educate" as one of the clichés that undermine serious study of education.[4] John Dewey and R. S. Peters affirm there is no such thing as an ultimate goal of education,[5] while Vatican II declares that a "true education aims at the formation of the human person with respect to his ultimate goal."[6] Peters aptly sums up the situation as he observes, "education has become rather like the kingdom of heaven in former times. It is both within us and among us, yet it also lies ahead. The elect possess it, and hope to gather in those who are not yet saved. But what on earth it is, is seldom made clear."[7]

The clarity needed is of the most fundamental sort. If I want to drive to Boston, I not only need directions but I need to know what Boston is, what a city is. Suppose I lacked an adequate concept of "city" and getting lost on the way I stopped to ask a farmer "Where's Boston?" and he replied, referring to one of his Jersey cows bearing that name, "She's in the barn." In my deficient conceptual state, how would I know whether or not I had arrived at my destination? Yet it often seems to me that our conceptions of education in the church are similarly deficient. We all know it has to do with what goes on between a teacher and a learner and a subject matter—but not always, since sometimes God is said to be the teacher, or perhaps you don't really need a teacher, but rather an enabler, a facilitator, or a resource person. Or it is popular to say that the medium is the message, the process is the subject matter. But at least it usually happens in a classroom—although not always there, or not only there, or some critics would say, especially not there, and Never on Sunday! When the process is over, the end result will be . . . well, quite literally, God only knows.

This concern for conceptual clarity is more than a trivial semantic game. Nationally we spend millions of dollars and billions of hours planning for and participating in the church's education and there is no way to calculate the devotion and goodwill put into this task. But if we are unclear about what it is or what we are looking for in the process, the best we can hope for is to get where we are going part of the time by accident. I would suggest both our people and our God are entitled to expect more of us than that.

THREE WAYS TO BE MISLED

In a search for greater clarity there are three ways people have been and can be misled. The first is to confuse education with schools. Just because a school can or should do some activity does not necessarily make that activity educational. Education can and does occur outside of, in the absence of, and even in spite of schools. Second, when thinking of education it is easy to begin thinking of it solely as a "discipline" like psychology or philosophy. But more fundamentally, education is one way of doing things with people. To gain basic conceptual clarity it is perhaps more important to compare education not with psychology or philosophy, but with other, noneducational ways of doing things with people. Third, perhaps most important for our present context, is the temptation to assume that because the church needs something, education can do it. In an emergency I could use a good heavy adding machine from my desk as a weapon to knock out a burglar, but needing it for that purpose and using it thus tells me nothing about what an adding machine is or what it is most appropriately used for. Yet, if I know what an adding machine is, how it works, what it can and can't do, then I can use it appropriately all the time, and unless I become rigid about its possible functions, I can also use it creatively in an emergency. So with education and the church. The church may need to convert people and bring them to a Christian way of living, and it has often been assumed that this is one of the tasks of education in the church. But the needs of the church do not establish the nature, structure, and function of education. For that we need to investigate education itself. *Then* we can ask, "Is this something the church has a need for or could make use of?"

CRITERIA OF "EDUCATION"

What then is educational about religious education? One useful tool for getting a handle on that question is by doing "conceptual analysis," that is trying to isolate the essential characteristics of something by finding out what are intrinsically necessary elements of the concept in question. Probably the most adequate and widely accepted conceptual analysis of "education" is that offered by R. S. Peters, who shows that there are two basic senses of "education," one a general term, which can refer to almost anything done with children in the process of bringing them into adulthood; and the other, a more specialized use, which he adopts and which we shall use here. In this more special sense, which has emerged since the middle of the nineteenth century, the term "education" does not refer to a specific activity, as for example, the term "gardening" might, but rather it is a general concept (rather like the concept "reform") which implies a series of criteria applied to any activity. That is, we look at some particular activity, and if we call it education, then we imply that it has met certain standards. Analysis helps us specify what these standards are. Peters claims that there are two basic criteria, and I will suggest four additional ones.[8]

First, to call something education implies that it is an *intentional* activity and that the result is not entirely accidental. We would think it most strange if someone were to say. "I am educated, but I didn't mean for it to happen." This means, for example, that education is not simply the same as learning, for one can learn things accidentally without intending to and without having taught, while education implies that there is intentionally directed learning.

Second, to call something education implies that it is of *value*. This implies that what is being done with people under the label "education" is improving them, much as one could not sensibly say that one has reformed and also say that he hadn't improved. This criterion implies that it would be a logical contradiction to say that one had been educated but that he had in no way changed for the better.

Third, to call something education implies that it involves *knowing and understanding in depth and breadth*. This entails the judgment that education is more than training, more than the acquisition of skills or memories, and more than having know-how or masses of facts. It suggests having the ability to see connections or relationships within a field and among different fields, and having a concern to gain a greater and greater understanding of more and more aspects of human experience. Peters and others claim that this criterion is the most distinctive aspect of education.

Fourth, there is a *time* criterion. When we use the concept "education" we typically do no refer to something that has just happened in the past ten minutes or even this afternoon. Rather we generally refer to a process which is understood to go on over a longish period of years.

Fifth, education is necessarily an *interpersonal interaction*, or better an interaction of interactions. Teaching is itself an interaction, or relationship between teacher, learner, and content. Learning is an interaction between learner and what is learned and whatever it was learned from. Education then implies the interaction of all these interactions over time. This criterion implies that strictly speaking there is no such thing as a totally self-educated person. Most of what anyone knows has been generated by someone else. Even if one learns from books privately, someone wrote those books, so there is relationship at least at second remove. This criterion also implies that introspection, by itself, is not an educational activity.

Sixth, perhaps implicit in all the above, there is a criterion of *wholeness*, that is, education necessarily involves the whole person, the whole of his or her life, and that it affects all of that person's relationships—with self, with others, and with things. Thus, to be educated means more than being an expert in one area of specialization. It means more than having gone to four years of college, and it is not the kind of thing one can just put aside when it is convenient.

These criteria do not so much provide us with a definition of education, as they do a way to recognize it. Perhaps it is a little like vodka—you can't describe its taste or smell, so you either have to do a chemical analysis, or better, drink it and see if it has recognizable effects.

DOES THE CHURCH NEED EDUCATION?

Clearly, conceptual analysis does not tell us what to do next. What conclusions one draws after the analysis is another matter. We might respond by saying, "Well, if that is what education is, the church doesn't need it." There are times when this might be an appropriate response, for education in this full special sense is sometimes preempted by the urgency of other needs. But I shall show below that these are limits beyond which the church cannot disown education in this sense.

Another response to this analysis might be, "If that is what education is, how might that affect our conception of education in the church?"

The most obvious effect is that strictly speaking it is contradictory to call what we are doing "religious education" or "Christian education," just as it is inappropriate to call my hand my body. The part is not the whole. On the other hand, the oddness of calling the part the whole directs attention to another important feature of terms like "religious education" and "Christian education." Note that we almost never speak of "chemistry education," or "English literature education," or "biology education," yet we commonly speak of such things as "driver education," "physical education," "sex education," "art education," and so on. All these latter terms designate areas which have had some difficulty justifying their place in the school curriculum. In fact, several of them are self-conscious attempts to "upgrade" the status of the subject by changing the name, for example from "driver training" to "driver education," or "religious instruction" to "religious education." Normally when there are obvious self-interest motives operating, such as a stranger claiming to be a cousin of a recently deceased millionaire without known relatives, we tend to be skeptical about taking things at face value. The same might be said about terms such as "religious education," since they often seem to have a persuasive function rather than a descriptive one, that is, they intend to convince people of their own respectability. Thus it would be a mistake to make too much, either positively or negatively, of the terms "religious education" or "Christian education."

On the other hand, the change of label for some people is an attempt to call attention to their own greater sense of awareness of the educational potential of their subject. By changing labels they are affirming their intent to function not simply as trainers, but to show that educational criteria can be legitimately applied to this subject. Precisely this has been happening recently in religious education.

Can we specify more fully what would be educational or noneducational ways of helping people in the area of religion? It might seem that the most obvious use of the criteria would be to rule some things out, and other kinds of activities "in" more or less permanently. But such is not the case. The criteria help us determine whether some activity is likely to have educative effects in the long run, or will it be more likely to inhibit "education" in the fullest sense? The criteria can help us become aware of the limitations of some sorts of activites and find ways to supplement them with others that will make them more beneficial.

Let's illustrate the use of the criteria by testing some forms of helping people change—either their behavior, or their thinking, or their feeling. Suppose Martha decided to learn the entire contents of the Encyclopedia Brittanica and persuaded Mary to hypnotize her to do it. This is a relatively efficient form of behavior change, and by her own values Martha is improved by this accomplishment, thus meeting the value criterion. She obviously meets the knowing criterion and the intentionality criterion since she wanted it to happen, and the interpersonal interaction criterion since she had Mary do it with her. She apparently meets the wholeness criterion for what could be more wholistic than the Encyclopedia Brittanica? She meets the time criterion, for the change lasts. Is this then a good example of education? By itself, I would say not, since there is considerable doubt whether this example does in fact meet the value and the knowing and understanding criteria. To the extent that Martha has succeeded in mastering the encyclopedia under hypnosis, to that extent she is reacting and not acting, that is, she is not doing something for which she has good reasons for performing, but is following a blind post-hypnotic compulsion which she cannot resist. She has been reduced to a voice, a mechanism for periodic displays of the contents of her memory bank. To that extent the value criterion has not been met, for it cannot be desirable that one who is at least potentially human, who is capable of actively deciding on alternative paths of behavior, has been reduced to a reactive mechanism who functions on cue. (The same observations apply to both conditioning and behavior modification   which are different only in the degree of control being exercised.) There is also some doubt about whether Martha could be said to have a knowing relation to the contents of her own memory in this case, since the contents of her "memory bank" are subconsciously reproduced using her vocal cords upon the triggering of the appropriate cue or stimulus.

Is this an irrelevant illustration, or are there forms of mechanistic reaction training occurring in "religious educatin?" It may be that there is little which is quite as efficient as hypnosis, but how have we arrived at the typically sudden hushed voice upon entering a church building, or the curious intonation a priest or pastor acquires while performing the liturgy? Why is it that in white churches, Roman Catholic or Protestant, prayers tend to be solemn, formal, softly spoken, or even silent, while in Black Baptist or Pentecostal churches prayers tend to be exhuberant and even shouted? Why is it that so many worshipers cannot allow themselves to laugh in church, let alone clap, shout, or dance—yet they speak of giving their whole being to God? Is it possible that these are all signs of conditioning and the reasons we offer for such behaviors are rationalizations which protect us from changing?

What about ways of dealing with people to help them improve their thinking? It is precisely here that so much so-called education in the church has fallen short by trying to substitute various forms of indoctrination for education. Many philosophers seem to assume that religious education is the classic form of indoctrination, and one seemingly sane author even claims that it is of the essence of Christian education that it be indoctrination. Brother Moran asserts, correctly, that religious education did not originate in the two fields of religion and education, but arose from the desire of confessional groups to indoctrinate, that is, to induce their children to follow the same path they have taken.[9] Indoctrination, more carefully defined, is the attempt to impose beliefs and belief systems on others by authority and by methods which allow little or no room for questioning, when the beliefs themselves more properly call for a free and critical acceptance.[10] Very often this is done by teachers with quite honorable intentions, but when students are offered only one position, given little or no opportunity to examine alternative understandings, and no time to examine critically the reasons offered for adopting various alternatives, then one is in danger of indoctrinating. This is a constant temptation in the church, because the beliefs involved are ones that people care deeply about, they regard them of ultimate importance, and they want desperately to have others share those beliefs. Indoctrination seems to fall short on both the knowing and understanding and the value criteria. Teaching in the fullest educational sense means

> at some points at least to submit oneself to the understanding and independent judgment of the pupil, to his demand for reasons, to his sense of what constitutes an adequate explanation. To teach someone that such and such is the case is not merely to try to get him to believe it; deception, for example is not a method or mode of teaching.[11]

Thus education implies a mutuality of relationship, insofar as possible, and a highly ethical respect for each other as persons and as thinking beings. What is being valued in the search for understanding is not simply the beliefs themselves, but also the integrity of the persons holding them and those seeking to acquire them (or resisting them). Education is not a matter of overpowering others intellectually, or coercing by forced options, or leading another to some position by any means necessary. Nor can the giving of reasons to learners simply be a veiled form of authoritarian imposition such as suggesting they believe something " . . . because I say so," or "because God and the Bible say so." Theologically, Christians make the same point by describing assent to God as a form of "radical obedience" which is given because one fully assents to what is being affirmed with all the human capabilities and not simply because someone else says so. To take the latter option as a form of Christian belief is to "pass the buck" to someone else's understanding, when what is being called for is my own understanding, as limited as that may be.

In other words, to approach religion educationally entails seeing that the learner is encouraged to reach as far in his or her understanding as he or she has reasons for reaching at that particular time—while at the same time not allowing anyone to stay permanently on one level of understanding.

At this point some might say. "That's all right for adults, but what about children? Recognizing their inability to understand religious matters at full depth is precisely why we must indoctrinate them, for these matters are so important they must not be without them." There is not space here to go fully into the nature of beliefs and the emotional and experiential base of beliefs which children can understand even without all the conceptual apparatus. Perhaps much of what we do with children would more appropriately be called "preeducational." The corollary of this is that we should perhaps pay much more attention to adults and adolescents in our education by the church. The virtually exclusive focus of the church's education on children has created the impression that religious education is "kid stuff," and perhaps even that Christianity is something to be outgrown as one becomes adult.

A related reason for not yielding to the temptation to indoctrinate is that one of the side effects of indoctrination is that it creates an impression that it's really quite simple— you either believe it or you don't. Yet being a Christian, or making informed decisions about Christian concerns, demands all the maturity, all the knowledge and under-

standing one can muster. We do our people a disservice if
we lead them to think it is quite simple.

Perhaps even more important is another indirect effect
of indoctrination which cuts at the heart of both education
and religion for the Christian, at least. Coercing people to
believe things which they should decide for themselves
creates a dependency in them which makes them more
reliant on dominant authority figures and thus more sus-
ceptible to the influence of others who are in a position to
persuade or offer more attractive appeals. It also tends to
make the learner less open-minded to new data and new
perspectives which could lead to new understandings and
commitments. In other words, indoctrination stifles the
source of intellectual life, curiosity and inquiry. The resulting complacent passivity inhibits education, and is hardly a
worthy offering to God.

Thus these criteria offer a way of sorting out activities so
as to maximize the effectiveness of what we do with people
in the name of education. They do not so much rule some
activities out as they do help us see the limits of some
approaches, and how they might be supplemented so as to
facilitate rather than inhibit the long range educational
process. Using these criteria helps us focus our energies,
while at the same time allowing extraordinary latitude for
experimentation and creativity in our attempts to "equip
the saints for the work of ministry."

It is perhaps here that the educational and the theological
come closest together, for the teacher expresses love for the
student in the passionate concern that the learner not allow
himself or herself to be less than he or she is capable of
becoming, especially in the use of the mind. If the question
were asked, "Why do you care? Why do you love me?" the
Christian does not simply respond "I just do," or "Because

you're you." Rather there is an ultimate reason for our loving, "We love because he first loved us" (1 John 4:19), and it is expected that we shall love with all our heart, soul *and mind* (Matthew 22:37). In other words, it is of the essence of our faith that our loving has a reason, that it is a joyful response to being loved and cared for by God. I would suggest that this also lies at the heart of the educational task, for we want others not to imitate but to think, not to respond on cue with the right phrases but to believe, and to believe not for our reasons but for their reasons, and to arrive at that place can only be done by something very like an educational process. Thus the church really does need education.

In a day when there are more and more things being offered to people as objects worthy of their commitment and their service, a religious educator especially must be deeply concerned that there are good reasons and bad reasons for holding certain things, persons, and beliefs more worthy than others. If we as educators are neglecting the task of helping people become more clear about and effective in all their creative cognitive functioning as it guides their decisions about what and whom we serve, then whatever else we may be doing, however exciting, we are not doing our central, unique distinctively educational task.

Risking An Answer: A Conclusion

JOHN H. WESTERHOFF, III

Seventy-five years in search of an identity and a constituency, or was it really seventy-five years of struggle for the acceptance of a single identity and following. I contend it was the later and, therefore, suggest that the future of the REA depends upon its ability to affirm, support, and bring together, for their mutual benefits, the various concerns which have previously vied for attention and acceptance.

Religious education, Christian-Jewish education, church-synagogue education and catechesis, are each important and need to have a place in the life and work of the Religious Education Association. Each must be understood individually. Each must be aided in its development. Each will have its own constituency and life.

RELIGIOUS EDUCATION

Education is an intentional, valuable, long-lasting, interpersonal activity of the whole person which involves knowing and understanding in depth and breadth. The religious is concerned with the depth dimensions of life, peoples ultimate concerns and commitments, and the search for the transcendent. Insofar as any educational effort deals with patterns of belief or commitment concerning goodness, truth or beauty it is religious. In one important sense, then, all education is religious. Similarly, a concern for religion implies a critical look at education. We need to seriously question the quality of life and educational processes within our educational institutions. What happens to the human spirit and sensibilities of persons cannot be neglected. Indeed, as Whitehead once wrote, "the essence of education is to be religious."

Further, religious studies or religious instruction is a special case of religious education in which religion and the religious are the object of investigation. It too is a proper field of endeavor. Our education is incomplete unless we learn about the literature, history, beliefs, and practices of the world's various religions. Religion and the religious are aspects of culture and any intelligent, well-educated person needs to understand both the world's religions and the religious in appropriate ways. For too long our public schools have ignored this important understanding of religious education and our parochial schools distorted it.

Surely religious education in these two senses is a proper concern of all citizens and educators. The REA should attempt, therefore, to unite all persons who share these concerns. The theory and practice of religious education and religious studies needs support. Research needs to be stimulated, the general public informed, legislatures influenced, teachers trained, and resources produced. This continuing need was once the major focus of the REA. Still, religious education, in this sense, has never been fully understood or accepted within our public schools and other educational agencies. The REA should assert greater leadership in this important dimension of national life. Indeed through the National Council on Religion and Public Education, it presently strives to do just that. Nevertheless, this concern needs to be broadened and made more central to the life of the REA. However, religious education can never become inclusive of all our concerns. Indeed, from a faith perspective it is not ultimately important at all.

CHRISTIAN-JEWISH EDUCATION

There is also good reason to reestablish the importance of what has been called Christian or Jewish education—not as it was used in the 40s but in an entirely different manner. I am referring to Christian education as any educational effort engaged in by Christians (or by Jews-Jewish education, Humanists-Humanist education, etc.) Each of us brings with us a world view and value system which informs our lives. We each need to be aware and understand the ways in which our faith influences our educational efforts. We also need to be informed by our faith when we consider the nature, purposes, and means of education. Further, we need to explore carefully the place and function of religious (Jewish, Christian, Humanist) educational institutions in a pluralist society. What should be the character of church or synagogue related elementary-secondary schools or colleges? How and for what ends should they educate? What is Christian or Jewish education?

Education is best understood as deliberate, systematic and sustained efforts to transmit, evoke, or acquire knowledge, attitudes, values, skills, or sensibilities as well as any outcomes of that effort. This definition stresses intentionality rather than context. To think comprehensively about education we must consider a wide variety of institutions that educate, not only schools and colleges, but libraries, museums, day care centers, radio and television stations, offices, factories and farms. Education must be looked at whole, across the entire life span and in all the situations and institutions in which intentional learning occurs. When we think this way, we realize the host of persons involved in education. We need to aid all such persons understand the implications of their faith for their vocations.

For too long we have all ignored such questions. Education, understood in this way, needs to be explored. Increased study, research, and writing needs to be done in this neglected area. The REA would be an appropriate body to assume leadership in this important area of investigation for it is essential that Christians, Jews, Humanists, and others discuss their various understandings and ways. Christian or Jewish education needs to have a distinctive identity and assume a new and important place in American life; only then can we have true pluralism.

CHURCH OR SYNAGOGUE EDUCATION

Church or synogogue schools have had a long, though rocky, history. There have been both those who have wanted to kill the church school and those who have believed it to be essential to the perpetuation of the faith. There are those who have predicted its death, but still it lives on. While in need of reform and revitalization there is an important place for church or synogogue education understood as schooling and instruction. Teaching and learning conducted within a schooling context can be beneficial. There is much, particularly in the adolescence years, which might be accomplished best through such means: for example, learning to reflect critically on the tradition, to think theologically, and to make moral decisions.

There a host of persons, mostly untrained, teaching in church and synogogue schools. A profession of directors, coordinators and ministers of education for churches and synogogues has emerged. Properly understood, church or synogogue education has an identity and a constituency. The REA needs to provide a place where those who are concerned with church and synogogue education can come together for mutual benefit. The field needs to be reformed. A new radical look at schooling and instruction is necessary. Roman Catholics, Protestants, and Jews need to stop passing each other in the night . . . we need to learn from and with each other.

CATECHESIS

Catechesis I have saved for last because I believe it is presently the most important, though perhaps the least clear of the four educational endeavors I recommend the REA support and encourage. Catechesis is a word that has no necessary religious bias. It can be used by Christians and Jews (with obviously different theological formulations) though in the following pages I will be confessional and refer to church and Christian.

Catechesis has a long history in Europe, especially among Roman Catholics, but it need not be a parochial word. Regretfully, however, it is somewhat unfortunate history among Roman Catholics which makes the word troublesome for many today. (Parenthetically, that could be said about all the words referred to in this article.) In particular, some Roman Catholics distorted catechesis through an over-emphasis on doctrine as right ideas and learning as indoctrination. It is important, therefore, to differentiate between catechetics—which typically emphasized content to the exclusion of persons and their experiences, i.e., catechesims—and catechesis a pastoral ministry uniting present experiences and the faith tradition. Consistent with this later emphasis, the General and National Catechetical Directories of the Roman Catholic Church have attempted to reform and reaffirm the centrality of catechesis. As a Protestant I recommend that we join them. Since catechesis is not a word commonly used in the history of the REA, I will expand on it in more detail than religious, Christian-Jewish and church-synogogue education.

Catechesis is a pastoral ministry which aims to help the faithful, individually and corporately, meet the twofold responsibilities which faith asks of them; community with God and community with one's fellow human beings. Catechesis aims to nurture an intimacy of life with God which expresses itself in social justice, liberation, and the political struggle for whole community, peace and the well-being of all persons. Catechesis is an endeavor which is never neutral in either content or process. Indeed, the content of the faith must influence the means used to communicate it, just as it must honor the present experience of persons and the community.

Knowledge and understanding are enough for education, but not catechesis. To understand means to appreciate how it is possible for a person to believe what he or she does, given the presuppositions that he or she holds. Catechesis is concerned with what persons believe, as well as the presuppositions which undergird those beliefs and make possible life in accord with them. To understand the experiential dimension of religion in religious education is not necessarily the same as providing persons with those experiences or expecting them to be committed to their importance. However, in catechesis the latter concerns are essential.

Catechesis is a life's work: it is a pastoral ministry shared by all those who participate in the life and mission of the Christian faith community. It values the interaction of faithful selves in community, striving to be Christian together, in-but-not-of the world.

Catechesis aims to enable the faith community to live

under the judgment and inspiration of the Gospel to the end that God's will is done and God's community comes. It's content is not religion, but faith in the conviction that Jesus is Lord. It's authority is not reason or experience, but the Word of God.

Like education, catechesis is: deliberate or intentional; it is systematic or whole; it is sustained or over time; it is of supreme value and concerned with interpersonal inter-actions. But catechesis is also unique; that is, catechesis focuses on the question: What is it to be Christian together in community and in the world? Catechesis is, therefore, interested in more than knowing and understanding in depth and breadth. Indeed, it is essentially concerned with conversion and nurture, commitment and behavior.

Faith is a total act of the personality. It is deeply personal and dynamic, it is directly related to life in a community of faith. It is expressed in symbol, myth and ritual. Faith is not tentative, a result of a purely rational process. Faith is an affectional relationship to God which embraces the whole person and about which it is difficult to be objective. Faith is a particular form of existence encompassing our spirits— our hearts, minds and wills; faith is expressed in and through our lives—in our actions. Religion is a witness to faith, and a stimulant to faith. But religion can never become an end in itself, not for the church. Only faith is a legitimate end for a community of faith. The knowledge and understanding of religion cannot save us or provide us with the meaning and purpose necessary for life. Only God's action in Jesus Christ can save us, and only faith can know, acknowledge, and witness to that truth.

But catechesis is rightfully not concerned with making someone else into a Christian. It is rather concerned with aiding the community to become Christian. Thus, the question parents need to ask is not, how can I make my child into a Christian, but rather how can I be Christian with my child. Catechesis demands that the church and its people ask first and foremost how they can be Christian with each other and with others in the world. Catechesis, therefore, includes all deliberate (intentional), systematic (related), sustained (over time) pastoral efforts within a community of faith which enable persons in a community to live under the judgment and inspiration of the Gospel to the end that God's will is done and God's community comes. (Jewish catechesis would obviously have a different end.)

Catechesis is founded upon revelation, but revelation is not a collection of facts or ideas of universal, immutable truth. Christian faith is not an appeal to ideas nor is it an appeal to religious experience. It is first and foremost an appeal to history. God communicates through God's Word—that is, through God's historical actions recounted through ritual and myth within tradition bearing communities of faith. That does not mean to imply that knowledge of God is limited to particular communities.

We need to distinguish between that revelation which is available to all and that which is acknowledged by a particular people. The first, general revelation, is available to all persons, at any time, in any place. It occurs wherever contemporary experience takes on a revelatory dimension. It is of great importante to affirm the primary (though not ultimate) nature of general revelation. We cannot believe or understand special revelation unless we have understood the general. First, the Lord of history is experienced as holy and then as the three persons of the trinity. Communities of faith, however, are not formed out of general revelation. They are rather the result of primordial or special revelation.

Catechesis is founded upon God's special self-revelation which breaks into the circle of human history from beyond. For some, of course, this claim to special revelation is a scandal. In principle, truth ought to be equally available to all. But the fact is that all truth is conditioned by history. We are historical beings, all that we experience and understand is shaped by our history and the communities to which we belong. The Christian claim is that the history of God's self-revelation is found in the Scriptures, in the form of a story of God's action with and for humans. God's desire is to reveal him/herself, his/her salvation, and his/her will to all persons. For the vocation of sharing the story of God's self-revelation every tradition bearing community exists.

The central claim of the Christian revelation is the good news that God acts in history, in and through the ministry, death, and resurrection of the man Jesus of Nazareth. God reveals to us our true condition and potential as individuals in community.

The authority of the church is God's action in Christ Jesus. Only that historical event itself is final authority. The Bible's words are not final authority, though the Bible is a collection of primary witnesses to this historical event; the living tradition of the church is not final authority, though it is an essential source for the interpretation of that event; personal experience or inner-conviction is not final authority, though they are important apprehensions of truth. All three, scripture, tradition, and religious experience are approximate authorities, each a corrective for the others. But the final authority to which all point and by which all are judged is the historic action of God in Jesus Christ.

Revelation is always an act, an act of unveiling that which was concealed. Revelation refers to that locus of experience through which we discover ourselves in relationship to

God. The Bible contains reports of revelation, the church as a community of faith testifies to the presence of revelation in the Scriptures, but unless and until persons perceive the significance of the biblical witness for themselves, it is not revelation for them. So it is that revelation to one person may not be for another. It is our faith, that basic stance which orients all our understandings and ways, which is necessary for revelation to be received. Revelation, therefore, is the process through which we are grasped and affirmed by that which is revealed, but the source is always outside us. All that anyone can do is testify to their faith, share their understandings of revelation, and strive to establish conditions whereby faith can be enhanced and revelation received by another.

Human nature is a paradox. In one sense we can all, through natural means, share in God's revelation. Indeed, at birth we inherit a potential for fullness of life as children of God. Thus each human being is religious by nature. The maturationists and developmentalists are correct (see: *Will Our Children Have Faith?*, Seabury 1977). A child is born with faith, understood as a centered activity which involves knowing, being, and willing in accordance with a persons growth and development. Faith can expand if the proper environments for growth and development are present, but faith cannot be given. Faith can only be shared, enlivened, enhanced, and encouraged to expand. Each of us is free: we influence, we shape, we determine our lives, and within each of us is the potential for creative humanness. We have a longing for wholeness and a potential for knowing truth, goodness, and beauty. All that we need are environments and experiences which enable us to use and develop to the fullest our God-given potential.

On the other hand, alone we can not know that primordial revelation out of which communities are formed and live. The content of our faith comes from life in the community of nurture. We must acknowledge, therefore, that we are also shaped by our community, we are determined by our experiences, we are taught right and wrong and what to believe, we are rewarded and punished for our actions and so taught how to behave, we are either given or denied the experience of love and so can or cannot share that emotion with others.

Locke and Hume were right, but so was Kant and Rousseau. It all depends on what question we ask. Only by asserting this paradox can we be morally responsible and responsive to ourselves and to others. Each of us becomes a self through social interaction with other selves. To deny that our peculiar behavior, beliefs, attitudes, and values are shaped through our experiences or to deny that we influence and shape the lives of others through our interactions with them can only result in irresponsible action. To be responsible is to know how much we do shape the lives of others. Only then can we live morally with them.

However, to deny the freedom and potential of another self and to act as if others are entirely dependent upon our influence is to deny their individuality and value as souls the co-equal of our own, determined but also free, a product of their culture, but also producers of culture—historical actors who act as well as react, influence as well as are influenced. Each person has a potential for self-actualization, possessing limitations but also possibilities that are striving to fulfill themselves. None of us needs to be captive to our experiences and environments. Each of us has a will and can determine our own future.

Catechesis is not the transmission of faith. Faith is a gift. Catechesis can only enhance and enliven faith, awaken and nourish faith. Catechesis can pass on a living tradition in the form of a story and vision; it can provide experiences and environments which aid in building community through sharing of life under the Lordship of Jesus Christ. Catechesis enables persons to live freely and humanly as followers of Jesus Christ. It is never a matter of pouring information into people's heads, nor is it indoctrinating persons into particular beliefs and doctrines.

Catechesis is transmitting the story of God's living revelation; catechesis is life in community consistent with that revelation; catechesis is judging individual and corporate life in the light of that revelation and catechesis is making decisions and acting in accordance with that revelation. Catechesis is concerned to help all of us know God, to love God, to obey God. Another way to say it is this: catechesis takes place whenever and wherever divine revelation is made known, faith is enhanced and enlivened, and persons in community are prepared and stimulated for their vocation in the world. Catechesis endeavors, among other things, to aid persons possess a personal knowledge and understanding of God's revelation and to be disposed and able to interpret its meaning for daily, individual, and social life. To achieve this aim we need to introduce persons to the biblical story of God's action in history as found in the stories of the Old and New Testament as our story; we need to provide experiences where persons can be involved in the historical and critical interpretation of the biblical story; and we need to provide experiences where persons can be engaged in reflection on personal and social issues in the light of the biblical story.

Catechesis also endeavors to make personal commitment to Jesus Christ as Lord and Savior possible. To achieve this aim we need to provide experiences which introduce persons to a community of persons who live their lives as an expression of faith in Jesus Christ as Lord and Savior; we need to provide experiences which confront persons with a clear intellectual understanding of the Gospel; and we need to provide opportunities for persons to make decisions for or against the affirmation that Jesus is Lord.

Catechesis further endeavors to help us be aware of our Christian vocation to make moral decisions in the light of faith and be disposed to act faithfully and responsibly in daily, individual, and social life. To achieve this aim, we need to provide experiences foundational to the development of Christian conscience and expose persons to role models of the Christian life; we need to be given opportunities to critically reflect upon, and apply Christian faith to individual and social life; and we need to be enabled to act and reflect faithfully and responsible in our individual and corporate lives to the end that God's will is done and God's community comes.

Catechesis as a pastoral ministry implies that people learn through their participation in any and every aspect of church life. Every aspect of the church's ministry has a relationship to catechesis. This does not mean that every activity and aspect of the church's life is catechesis. Social action is the church engaged in political action on behalf of God's community coming. Evangelism is the church proclaiming through word and deed God's good news. Stewardship is the church expressing God's will for individual and corporate life in the world. Worship is the church celebrating its faith and being empowered for mission. Pastoral care is the church meeting the material and spiritual needs of all persons. Administration is the church planning, organizing, and directing its life so that it can best fulfill its mission and ministry for others.

In terms of ministry, catechesis is the means by which the community critically shares the Christian tradition and acquires a knowledge, understanding, and commitment to its truth. Catechesis is the means by which the community judges and evaluates its ministry. And catechesis is the means by which the community prepares and stimulates persons for faithful ministry.

Designing catechesis for social action implies providing opportunities (1) to understand the requirements of Christian faith for action in the world; (2) to evaluate and judge our individual and corporate actions in the world in the light of our faith; and (3) to equip the church in mind, heart, and will to act reflectively in the world on behalf of the Gospel. Catechesis is not social action, but catechesis is related to social action. Likewise, catechesis needs to play an integral role in every aspect of the church's ministry.

Catechesis is an important endeavor and needs to become central in the life bf faith communities. Priests, ministers, and rabbis need to be trained to lead in this field. Further, catechesis—education as a pastoral ministry—needs to become a central aspect of the education of all clergy. A new constituency of rabbis, priests, pastors, and laypersons who share responsibility for catechesis needs to be attracted and served by the REA. Only if we can acknowledge the distinctive differences between catechesis, church-synogogue education, Christian-Jewish education and religious education will we be able to move ahead. Each has its own identity and constituency. Each is valuable. All are legitimate and important concerns of the REA.

Notes for Chapter 8

1. American title, *The Word of God and the Word of Man*, published by the Pilgrim Press, 1928.
2. *The Barthian Theology and the Man of Today* (Harpers, 1933), p. 184.
3. *The Epistle to the Romans*, translated by E. C. Hoskyns (Oxford University Press, 1933), p. 63.
4. *Natural Law in the Spiritual World* (A. L. Burt Co.), p. 7.
5. Ibid, p. 67.
6. *The Epistle to the Romans*, p. 89.
7. *The Epistle to the Romans*, p. 87.
8. *What is Christianity?* (G. P. Putnam, 1904), p. 8.
9. Quoted by Pauck, *Karl Barth* (Harpers, 1931), p. 32.
10. Quoted by Pauck, Ibid. p. 32.
11. *The Theology of Crisis* (Scribner's, 1927), p. 23f.
12. *The Theology of Crisis*, 29.
13. *The Epistle to the Romans*, 98.
14. Brunner, *The Word and the World* (Scribner's 1931), p. 37.
15. *The Word and the World*, p. 95
16. *The Word and the World*, p. 82.
17. Ibid, 101f.
18. *The Word and the World*, p. 95.
19. McConnachie, *The Barthian Theology and the Men of Today* (Harpers, 1933), p. 87.
20. *Barthian Theology and the Man of Today*, p. 85.
21. *Barthian Theology and the Man of Today*, p. 186.

Notes for Chapter 11

1. See W. Jaeger, *Early Christianity and Greek Paideia*, the Belknap Press of the Harvard University Press, 1961; and also his *Paideia: the Ideals of Greek Culture*, Oxford University Press, 1945, Vol. I, pp. 4-5.
2. Chave, Ernest J., *A Functional Approach to Religious Education*, University of Chicago Press, 1947, p. 127.
3. Ibid., p. 3.
4. While definitions of God as the "creative order" reflect influence of the early Wieman, I am not sure the way Chave speaks about religious education as "making religion . . . opera-

tive in the individual" would be acceptable to Wieman. Wieman always retained an element of transcendence in his descriptions of God which would resist this language of causality and conditionality.

5. *Principles and Objectives of Religious Education*, International Council of Religious Education, Chicago, 1932, pp. 10-16.

6. Quoted in Taylor, Marvin K., *Religious Education, a Comprehensive Survey*, New York, Abingdon Press, 1960.

7. Wyckoff, D. Campbell, *The Task of Christian Education*, Westminster Press, 1955, p. 163.

8. Cully, Iris V., *The Dynamics of Christian Education*, The Westminster Press, 1958, p. 76.

9. Ibid., p. 109.

10. Ernsberger, David J., *A Philosophy of Adult Christian Education*, Westminster Press, 1958, p. 76.

11. Hunter, David R., *Christian Education as Engagement*, The Seabury Press, 1963, p. 31.

12. Ibid., p. 39.

Notes for Chapter 12

1. Webster's 3rd New International Dictionary. Springfield, Mass., 1961. Definitions of: instruct, education, nurture.

2. Phenix, Philip, *Realms of Meaning*, McGraw-Hill, 1964, p. 83f. The descriptions under "non-discursive symbolic forms" was suggestive here.

Notes for Chapter 13

1. Paul Ramsey, ed., *Religion*, Englewood Cliffs, N.J.: Prentice-Hall, 1965, p. *VIII* .

2. Englewood Cliffs, N.J.: Prentice-Hall, 1963.

3. Madison: University of Wisconsin Press, 1963.

4. Op. cit., p. 5.

5. J. Gordon Chamberlin, *Freedom and Faith, New Approaches to Christian Education*. Philadelphia: Westminster Press, 1965, pp. 19-20.

Notes for Chapter 14

1. For the development of this custom see: Nehemiah, 8:8; *Yoma* 68b; *Sotah* 40b; *Baba Kama* 82a; *Megillah* 29a, 30b.

2. *Sotah*, 22a; see also *Sanhedrin*, 17b; *Shabbat*, 119a.

3. *Yoma*, 35a.

4. *Shabbat*, 119a.

5. *Shabbat*, 119b.

6. *Kiddushin*, 40b.

7. *Rosh Hashannah*, 18a.

9. *Peach*, 1a.

9. *Avot (Ethics of the Fathers)*, 1:4., 1:6.

10. *Sanhedrin* 17b; *Baba Batra* 21a; *Berachot* 2a, 47b; *Taanit* 9b. Concerning compulsory education, see Drazin, Nathan, *History of Jewish Education From 515 B.C.E. to 22 C.E.*, Baltimore, John Hopkins Press, 1940, p. 46-49.

11. *Jerusalem Talmud, Ketuvot*, Chapter 8.

12. *Baba Batra* 8b; see also *Ketubot* 66a.

13. *Nedarim* 37a; also, *Avot*, 4:5, and *Derech Eretz Zuta* 4:2.

14. *Avot*, 4:15.

15. *Baba Mezia*, 33a.

16. Pupils are compared to the flowers of the golden candle-stick in the Sanctuary. *Pesichta Rabbah*, 29b. Moreover, the teacher was enjoined to hold his pupils as dear as he holds himself. *Mechilta, Beshallah*, 1. See also *Shabbat* 119a.

17. Marvin Fox, "Day Schools and the American Educational Pattern," *The Jewish Parent*, September 1953.

18. Abraham J. Tannenbaum, New York, Columbia University Press, 1962.

19. Bernard Revel (founder and first president of Yeshiva University), *Yeshiva College*, (address delivered at opening exercises, 1929), New York, Archives of the Department of Public Relations, Yeshiva University.

20. Immanuel Jakobovitz, "The Religious-Secular Dilemma," *Tradition and Modern Society* (Alvin I. Schiff, editor); Yeshiva University and Jewish Education Committee Press, Publication date 1969, p. 179.

21. Immanuel Jakobovitz, o. cit., p. 180.

22. Samuel Belkin, *Essays in Jewish Traditional Thought*, New York: Philosophical Library, 1956.

23. Emanuel Rackman, "Diversity of the American-Jewish Experience," *Tradition and Modern Society*, (Alvin I. Schiff, editor),

Yeshiva University and the Jewish Education Committee Press, publication date 1969, p. 141.

24. Emanuel Rackman, op. cit., p. 142.

25. *Ruth Rabbah*, 19.

Notes for Chapter 15

1. Oscar J. Hussel and Gerald L. Klever, *Church School Teachers of the United Presbyterian Church*, 1967, pages 14-19; 122-125.

2. Erik Erikson, *Insight and Responsibility*, 1964, p. 204.

3. *The Church, the University, and Social Policy*, Wesleyan University Press, 1969.

4. Ibid., p. 92.

5. Ibid., p. 93.

6. Ibid., p. 19.

Notes for Chapter 16

1. William H. Grie, M.D. and Price M. Cobbs, *The Jesus Bag* (New York: McGraw-Hill, 1971), p. 167.

2. The Mission of the Church from the Black Perspective," unpublished statement from the August 1969 Krisheim Conference on "The Educational Role of the Black Church in the '70s." Used by permission of the Department of Educational Development, National Council of Churches, New York, N.Y.

3. Paulo Freire, *Pedagogy of the Oppressed* (New York: Herder and Herder, 1971), p. 58.

4. Ibid., p. 60.

5. Ibid., pp. 71-73.

6. John Hurst Adams, "Saturday Ethnic School: A Model," *Spectrum, International Journal of Religious Education*, July-August, 1971, pp. 8-9, 32.

Notes for Chapter 18

1. William B. Williamson, *Language and Concepts in Christian Education* (Philadelphia: Westminster, 1970), p. 144.

2. John Wilson, *Education in Religion and the Emotions* (London: Heinemann, 1971), pp. 6, 11, 105-111.

3. James Michael Lee, *The Shape of Religious Instruction* (Dayton, Ohio: Pflaum, 1971), pp. 6-7.

4. Marc Belth, *Education as a Discipline: A Study of the Role of Models in Thinking* (Boston: Allyn and Bacon, 1965), pp. 51-54.

5. R. S. Peters, *Authority, Responsibility and Education* (London: George Allen and Unwin, Third edition, 1973), pp. 122-131. John Dewey, *Democracy and Education* (New York: Macmillan, 1916), pp. 109-110.

6. Declaration on Christian Education," *The Documents of Vatican II*, Walter M. Abbott, S. J., ed. (New York: America Press, 1966), p. 639.

7. "Education as Initiation," in *Philosophical Analysis and Education*, R. Archambault, ed. (London: Routledge & Kegan Paul, 1965), p. 88.

8. Peters identifies the second and third criteria in the following list. See especially Peters and P. H. Hirst, *The Logic of Education* (London: Routledge and Kegan Paul, 1970), pp. 19-25.

9. Gabriel Moran, *Design for Religion: Toward Ecumenical Education* (New York: Herder and Herder, 1970), pp. 18-19.

10. Barry Chazan, "Indoctrination' and Religious Education," *Religious Education*, Vol. LXVII, No. 4 (July-August, 1972); pp. 250-252.

11. Israel Scheffler, *The Language of Education* (Springfield, Ill.: Charles C. Thomas, 1960), p. 57.